ROGET'S THESAURUS

1994 EDITION

Paradise Press Inc.
12956 SW 133 Court
Miami, FL 33~

D0973717

CONTENTS

Synonyms . . .

Are those words which appear under the
alphabetical listing
All have the same meaning

Antonyms . . .

Are those words which appear under the
alphabetical listing in parentheses
All have the opposite or different meanings

Parts Of Speech . . .

Abbreviations:

n - noun
v - verb
adv - adverb
adj - adjective

1994 EDITION

COPYRIGHT © 1993 BY P.S.I. & ASSOCIATES, INC.
ALL RIGHTS RESERVED PRINTED IN THE U.S.A.
ISBN# 0-938261-08-X

41981

A

abandon-*v* depart, go, quit, vacate, evacuate, exit, retire, withdraw, remove, (spring, fly, embark, reach, attain, advent, arrive, join, return, land, get to)

abate-*v* decrease, diminish, lessen, wane, ebb, decline, descend, subside, melt, die away, subtract, decay, (advance, gain strength, grow, add, enlarge, increase, augment)

abdicate-*v* resign, give up, vacate, retire, renunciate, abjuration, renounce, disclaim, anarchy, relaxation, loosening, remission, (authorize, influence, despotism, command)

abduct-*v* take, catch, hook, nab, bag, clutch, sequester, distress, capture, extortion, rapacity, receive, evict, (unclench, release, replevin, return, give, restore, render)

aberrant-*adj* abnormal, stray, exceptional, deviant, diverge, irregularity, variety, exemption, qualification, (illustrate, conform, adapt, follow, conventional, normal)

abet-*v* aid, help, support, sustain, uphold, further, advance, nurture, cradle, suckle, relief, rescue, (bar, clog, drag, hinder, stop, impede, obstruct, thwart, frustrate)

abhor-*v* dislike, loathe, hate, detest, abominate, repel, sicken, reluctance, unwillingness, repugnance, animosity, (care for, like, desire, take to, want, need)

abide-*v* persist, remain, stay, endure, maintain, keep, continue, sustain, uphold, carry on, keep one's course, (desist, cease, discontinue, halt, pause, rest)

ability-*n* ableness, cogent, competency, validity, skill, adroitness, craft, proficiency, knack, (bungle, fumble, botch, incompetent, raw, green, disability, impotent)

ablaze-*adj* afire, burning, fiery, shining, bright, heat, caloric, temperature, warmth, spark, fever, bonfire, (cool, cold, icy, dark, obscure, gloomy, somber, lightless)

able-*adj* ability, competent, efficient, enablement, capable, competent, dexterous, proficient, (incompetent, unskilled, awkward, clumsy, helpless, exhaust)

abnormal-*adj* unconventional, oddity, rarity, freak, bizarre, aberration, individuality, idiosyncrasy, (normal, conform, regular, usual)

aboard-*adv* inhabit, dwell,
reside, stay, lodge,
presence, occupancy,
attendance, inhabit,
moored, roost, (absent,
void, vacuum, away, gone,
missing, lost, elsewhere)

abode-*n* dwelling, lodging,
domicile, residence,
address, home, fatherland,
quarters, roost, camp,
household, native land,
inhabit, bivouac, native,
cottage, hermitage

abolish-*v* destruction,
dissolution, annihilation,
nullify, annul, put an end
to, tumble, topple, smash,
destroy, break, undo,
(produce, do, make,
construct, form, fabricate)

abominable-*adj* evil, bad,
sinister, dreadful, dire,
horrid, foul, rotten,
offensive, hurt, injure,
abuse, maltreat, damnify,
(super, excellent, good,
best, good as gold)

abortion-*n* failure, fault,
miscarriage, blunder,
botch, fail, unsuccessful,
lost, cast away, wrecked,
addle, stillborn, fruitless,
lame, (succeed, triumph,
gain, attain)

about-*adv* reference, refer,
analogy, pertaining,
related, connect,
associate, near, close,
nigh, approximate, around,
(disconnected,
independent, no relation,
irrelevant, remote, far, out

of the way)

above-*adv* superior,
exceed, transcend, out-do,
pass, surpass, top, beat,
over, eclipse, precede,
ultra, supreme, aloft,
overhead, elevated, lofty,
upper, (below, underlie,
down, ebb, inferior, less,
smaller)

abroad-*adv* remote,
removed, afar, distant,
away, off, yonder, farther,
further, beyond, apart,
asunder, (earshot, close,
near, nigh, bordering,
contiguous, adjoining,
adjacent, proximate, home,
intimate, beside, here)

abrupt-*adj* instantly,
sudden, moment, flash,
burst, hasty,
instantaneously, presto,
(eternity, ever, perpetual,
flowing, everlasting,
continued, evergreen,
immortal, undying)

absence-*n* alibi, emptiness,
vacuum, void, exemption,
hiatus, truant, absent,
vacate, withdraw, gone,
missing, lost, wanting,
omitted, empty, devoid,
(presence, occupancy,
attendance, fill, pervade,
permeate)

absolute-*adj* infinity,
greatest, transcend,
intense, profound, rank,
consummate, supreme,
grand, majestic, extreme,
towering, perfect,
unlimited, stark, complete,

unrestricted, entirely,
entirety, perfection, ideal,
unity, whole, (incomplete,
short, meager, uncertain,
doubt, hesitation, fallible)

absolve-*v* forgive, pardon,
amnesty, conciliation,
excuse, exonerate,
release, forget acquit,
discharge, free, liberate,
immune, clear, (revenge,
vengeance, avenge,
vendetta, vindictive)

absorb-*v* combine, mix,
join, union, unify,
synthesize, incorporate,
fusion, blending, embody,
amalgamate, blend,
merge, fuse, consolidate,
import, (disperse,
disembody, disintegrate,
break up, unravel, evict,
expel)

abstain-*v* avoid, forbear,
evade, elude, reject,
eschew, shun, do without,
dispense with, do nothing,
wait, refrain, (pursue,
quest, chase, hunt, follow,
engage in, use, consume,
employ, perform, operate,
do, execute)

abstract-*adj* sole, single,
lone, solitary, desolate, by
itself, epitome, analysis,
digest, brief, summary,
draft, note, excerpt,
synopsis, textbook,
prospectus, (accompanied,
appendage, coexistence,
company)

abuse-*v* hurt, ill-treat,
molest, persecute, harm,
injure, victimize, maul,
maltreat, do violence,
misuse, desecrate, (good,
value, virtue, benefit, profit,
do a good turn, do no
harm, be good)

abut-*v* contiguous, contact,
border, adjoin, touch,
come in contact with,
adhere, end to end, close
to, prop, stand, support,
bolster, (interspace, gap,
hole, opening, far
between)

abyss-*n* space, infinite
space, roomy, spacious,
boundless, vast,
bottomless pit, hell,
(definite space, region,
sphere, area, realm,
domain, tract, territory,
spot, point, niche, nook,
compartment, heaven,
paradise, eden)

academic-*adj* teaching,
instruction, education,
discipline, lesson,
curriculum, course of
study, school, academy,
scholastic, collegiate,
educational, (misinform,
render unintelligible,
uncertain, conceal)

accelerate-*v* sharpen,
quicken, excite, urge,
stimulate, foment, speed
up, spurt, rush, dash, bolt,
dart, swiftly, hurry, (slow,
languor, drawl, creeping,
delay, move slowly, creep,
crawl, lag, linger, dawdle,
apply the brake, reduce
the speed)

accept-_v_ assent, admit, agree, concur, avow, own, acknowledge, ratify, approve, consent, comply, concede, confirm, allow, grant, give in, embrace an offer, satisfy, receive, take, (denial, contradiction, refuse, give, donate, bestow, cede, deliver, endow, invest, award, bequest, contribute, hand, pass)

access-_n_ approach, path, route, near, pursue, approximate, impending, method, manner, procedure, track, (recession, withdrawal, deadlock, retirement, departure, recede, remove)

accessible-_adj_ possible, feasible, practical, possible, conceivable, credible, likely, performable, achievable, surmountable, capable, easy (impossible, no chance, absurd, contrary, unlikely, impracticable, inaccessible, impassable, difficult, hard)

accessory-_n_ addition, add, annexation, tack to, append, also, too, complement, addendum, supplement, adjunct, accompany, associated, with, auxiliary, partner, colleague

accident-_n_ occurrence, misfortune, act of God, mishap, mischance, disaster, calamity, contingency, fortune, haphazard, casualty, tragedy, adversity, (well, alert, satisfactory, remedy, utility, happiness)

acclimatize-_v_ habituate, accustom, naturalize, inure, season, tame, domesticate, breed, tend, break in, train, cage, bridle, restrain, harden, familiarize, educate, (unaccustomed, disuse)

accomodate-_v_ fit, suit, conform, adjust, adapt, oblige, furnish, supply, unison, harmony, concord, concert, congruity, keeping, fitness, aptness, relevancy, adaptation, (discord, dissidence, conflict)

accompaniment-_n_ adjunct, accessory, appendage, concomitant, attribute, context, concomitance, affix, augment, garnish, sauce, complement, (remainder, residue, remnant, rest, relic, leavings)

accomplice-_n_ confederate, ally, abettor, accessory, assistant, colleague, recruit, adjunct, help, partner, mate, collaborator, friend, confidant, (opponent, antagonist, adversary, wrangler)

accomplish-_v_ fulfill, do, achieve, effect, execute,

perform, attain, feat,
acquirement, fulfillment,
performance, realization,
achievement, (destruction,
waste, dissolution,
downfall, ruin, fall, crash)
accord-v tally, harmonize,
concur, grant, bestow,
acquiesce, conformity,
uniformity, agreement,
constancy, level, smooth,
dress, (diversified, varied,
irregular, uneven, rough)
accost-v speak, salute,
hail, address, greet,
speech, appeal,
invocation, salutation,
make up
account-n score, record,
recital, narration,
description, answerable,
explicable, liable,
responsible, amenable,
money matters, finance,
bill, budget, tally,
(unaccountable)
accretion-n concretion,
adhesion, increment,
growth, accumulation,
increase, enlargement,
extension, development,
augment, (decrease,
lessening, subtraction,
reduction, shrinking, ebb)
accrue-v bring in, yield,
result, arise, annexation,
increase, supplement,
insertion, affix, additive,
extra, plus, further, also,
(deduction, retrenchment,
amputation, curtailment,
abrasion, deduct)
accumulate-v collect,

gather, hoard, increase,
assemble, amass,
collection, compilation,
levy, gathering, muster,
assembly, (dispersion,
divergence, scattering,
dissipation, spread)
accuracy-n preciseness,
precision, verity,
correctness, just, proper,
true, correct, exact, fact,
truth, gospel, authenticity,
veracity, honest, sober,
(error, fallacy, inexactness,
report, mistake, fault)
accursed-adj fated,
doomed, detestable,
damnable, diabolic,
charge, slur, incrimination,
imputation, recrimination,
blame, censure,
denunciation, inculpation,
plaint, accusation,
(congratulate, compliment,
commendation, praise,
eulogy)
accustom-v inure, season,
familiarize, habituate,
common, general, natural,
ordinary, track, practice,
rut, groove, precedent,
(newness to, leave off,
cast off, break off, violate,
infringe)
ache-v smart, shoot,
twinge, hurt, pain,
discomfort, suffering,
twitch, headache, spasm,
cramp, crick, thrill, sharp,
gnawing, torment,
(pleasure, physical,
sensual, sensuous,
comfort, luxury)

achievement-*n*
performance, fulfillment,
accomplishment, exploit,
feat, trace, vestige,
courage, bravery, valor,
boldness, spirit, defiance,
(cowardice, timid,
baseness, fear, faint heart)

acknowledge-*v* grant,
concede, confess, admit,
own, assent, disclose,
answer, response, reply,
retort, repartee, discover,
conclusive, satisfy,
(inquiry, search, pursuit,
review, scrutiny, analysis)

acquaint-*v* familiarize,
notify, apprise, inform, tell,
communicate, intimation,
represent, round robin,
present, case, estimate,
specification, report,
(conceal, hiding, secret,
screen, disguise,
masquerade)

acquiesce-*v* agree, concur,
accede, comply, close
with, admit, to deign,
acquirement, obtainment,
grant, gift, inheritance,
donation, purchase,
(expenditure, loss, penalty,
dissent, refusal)

acquittal-*n* exculpation,
clearance, clearing,
exoneration, discharge,
absolution, quietus,
reprieve, pardon, absolve,
release, liberate, let off,
(condemnation, accuse,
conviction, restraint)

acrid-*adj* acrimonious, tart,
pungent, bitter, severe,
caustic, biting, keen,
sharpness, roughness,
mustard, pepper, brine,
stinging, unsavory,
virulence, spleen, asperity,
(condiment)

act-*n* ordinance, decree,
deed, exploit, statute, law,
edict, scene, perform, do,
operate, behave, play,
feign, simulate, action,
doing, (inaction,
passiveness, idle,
misbehave, lax)

advocate-*v* recommend,
counsel, suggest,
prescribe, to advise, to
support, advise,
instruction, charge,
enforce, enjoin, (intendant,
husband, moderator,
speaker, proctor)

aeronaut-*n* pilot, flyer,
navigator, aviator, airman,
aviatrix, scout, balloonist,
Icarus, seaman, skipper,
marine, (wayfarer,
voyager, passenger,
tourist, explorer, straggler,
rambler)

aesthetic-*n* artistic, refined,
cultured, cultivated,
appealing, sensibility,
physical, feeling,
sensation, impression,
cultivate, tudor, (opium,
insensible, paralyze, blunt,
callous, dull)

afar-*adv* aloof, abroad,
away, distant, distance,
horizon, reach, spread,
remote, mundane, away,
yonder, farther, apart,

(nearness, proximity,
adjacency, breadth, span,
close, handy, home)
affable-adj approachable,
sociable, gracious, friendly,
amiable, humility, meek,
resignation, modesty,
confusion, humble, submit,
diminish, (starch, perked,
lofty, haughty, mighty,
dignified)
affair-n event, business,
occurrence, matter,
concern, question,
eventuality, incident,
transaction, proceeding,
phenomenon, advent,
(impending, destined,
loom, threaten, await)
affectation-v insincerity,
pretension, airs,
modishness, charlatanism,
quackery, artificiality,
(modesty, diffidence,
timidity, shyness, humility,
demureness)
affection-n bent, quality,
malady, ailment, fondness,
tenderness, devotion,
nature, spirit, tone, temper,
habit, soul, turn, bosom,
breast, heart, (experience,
response, impression,
emotion)
affirmation-n ratification,
corroboration, allegation,
confirmation, assertion,
profession, avowal,
emphasis, positiveness,
dogmatism, (negation,
uncertainty, refutation,
disclamation)
afraid-adj apprehensive,

fearful, timorous, alarmed,
cowardly, terrified,
uncertainty, demure,
suspense, caprice, levity,
dilly dally, boggle,
(determination, resolve,
conclude)
agency-n causality, method,
impelling force, force,
function, office, exercise,
maintenance, work, swing,
action, official, acting,
operant, (inaction,
powerlessness)
agent-n servant, proxy,
doer, actor, operator,
perpetrator, executor,
representative, go-
between, mediate, deputy,
consignee, trustee,
nominee, (deputy,
substitute, vice, proxy,
minister)
aggravation-n heightening,
intensification, vexation,
annoyance, acridity,
irritation, render worse,
acerbate, worsen, (relief,
alleviation, mitigation,
assuagement)
aggregate-adj sum total,
sum, all, complete, whole,
assemblage, compilation,
gathering, muster,
meeting, assembly, mob,
body, tribe, crew,
(divergence, scattering,
diffusion, dissipation)
aggression-n inroad,
encroachment, invasion,
attack, assault, charge,
offense, incursion,
invasion, against, impugn,

assume, harry, invade,
(defense, guard,
resistance, safeguard)

agile-*adj* quick, lithe, active,
nimble, spry, brisk, activity,
liveliness, spirit, dash,
energy, smartness,
alacrity, industry,
movement, bustle, stir,
fuss, (inactivity, inertness,
dullness, languor, sleep,
sound)

agitation-*n* jar, jolt, shake,
trepidation, shock, flutter,
perturbation, disconcertion,
confusion, turmoil,
turbulence, tumult, stir,
ripple, jog, dance, flutter,
(order, rest, stability)

agony-*n* anguish, pain,
suffering, torment, torture,
smart, twitch, spasm,
headache, cramp,
discomfort, throb, piercing,
rack, (pleasure, sensual,
comfort, luxury, enjoy, at
ease, cozy, snug)

agreement-*n*
understanding, accord,
keeping, unison,
reconcilement, union,
harmony, consonance,
(disagreement, dissent,
inequality, disharmony,
unconformity, discord)

agriculture-*n* agrarian,
rural, farming, husbandry,
cultivation, tillage,
gardening, florist, field,
meadow, flower,
plantation, (taming,
breeding, aviary, fishery,
trainer)

aid-*v* assistance, help,
succor, promotion,
cooperation, furtherance,
advocacy, defense,
patronage, countenance,
alleviation, support, lift,
advance, relief, rescue,
(hindrance, opposition,
neglect)

ailment-*n* affection, illness,
disorder, disease, malady,
sickness, infirmity,
complaint, attack, seizure,
stroke, canker, virus,
plague, pestilence, (health,
soundness, vigor, perfect,
robust, bloom, recover)

alarm-*n* fear, dread, scare,
fright, panic, warning,
signal, summons, excite,
agitate, arouse, startle,
affright, terrify, appall,
caution, prediction, omen,
beacon, give notice,
beware, sentinel,
watchman

allay-*v* ease, assuage,
lessen, mitigate, slacken,
pacification,
accommodation,
arrangement, adjustment,
terms, compromise,
armistice, suspension of
hostilities, (warfare,
fighting, crusade)

allegiance-*n* duty, homage,
obedience, loyalty,
observance, compliance,
submission, passiveness,
devotion, obey, control,
follow, service,
(insubordination, violation,
non compliance)

alliance-*n* connection,
affinity, compact, league,
cooperation, concurrence,
complicity, collusion,
union, concur, (opposition,
antagonism, counter
action, cross-fire, clashing)
allot-*v* divide, share, assign,
distribute, apportion,
appropriation, portion,
contingent, lot, measure,
dole, pittance, ration, ratio,
quota, allowance
allow-*v* admit, concede,
grant, tolerate, let, suffer,
permit, permission, leave,
concession, grace,
dispensation, release,
authorization, warranty,
(inhibition, disallowance,
interdict, embargo)
allowance-*n* salary, grant,
stipend, concession, pay,
contribution, reward,
remittance, discount,
apportion, allot, consign,
dispensation, division,
deal, cast, share, portion,
administer
allude-*v* connote, imply,
infer, suggest, declaratory,
intelligible, literal,
synonymous, implied,
explicit, latent, expressive,
understand, interpret,
(nonsense, jargon,
gibberish, jabber, mere
words)
allure-*v* tempt, attract,
draw, desire, wish, fancy,
fantasy, want, need,
exigency, leaning, bent,
partiality, propensity,

willingness, liking, love,
fondness, relish, (neutral,
indifferent, cold, frigid)
almighty-*adj* omnipotent,
all-powerful, potency,
might, force, energy, arm,
authority, strength, ability,
ableness, enablement,
influence, pressure,
(impotence, disability,
incapacity, ineptitude,
palsy)
alms-*n* charity, gratuity,
grant, dole, giving,
bestowal, donation,
presentation, delivery,
consignment,
dispensation, investment,
award, (receiving,
acquisition, acceptance,
admission)
alongside-*adv* beside,
abreast, side by side,
broadside on, neck and
neck, on a level, parallel,
nearness, proximity,
adjacency, (distance,
remoteness, elongation,
offing, background)
aloof-*adj* distant, remote,
reserved, unneighborly,
secluded, away, afar,
beyond, further, abroad,
(near, nigh, close,
adjoining, handy, intimate)
alternate-*v* periodically,
recurrence, succession,
taking of turns,
changeable, inconsistency,
instability, mobility,
unstable, (stability,
unchangeable, consistent)
altitude-*n* tallness, height,

loftiness, perpendicular,
distance, elevation, giant,
eminence, pitch, loftiness,
prominence, (low, flat,
level, squat, prostrate)

amateur-*n* novice,
dilettante, volunteer,
nonprofessional,
unaffected, bad taste,
dowdy, shabby, ill bred,
untamed, (refined,
professional, tasteful, pure,
dainty)

amatory-*adj* erotic, ardent,
amorous, loving, fondness,
liking, regard, cherish, hug,
prize, adore, suitor,
admirer, sweetheart,
(hatred, coolness, grudge,
bitterness)

ambiguous-*adj* obscure,
vague, undefined,
equivocal, uncertainty,
doubt, hesitation,
suspense, dubious,
indecisive, confused,
(certainty, surety, reliable,
positive)

ambition-*n* resolve, design,
aspiration, longing, zeal,
pretentious, bold, desirous,
zealous, soaring, aspiring,
intent, purpose,
(speculation, venture,
chance, risk)

ambush-*n* ambuscade,
trap, pitfall, lurking place,
screen, cover, recess,
shade, curtain, blind,
cloak, cloud, (reveal, lift
up, remove, acknowledge,
expose, bear)

amenable-*adj* liable,

responsible, yielding,
accountable, answerable,
duty, morality, conscience,
decalogue, (fault,
nonobservance,
nonperformance)

amend-*v* improve, correct,
rectify, change, mend,
promote, cultivate,
advance, forward,
enhance, foster, bolster,
brighten, (wreck, decay,
decline, erosion, blight)

amiable-*adj* kindly, affable,
agreeable, pleasant,
courtesy, respect,
behavior, politeness,
gentility, polish, presence,
(rude, insult, ill breeding,
discourtesy)

ample-*adj* roomy, spacious,
large, abundant,
considerable, greatness,
magnitude, size,
immensity, enormity,
might, strength, fullness,
(smallness, little,
diminutive, paltry)

amusement-*n* pleasure,
sport, solace, pastime,
entertainment, diversion,
distraction, relaxation,
solace, fun, frolic,
merriment, (tedious,
weariness, disgust,
nausea)

anachronism-*n* error in
time, error in chronology,
prolapses, misdate,
anticipation, disregard,
neglect, (chronicle, journal,
diary, clock)

analogy-*n* resembling, like,

associated, related,
correspondent, parallel,
similar, semblance, affinity,
agreement, look like,
(diversity, disparity,
difference, novelty)

analysis-*n* decomposition,
inquiry, consideration,
study, disintegration,
break-up, investigation,
dissection, resolution,
dissolve, (combination,
mixture, union,
incorporation)

analyst-*n* recorder,
historian, chronicler,
compiler, notary, clerk,
registrar, secretary, scribe,
biographer, time keeper,
almanac, calendar, journal

anarchy-*n* rebellion, chaos,
terrorism, lawlessness,
disorder, turmoil,
confusion, disarray,
jumble, huddle, muddle,
hash, (order, regularity,
uniformity, symmetry)

ancestry-*n* line, lineage,
family tree, family, race,
descent, parent, father,
dad, pedigree, tribe, clan,
descent, parental,
forefathers, maternity,
mother

anchor-*n* stay, grapnel,
safeguard, protection,
hold, kedge, killick, link,
connective, hyphen,
bracket, bridge,
(separation, parting,
segregation, divorce,
break)

anchorage-*n* harbor, safety,
roadstead, mooring,
refuge, lodgement,
establishment, settlement,
place, station, (displace,
dislodge, exile, remove,
unload)

ancient-*adj* aged, hoary,
antique, archaic, old,
venerable, antiquated,
maturity, decline, decay,
primitive, classic,
(newness, novelty, youth,
modernism)

anecdote-*n* story, tale,
sketch, account, narrative,
description, statement,
report, summary, brief,
relate, recite, recount, sum
up, tell, give, graphic, epic

angel-*n* divine messenger,
ministering spirits, invisible
helpers, good man, worthy,
model, paragon, hero,
demigod, innocent, saint,
(bad man, evil doer,
sinner, wicked)

anger-*n* enrage, inflame,
arouse, irritate, annoy,
exasperate, provoke,
offend, infuriate,
resentment, displeasure,
wrath, indignation,
(favorite, pet, idol,
fondness, love, dear)

angle-*n* guise, aspect,
phase, crook, fork,
obliquity, cusp, bend,
notch, ankle,
measurement, elevation,
distance, triangle, square,
diamond

animate-*v* actuate, excite,
cheer, enliven, encourage,

inspire, motion, action,
intention, inducement,
draw, inspire, (dissuade,
reluctance, detour, hold,
repel)

annex-v add, attach, join,
affix, junction, union, unite,
lump, fix, bind, fasten,
stitch, buckle, button, knit,
lock, (disjoined,
disconnect, disengage,
divorce, cut, adrift)

annihilate-v exterminate,
eradicate, destroy, end,
wreck, demolish,
extinction, blow, doom,
ravage, sacrifice, abolish,
perish, (evolve, bring forth,
birth, produce, perform)

announce-v report,
declare, predict, foretell,
tell, inform, proclaim,
assert, notice,
communicate, acquaint,
(conceal, hide, mystify,
masquerade, cunning)

annoy-v trouble, bother,
vex, harass, molest,
disturb, irritate, tantalize,
worry, badness, hurtful,
inflict, harm, injure,
oppress, persecute,
(produce, profit, benefit,
goodness, merit)

annul-v nullification,
diffuseness, cancellation,
counter order, invalidation,
retraction, repeal,
abolishment, rescission,
abrogation, (commission,
delegate, consign, assign)

anoint-v rub, lubricate,
salve, oil, divinity, wisdom,

goodness, justice, truth,
unity, eternity,
preservation, (scourge,
halter, stake, truncheon,
stocks)

anonymous-adj
unacknowledged,
unknown, unnamed,
misnomer, alias,
pseudonym, nickname,
(nomination, designation,
title, head, namesake)

answer-n reply, response,
acknowledgment, rebuttal,
retort, return, respond,
say, rebut, acknowledge,
echo, replication,
(question, inquiry, request,
search)

antagonism-n animosity,
antipathy, hostility,
opposition, enmity,
counteraction, polarity,
clashing, collision,
resistance, (concurrence,
cooperation, agreement)

antecede-v preexist,
precede, go before,
precedence, first, head,
lead, introduce, prefix,
prelude, preface, former,
before, (sequence, after,
succeed, follow, suffix)

anteroom-n hall, lobby,
antechamber, receptacle,
enclosure, receiver,
apartment, vessel, portico,
porch, veranda, lobby, hall,
vestibule, chamber, bower

anticipate-v expect, await,
forestall, be early, surmise,
predict, preparation,
provide, disposition,

forecast, cultivate,
(disqualify, unfitted,
shiftless, unprepared)
antidote-*n* emetic, remedy,
counter poison, help,
antiseptic, corrective,
sedative, recipe,
prescription, (poison, virus,
venom, scourge)
antipathy-*n* repugnance,
clashing, opposition,
abhorrence, detestation,
dislike, incompatibility,
reluctance, backward,
disgust, (desire, wish,
want, need, longing)
apathetic-*adj* insensible,
indifferent, cold, unfeeling,
impassive, insensibility, no
desire, disregard, no
interest, (sensible, morale,
softness, warm, tender)
ape-*n* simian, monkey,
mimic, mock, simulate,
imitate, copying,
simulation, semblance,
mirror, reflect, repeat,
echo, match, follow,
counterfeit
apostasy-*n* renunciation,
abjuration, recantation,
defection, retraction,
disavowal, revocation,
abandonment, recreancy,
relapse
appall-*v* nauseate, revolt,
disgust, terrify, putrefy,
painful, trouble, curse,
hurt, displease, annoy,
perplex, tease, irk, vex,
(refresh, comfortable,
cordial, genial)
apparatus-*n* machinery,

outfit, equipment,
contrivance, instrument,
engineer, mechanism,
organ, appliance, gear,
tackle, implement, utensil
apparent-*adj* perceptible,
obvious, seeming, clear,
patent, manifest, visible,
appearing, conspicuous,
distinct, evidence,
(invisible, dim, mysterious,
confused)
appearance-*n* sight, show,
phenomenon, prospect,
representation, display,
stage setting, exposure,
(vanishing, fading,
evanescence, departure,
occultation, withdrawal)
appease-*v* satisfy, allay,
pacify, placate, quiet,
soothe, mollify, pleasure,
moderate, soften,
tranquilize, swag, lull,
compose, (violent, sharp,
quicken, excite, incite)
append-*v* subjoin, add,
affix, attach, annex,
supplement, subjoin,
reinforce, augment,
accrue, introduce, insert,
more, include, (subtraction,
amputate, abscind, pare)
appetite-*n* passion,
craving, want, hunger,
longing, desire, wish,
need, exigency, inclination,
greed, covetous, ravenous,
(anorexia, apathy, listless)
applause-*n* acclamation,
praise, plaudit, acclaim,
clapping, approbation,
commendation, cheer,

good word, blessing,
approval, (dislike,
reprehend, chide,
admonish)

applicable-*adj* convenient,
pertinent, suitable,
appropriate, relevant,
adequate, service,
available, ready, tangible,
advantageous, (useless
inefficacy, worthless)

appoint-*v* nominate,
ordain, assign, establish,
prescribe, commission,
delegate, consign,
authorize, accredit,
engage, hire, (annulment,
nullification, conceal,
cancel)

apportionment-*n* allotment,
assignment, consignment,
partition, allocation,
division, distribution,
disperse, spread,
intersperse, (crowd,
muster, levy, gather, flood)

appraise-*v* rate, judge,
estimate, assess, value,
survey, reckon, measure,
standard, rule, compass,
gage, gauge, yard, meter,
coordinates, ordinate,
latitude

apprehend-*v* arrest, seize,
imprison, dread, distrust,
perceive, see, understand,
known, ascertain,
recognize, realize,
(ignorant, unexplored,
bewilderment)

approach-*v* drawing near,
advance, access, advent,
admission, convergence,

pursuit, drift, gain upon,
converge, (avoidance,
recession, go away)

approbation-*n* sanction,
approval, advocacy, favor,
renown, kudos, popularity,
commendation, eulogy,
homage (detraction,
disrepute, disapprobation)

appropriate-*adj* becoming,
fit, suitable, timely, proper,
adapted, agreeable,
expedient, advisable,
convenient, worthwhile,
applicable, (undesirable,
unfit, clumsy, awkward)

apt-*adj* clever, quick,
dexterous, skillful,
influence, important,
rampant, dominant,
regnant, predominant,
support, (powerless,
uninfluential, irrelevant,
inertness)

arable-*adj* productive,
fertile, tillable, farming,
georgic, agronomy,
horticulture, florist, field,
meadow, garden,
ornamental

arbitrary-*adj* overbearing,
imperious, harsh,
tyrannical, dictatorial,
peremptory, domineering,
despotic, austere, (lenient,
mild, gentle, tolerant,
forbearing)

argument-*n* data, case,
discussion, debate,
controversy, wangling,
contention, dispute,
examine, pros and cons,
(deceptive, sophistical,

irrelevant, evasive)

aristocrat-*n* patrician, lord,
noble, nobleman, empire,
monarchy, royalty,
(democracy, demagogy,
republic, magistrate,
socialism, anarchy,
relaxation, toleration,
freedom)

arrangement-*n* provision,
preparation, array,
assortment, allotment,
distribution, analysis,
organize, sort, distribute,
(disorder, disarrangement,
disturb, confuse)

arrive-*v* advent, coming,
debarkation, landing,
reception, welcome, goal,
destination, harbor, haven,
port, (egress, departure,
embarkation, exit, leaving)

arrogant-*adj* airs, swagger,
haughtiness, pretension,
ostentation, insolence,
take, demand, usurp,
appropriate, seize,
assume, dignity, pride,
self-respect

arsenal-*n* armory, depot,
magazine, storehouse,
arms, weapons,
armament, partisan,
battery, gunnery, missile,
shrapnel

artful-*adj* adroit, tricky,
crafty designing, sly,
shrewd, dexterous, falsity,
deception, untruth, lying,
misrepresentation, perjury,
forgery, (frankness,
truthfulness, sincerity)

artificial-*adj* false, sham,
unnatural, affected,
counterfeit, imitation,
deception, untruth,
delusion, collusion,
treachery, trick, cheat,
(truthfulness, veracity,
frankness, honesty)

artistic-*adj* talented,
beautiful, graceful,
accomplished, cultural,
exquisite, aesthetic, skillful,
clever, ability, ingenuity,
capacity, (unskillful,
stupidity, indiscretion)

asceticism-*n* austerity,
penance, puritanism,
abstinence, cynicism,
mortification, maceration,
flagellation, fasting,
ascetic, cynical

ascribe-*v* assign, impute,
attribute, refer, theory,
reference, pedigree,
rationale, (accident,
fortune, hazard, chance,
random, luck, casualty)

ask-*v* implore, beseech,
inquire, interrogate, beg,
entreat, request, question,
search, research, pursuit,
review, scrutiny, sifting,
(answer, respond, reply,
rebut, retort)

askew-*adj* oblique, crooked,
awry, distorted, inclination,
slope, slant, leaning,
beveled, tilt, bias, twist,
swag, oblique, descend,
decline

ass-*n* dolt, booby, donkey,
fool, idiot, wiseacre,
simpleton, ninny, oaf, lout,
loon, addle, innocent,

babbler, (sage, wise man, mastermind, thinker, authority)

assassin-*n* cutthroat, killer, murderer, slayer, homicide, manslaughter, slay, butcher, victimize, massacre, strangle, stifle, (alive, breathe, respire)

assemblage-*n* collection, concourse, conflux, gathering, mobilization, meet, concentration compilation, (disjunction, dispersion, divergence)

assert-*v* allege, claim, avow, maintain, state, affirm, belief, credence, credit, assurance, faith, trust, confidence, dependence, (misbelief, discredit, infidelity, dissent, retraction)

astringent-*adj* styptic, sour, tart, austere, binding, contraction, reduction, lessening, shrinking, collapse, decrease, (large, expand, widen, enlarge, grow)

astute-*adj* acute, bright, shrewd, quick, intelligent, capacity, comprehension, intellect, sagacity, judgment, cunning, brains, (imbecility, dull, incompetence, idiocy)

athletic-*adj* acrobatic, strong, robust, powerful, gymnastic, strength, energy, vigor, force, main, spring, elasticity, tone, (weakness, debility, relaxation, languor)

atonement-*n* indemnification, expiation, redemption, conciliation, propitiation, recompense, compromise, (impenitence, obduracy, callousness)

attack-*v* encroachment, onset, onslaught, encounter, assault, charge, aggression, thrust, kick, punch, assail, invade, (defense, protection, guard, shield)

attention-*n* alertness, heed, observance, intentness, scrutiny, study, mindfulness, thought, consideration, reflection, (inattention, neglect, oversight, disregard)

audacity-*n* overconfidence, gall, impudence, temerity, insolence, rashness, imprudence, indiscretion, presumption, (caution, discretion, calculation, deliberation)

auspicious-*adj* fortunate, favorable, propitious, promising, expedient, occasion, opportunity, suitable, proper, (unsuitable, improper, lose, waste)

authority-*n* authorization, power, warrant, right, dominion, dictation, command, influence, facts, evidence, collateral, (laxity, obedience, servant, submission)

auxiliary-*adj* assistant,

collaborator, adjuvant,
helping, aiding, ancillary,
support, lift, favor, relief,
rescue, ministry, aid,
(prevention, stoppage,
enemy, opponent)

avail-*v* benefit, profit, serve,
succeed, suffice,
usefulness, adequacy,
conduce, gainful,
advantageous, valuable,
(inadequacy, unskillful,
lost, seek)

averse-*adj* reluctant, loath,
opposed, counter,
unwillingness, renitency,
reluctance, indifference,
backward, slowness,
(willing, mind, heart,
incline, eager)

await-*v* contemplate,
impend, anticipate,
expectation, approach,
future, coming, heritage,
posterity, close, next,
eventual, (past, gone,
former, ancient, antiquity)

award-*v* adjudication,
compensation, bestowal,
conferment, decision,
giving, donation,
presentation, accordance,
delivery, endowment,
(receiving, acquisition,
acceptance, admission)

awkward-*adj* unskillful,
ungainly, clumsy,
ungraceful, incompetency,
inability, inexperience,
fumble, boggle, blunder,
flounder, stumble, (skill,
expert, craft, competence)

axiom-*n* aphorism, truism,

postulate, rule, proposition,
saying, adage, saw,
proverb, sentence, motto,
word, morale, reflection,
(absurdity, imbecility,
nonsense, paradox,
muddle)

axle-*n* arbor, pivot, axis,
spindle, rotation,
revolution, gyration, whirl,
surge, screw, gimbals,
gyrate, twirl

B

babble-*v* chatter, prattle,
rave, gibber, murmur,
gurgle, gossip, empty
sound, nonsense, jargon,
gibberish, jabber, bombast,
(meaning, expression,
bearing, substantial)

backsliding-*v* apostasy,
retrogression, lapse,
countermovement,
regression, retreat,
withdrawal, retirement,
recession, reflection,
(progression, advance,
ongoing, headway)

backward-*adv* delayed,
dull, stagnant, tardy, loath,
disinclined, reluctant,
remiss, retrograde,
unwillingness, reluctance,
(willingness, punctual,
inclination, leaning)

bad-*adj* sinful, imperfect,
rancid, unsuitable, wicked,
tainted, hurtful, virulence,
injurious, deleterious,
noxious, aggrieve,
oppress, (good,

excellence, merit, virtue, worth)

baffle-*v* outwit, confound, check, balk, frustrate, foil, nonplus, restrict, restraint, blockade, hindrance, obstacle, drawback, (assistance, help, support, lift, advance)

bag-*n* container, pouch, sack, protrude, sag, capture, entrap, catch, receptacle, enclosure, receiver, compartment, sac, pocket, sheath

bait-*n* worry, badger, lure, trap, decoy, harass, deception, falseness, untruth, fraud, deceit, misrepresentation, delusion, juggling, (veracity, truthfulness, sincerity)

balance-*n* evenness, scales, equilibrium, steadiness, parallel, match, compare, contrast, identification, collate, confront, (crooked, uneven, unbalanced)

balk-*v* shy, stop, back, thwart, disappoint, foil, frustrate, hindrance, deception, falseness, untruth, fraud, deceit, trick, cheat, (true, frank, open, candor, sincerity)

ball-*n* hop, dance, party, shot, sphere, globe, projectile, roundness, cylinder, drum, rotund,

balm-*n* ointment, balsam sedative, moderation,

gentleness, calmness, relaxation, mitigation, lullaby, (violence, vehemence, might, turbulence)

banish-*v* expatriate, exile, dismiss, expel, eject, exclude, punish, emission, evacuation, drainage, reject, discard, cut, (admit, introduce, inject, insertion)

bare-*adj* simple, mere, nude, naked, undraped, empty, destitute, unfurnished, disclose, uncover, reveal, expose, (cover, screen, shake, full, furnish)

bark-*n* skin, rind, shell, cortex, howl, yelp, yap, bay, cry, growl, yip, roar, bellow, grunt, snort, squeak, purr, mew, croak

barren-*adj* arid, sterile, unfertile, unprofitable, fruitless, worthless, impotence, waste, desert, unproductive, inoperative, (fertility, multiplication, productive, generate)

barter-*v* trade, exchange, bargaining, swap, traffic, marketing, interchange, reciprocation, shuffle, retaliate, (substitution, supplanting, alternative)

base-*n* groundwork, footing, foundation, foothold, substratum, basic, lowest, fundamental, platform, dishonesty, disgrace, shabbiness, (integrity, rectitude, honesty, faith)

bashful-*adj* sheepish, modest, timid, diffident, shy, constrained, humility, difference, reserve, nervous, (conceit, confidence, approbation)

bear-*v* yield, hold, sustain, suffer, feel, tolerate, carry, transport, convey, transfer, deportation, carriage, conveyance, delegate, consign

beat-*v* defeat, conquer, pulsate, throb, hit, strike, bruise, batter, overcome,accent, rhythm, pulse, track, course, (break down, collapse, fail, lose ground)

beatify-*v* bless, hallow, consecrate, sanctify, piety, faith, reverence, humility, believe, convert, veneration, holy, revere, inspire, (bigot, fanatic, irreverence)

beauty-*n* loveliness, grace, elegance, symmetry, comeliness, fairness, attractiveness, (ugliness, deformity, inelegance, distortion)

becoming-*adj* proper, fit, attractive, seemly, ornamental, decorous, beam, bloom, grace, (unfit, clumsy, awkward, objectionable)

beg-*v* plead, petition, ask alms, implore, beseech, crave, request, motion, overture, appeal, (depreciation, protest, receive, mediation)

beginning-*n* start, onset, commencement, introduction, prelude, prologue, debut, outbreak, outset, source, rudiment, genesis, cause, introductory, prefatory, initiative, inaugural, (end, rear, sequel)

belief-*n* faith, assurance, credence, trust, hope, dependence, conviction, persuasion, conclusion, dogma, theory, principle, (doubt, unbelief, uncertainty)

belligerent-*adj* disputatious, pugnacious, quarrelsome, warlike, fighting, hostilities, mobilize, armed, combative, (pacify, composed, reconcile)

benefactor-*n* protector, savior, patron, guardian, guardian angel, altruist, supporter, (evildoer, opponent)

benefit-*n* avail, behalf, gain, profit, advantage, aid, assist, serve, improve, helpful, valuable, useful, utility, (useless, inadequacy, lose, waste)

benevolence-*n* charity, love, kindness, unselfishness, philanthropy, humanity, tenderness, amiability, mercy, (malevolence, misanthropy)

bereavement-*n* destitution, loss, deprivation, affliction,

death, decease, release,
departure, perish, expire,
(alive, respire, living, lively)
besiege-v circumscribe,
storm, surround, hedge,
beleaguer, attack, request,
ask, beg, crave, prey,
petition, invite,
(depreciation, intercession,
protest, receive)
betray-v deceive, divulge,
ensnare, trick, reveal, let
slip, disclosure, discover,
breathe, break, split,
acknowledge,
(concealment, cover,
screen, mask, shade)
bewilder-v stagger, daze,
dazzle, perplex, confuse,
mystify, confound, puzzle,
wonder, marvel, astonish,
amaze, (expectance,
common, ordinary)
bewitch-v hypnotize,
charm, fascinate, enchant,
inveigle, incentive,
provocation, induce,
inspire, stimulate,
(discouragement, damper,
dissuade)
bias-n prejudice, tendency,
inclination, warp, slope,
prepossession, proneness,
bent, turn, tone, conduce,
dispose
bid-v invite, ask, proffer,
direct, order, enjoin,
instruct, summon, call,
offer, presentation, tender,
motion, present, move,
(refusal, rejection, decline,
repulse)
bigot-n fanatic, dogmatist,

iconoclast, formalist,
Pharisee, misconception,
bias, warp, twist, partial,
narrow, (result, conclusion,
judge, deduce, derive)
bind-v restrain, secure,
tighten, force, fasten, join,
union, junction, associate,
closeness, attach, affix,
link, fetter, (sunder, divide,
sever, cut, cleave)
bisection-n divergence,
bifurcation, branching, half,
separation, split,
(duplication, iteration)
biting-adj nipping, keen,
pungent, piquant, sharp,
telling, forceful, irritate,
pinch, prick, gripe,
painfulness, trouble,
(pleasurable, agreeable,
flatter, enchantment)
blacken-v defame, blot,
malign, besmirch, smudge,
detract, defamation,
scandal, slander, liable,
criticism, decry, derogate,
(flattery, humor, smooth)
blemish-n deformity, taint,
disfigurement, failing,
defacement, defect,
imperfection, mar, sully,
damage, deform, tarnish,
(improvement, ornament,
perfection)
blend-v compound,
combine, mix, fuse,
amalgamate, cross,
merge, interbreed, union,
synthesis, unite,
consolidate, (analysis,
dissection, decompose,
resolve)

blessing-*n* approbation, boon, Godsend, benefit, benediction, approval, sanction, advocacy, esteem, (dislike, censure, object, disapprove)

blight-*n* rot, corruption, decay, impairment, foil, blast, thwart, deterioration, recession, decrease, degenerate, (improvement, mend, elevation, build)

blind-*adj* sightless, unseeing, inattentive, shade, screen, artifice, ruse, pretext, ambush, subterfuge, (luminary, light, flame, see, sight, candle)

bloat-*v* puff up, swell, expand, dilate, distend, increase, extend, spread, obesity, inflation, larger, (reduction, lessening, shrinking, collapse)

block-*n* street, terrace, row, lump, mass, hinder, impede, check, obstruct, prevent, preclude, hindrance, stricture, (support, lift, advance, favor, rescue)

bloom-*n* prosper, blossom, flower, glow, flourish, thrive, be in health, prosperity, welfare, affluence, luck, (adversity, failure, mishap, rot, disaster)

bluff-*v* brusque, abrupt, ungracious, unceremonious, bank, cliff, headland, brag, hoax, mislead, (lowness, below,

debased, down)

blusterer-*n* braggart, boaster, blower, bluffer, ranter, braggadocio, fanatic, dogmatist, swagger, bully, terrorist

bodily-*adj* material, physical, corporeal, substantial, entirely, completely, wholly, en masse, (immaterial, spiritual, unearthly)

bogus-*adj* sham, fake, false, counterfeit, spurious, fraudulent, pretended, deception, untruth, deceit, trick, cheat, (veracity, truth, sincerity, honesty)

bold-*adj* daring, intrepid, courageous, fearless, forward, dauntless, project, prominence, protrude, (depress, hollow, concave, vaulted)

border-*n* boundary, brim, rim, margin, frontier, edge, verge, brink, flange, side, lip, threshold, portal, fringe, (enclosure, wrapper, barrier)

bore-*v* pierce, drill, cloy, annoy, diameter, caliber, dullard, pest, hole, puncture, perforation, passage, canal, (close, blockade, plug, stop)

bottomless-*adj* unending, abysmal, unfathomable, depth, depression, shaft, well, crater, deepen, buried, (shallowness, shoals, superficial)

bound-*adj* spring, vault,

jump, confine,
circumscribe, limit,
restrain, swiftness, spurt,
rush, dash, race, lively,
gallop, (slowness,
creeping, loiterer, retire)

bounty-*n* subsidy, grant,
generosity, liberality,
munificence, benevolence,
giving, donation,
consignment, charity,
(receiving, acquire,
assignee)

braid-*v* plait, interweave,
interlace, intertwine,
joining, union, unite, bind,
attach, fix, splice, truss,
tether, (disjoin, disconnect,
disengage, separate)

branch-*n* wing, arm,
member, ramification,
offshoot, limb, bough, twig,
fork, divide, bifurcate,
diverge, radiate

brand-*n* stamp, stain, sort,
kind, grade, stigma,
firebrand, burning,
cauterization, ignite,
(cooling, refresh, congeal,
starve)

bravado-*n* boasting, bluster,
vaunting, braggadocio,
flourish, bombast, brag,
resonance, exult, crow

breadth-*n* broadness, width,
expanse, amplitude,
spaciousness, tread, span,
reach, bore, caliber,
thickness

break-*v* fracture, shatter,
sever, rend, violate, tame,
transgress, infringe,
subdue, interruption,

interval, gap, (adjoin,
touch, contact, adhere,
coincide)

breathe-*v* inhale, respire,
live, exist, divulge, utter,
whisper, disclose, puff,
blow, dust, blast, breeze,
gale, blowing, fanning

brevity-*n* briefness,
shortness, succinctness,
terseness, conciseness,
little, curtail, abridge, curt,
compact, stubby, (long,
length, span, elongate)

bribe-*n* graft, price,
allurement, seduction,
hush-money, recompense,
fee, corrupt, suborn, tempt

brigand-*n* thief, bandit,
thug, robber, highwayman,
freebooter, filcher,
buccaneer, swindler,
forger, fence

bright-*adj* vivid, intense,
deep, intelligent, apt,
clever, lustrous, radiant,
luminous, flashing,
glistening, glowing, brilliant

brisk-*adj* alert, lively, swift,
quick, nimble, velocity, fly,
gallop, vanish, brief, quick,
sudden, short, spasmodic,
cursory, (long, eternity,
persistence)

bristling-*adj* sullen, angry,
perverse, thorny, spiny,
spiked, sharpness, barbed,
horned, nib, tooth, (dull,
bluntness, obtuse, bluff)

brittleness-*n* frailness,
fragility, delicateness,
splintery, crack, snap, split,
splinter, crumble,

(toughness, strength,
tenacious, resisting)
broadcast-v diffuse, scatter,
disseminate, utter, spread,
disperse, sow, dispense,
disband, dispel,
(assemblage, collection,
levy, gathering)
broken-v shattered, divided,
disconnected, docile,
infirm, gentle,
domesticated, weakness,
languor, fragility, (strength,
power, energy, vigor)
bubble-n sparkle, gurgle,
effervescent, foam, boil,
nothingness, zero, never,
unsubstantial, burp,
(substantial, article,
something, substance)
buckle-n twist, bend, warp,
fastening, fastener, clasp,
link, junction, union, unite,
bond, bridge, braid, hook,
girdle, (disjoin, disconnect,
divorce, cut)
buffoon-n pantomimist,
fool, jester, clown,
mummer, comedian,
humorist, wag, wit, dandy,
joker, charlatan, mime
bulk-n amount, volume,
measure, largeness, mass,
expanse, greater part,
whole, integrity,
collectiveness, lump,
(division, segment,
fragment, piece)
bulletin-n statement, report,
journal, news, information,
word, advice, dispatch,
publicity, notice, (secret,
mystery, riddle,

conundrum)
bully-n brawler, tyrant,
roisterer, swaggerer,
threaten, bluster,
domineer, browbeat,
combatant, litigant,
competitor, rival,
(submissive, surrender,
resignation)
bulwark-n rampart, barrier,
fortification, safeguard,
defense, protection, guard,
shield, self defense, ditch,
dike, (attack, assault,
charge, thrust)
bungler-n muddler, lout,
blunderer, fumbler, clown,
duffer, novice, clod, lubber,
muff, swab, yokel,
greenhorn, (proficient,
master, veteran, soldier,
experienced)
buoyant-adj light, floating,
resilient, springy,
sanguine, foamy, rise,
hover, spire, soar, tower,
swim, surge, (descent, fall,
drop, downfall, tumble)
bureaucracy-n officialism,
red-tape, authority,
influence, power,
command, empire, sway,
(laxity, loose, freedom,
tolerate)
burglar-n bandit, robber,
housebreaker, thief, filcher,
swindler, forger, coiner,
fence, smuggler, wrecker
burlesque-n buffoonery,
farce, take-off, parody,
comedy, drollery,
ridiculous, ludicrous,
preposterous, monstrosity,

(formality, prudery, demureness, modesty)

burn-*v* sear, parch, char, destroy, blaze, flame, hot, swelter, boil, torrid, tropical, sultry, stifling, stuffy, suffocating, oppressive, (cold, cool, chill, frigid, inclement)

burrow-*n* tunnel, mine, dig, excavate, penetrate, rooted, inhabit, domesticate, moored, anchored, established, lodged, (displacement, banishment, removal, dislocate)

bushy-*adj* shaggy, hairy, clumpy, dense, jungle, prairie, grass, hedge, rush, week, foliage, growth, woody

business-*n* employment, occupation, undertaking, pursuit, avocations, financial activities, affair, concern, case, interest, (inaction, inactivity, leisure)

busy-*adj* occupied, active, engrossed, employed, engaged, industrious, diligent, officious, flurry, rustle, stir, perturbation, (idle, dawdle, mope, inactivity, relaxation)

buttress-*n* abutment, prop, truss, brace, support, aid, block, anvil, shore, jamb, beam, rafter, (suspend, hand, fast to, pensile, hanging)

buy-*v* procure, purchase, acquire, invest, shop,

market, buyer, vendee, patron, customer, client, pay, market, (sell, sale, dispose of, mortgage, auction)

bygone-*adj* old, former, departed, antiquated, obsolete, gone by, past, yore, away, latter, look back, ancestry, lapse

byword-*n* proverb, saying, object of scorn, nickname, pet expression, by-name

C

cab-*n* carriage, hansom, taxicab, hackney, hack, vehicle, conveyance, van, wagon, cart, coach, caravan, car

cabinet-*n* closet, room, repository, case, ministry, council, committee, chamber, board, bench

cackle-*v* chuckle, giggle, cluck, clack, gabble, chit-chat, small talk, babble, gossip, converse, tattle, verbal intercourse, (soliloquize, say, think aloud)

cage-*n* confine, restrain incarcerate, imprison, enclosure, receptacle, reservatory, compartment, hole, nook, stall

cajole-*v* coax, wheedle, deceive, delude, flatter, praise, soothe, humor, exaggerate, charm, (scandal, defamation, slander, derogate)

calamity-*n* catastrophe, disaster, affliction, casualty, adversity, failure, mishap, accident, trial, tribulation, reverse, (welfare, well being, luck, success)

calculate-*v* estimate, count, reckon, compute, numerate, numbering, enumeration, summation, poll, recite

calefaction-*n* torrefaction, heating, melting, warming, fusion, liquefaction, scarification, cremation, incineration, (cooling, refrigeration, liquefying)

calendar-*n* register, list, almanac, schedule, chronicle, clock, watch, hour glass

caliber-*n* bore, diameter, gauge, capacity, ability, power, force, dimension, bulk, magnitude, big, great, considerable, (smallness, dwarf, pygmy, minute)

call-*v* muster, assemble convene, convoke, elect, appoint, summon, invite, shout, yell, designate, signal, invitation, offer, visit, urge, impulse

calling-*n* vocation, outcry, profession, notice, business, occupation, employment, pursuit

callous-*adj* stiff, unfeeling, hardened, obdurate, insensibility, unfeeling, senseless, thick-skinned, dull, numb, dead, (sensible, moral, cultivate, impress)

calm-*adj* placid, serene, impassive, peaceful, composed, tranquil, quiet, rest, still, stagnation, silence, (motion, volatile, restless, mobility, shift)

camouflage-*n* screen, cloak, disguise, concealment

camp-*n* shack, encampment, quarters, tent, locate, encamp, lodge, abode, dwelling, lodging, domicile, nest, (settler, squatter, indigent)

cancel-*v* abolish, repeal, delete, revoke, overrule, abrogation, annulment, stop, disclaim, dismiss, discard, (initiate, commission, start, delegate, consign)

candid-*adj* unaffected, frank, artless, sincere, blunt, outspoken, veracity, sincerity, candor, honesty, fidelity, truthful, (falsify, deception, untruth, lying)

cannibal-*n* anthropophagite, savage, man-eater, brute, ruffian, terrorist, desperado, bully, dangerous, (benefactor, good savior, saint)

canon-*n* law, charge, code, rule, precept, courage, bravery, valor, boldness, gallantry, rashness, confidence, (cowardice, timidity, cower, week-minded)

canopy-*n* tester, awning, overhanging, shelter, dome, vault, sky, cover, tent, umbrella, parasol, sun-shade, envelope

canvas-*n* tent, sailcloth, tarpaulin, painting, picture, covering, gather way, spread sail

canvass-*v* solicit, seek, examine, discuss, request, address, overture, asking, begging, invite, beseech, plead, (depreciate, mediation, protest, intercessory)

cap-*n* headpiece, headdress, skullcap, barrette, fez, completion, achieve, fulfillment, execution, finish, attain, reach, (shortcoming, incomplete)

capital-*n* admirable, first-class, excellent, primary, principal, resources, assets, riches, opulence

caprice-*n* humor, notion, fancy, quip, conceit, whim, (permanence, stability)

captious-*adj* fault-finding, hypercritical, carping, sophistical, specious, moodiness, obstinacy, sulk, frown, pout, (endearment, caring, salute, fondle)

captivate-*v* delight, charm, fascinate, enchant, pleasant, pleasurable, agreeable, enrapture, indulge, beatify, (painful, infliction, annoyance, grievance)

capture-*v* apprehend, seize, catch, arrest, secure, taking, hook, nab, bag, receive, accept, distraint, (return, release, replevin, restore)

career-*n* progress, course, path, passage, success, occupation, business, employment, pursuit, undertake, serve

careless-*adj* nonchalant, heedless, easy-going, negligent, thoughtless, reckless, impulsive, indiscreet

caress-*n* fondle, hug, pet, embrace, clasp, cling-to, endearment, kiss, smack, hug, cuddle, gallivant, ogle, sweet upon, (moodiness, sullen, sulky, ill-tempered)

caricature-*n* ridicule, parody, satirize, take-off, repetition, duplication, copy, simulate, mimic

carnage-*n* slaughter, bloodshed, massacre, butchery, killing, homicide, murder, assassination

carouse-*n* feast, debauch, make merry, revel, riot, diversion, reaction, relaxation, pleasure, fun, frolic, prank, (weary, stupid, dry, monotonous, dull)

carry-*v* bear, convey, uphold, sustain, support, purchase, stand, foundation, buttress, stanchion, main stay

cart-*n* wagon, pushcart, dray, tumbrel, vehicle, transport, displace, displant, unload, empty, transfer, vacate, (lodgement, stow, installation, localize)

carve-*v* quarter, slice, dissect, mold, hew, cut, disjunction, separation, parting, divorce, detach, divide, split, (join, unite, close, together)

castrate-*v* neuter, spay, geld, emasculate, purify, cleanliness, lavation, clear, purgative, (impurity, contamination)

casual-*adj* random, accidental, occasional, incidental, contingent, external, conditional, fortuitous

casualty-*n* misfortune, disaster, calamity, mishap, accident, event, adventure, crisis, emergency, contingency, consequence, (loom, await, impend)

cause-*v* birth, beginning, origin, prime, principle, producer, generator, creator, determinant, motive, root, basis, foundation

caustic-*adj* pungent, biting, burning, acrimonious, corroding, mordant, repulsive, discourteous, blunt, gruff, harsh, austere, (courtesy, politeness, compliment)

caution-*n* discretion, heed, circumspection, wariness, forethought, vigilance, watchfulness, admonition

cave-*n* grotto, den, cavern, lair, hole, abode, dwelling, domicile, lodging, nest, arbor, cell, retreat, roost

cavil-*v* quibble, haggle, carp, mangle, dissent, dislike, object, to, disvalue, outcry, (sanction, advocacy, esteem, repute)

cavity-*n* opening, hole, dent, depression, hollow, excavation, dip, scoop, excavate, tunnel, burrow, (projection, bulge, swell, nob)

cease-*v* discontinue, halt, end, stop, terminate, refrain, closure, desist, pause, rest, interrupt, suspend, cut, (start, continue, initiate, sustain, uphold)

cede-*v* surrender, give up, concede, yield, relinquish, submission, resignation, homage, succumb, submit, (combatant, belligerent, competitor)

celebration-*n* observance, commemoration, jubilation, ovation, triumph, inauguration, honor, installation, coronation

celestial-*adj* holy, unearthly, divine, beatific, Elysian, heavenly, solar, empyreal, starry, otherworldly

celibacy-*n* misogyny, purity,

singleness, bachelorhood, virginity, maidenhood, spinster, unmarried, (marriage, wedlock, union, mate)

censure-n faultfinding, hypercritical, carping, condemnatory, disesteem, dislike, disapprove, object to, frown, (approval, sanction, esteem, praise)

ceremonial-adj ritualistic, formal, pompous, solemn, display, show, parade, ostentatious, showy, grand, flashing

certainty-n sureness, certitude, assuredness, safety, inevitable, fact, infallibility, dogmatic, (unbelief, uncertainty)

cessation-n discontinuance, interruption, respite, intermission, interval, recess, impediment, halt, lull, suspension, truce

chafe-v vex, fret, gall, annoy, rub, warm, pain, suffering, twitch, soreness, crick, sharp, piercing, gnawing, (pleasure, sensual, comfort, luxury)

chaff-v refuse, husk, persiflage, raillery, ridicule, deride, travesty, mock, sarcastic, ironical, banter, rally

chagrin-n vexation, mortification, painfulness, anxiety, annoyance, irritation, worry, ordeal, trouble, fret, (happiness,

enjoyment, comfort, ease)

chance-n luck, fortune, unforeseen occurrence, fate, lot, destiny, fortuity, risk, gamble, uncertainty, jeopardy, happen, come, arrive, befall, turn up, (attribution, intention)

channel-n duct, waterway, conduit, canyon, chasm, aqueduct, canal, moat, ditch, water gate

chant-n melody, song, psalm, canticle, hymn, vespers, mass, prayer, service, vigils

chapter-n part, section, division, passage, branch, portion, segment, parcel, piece, detachment, verse, clause, (totality, collectiveness, completeness, bulk)

char-v parch, sear, burn, carbonize, scorch, boil, heat, fusion, inflame, roast, toast, cauterize, incinerate, (refrigerate, cool, fan, refresh)

charitable-adj unselfish, generous, liberal, kind, altruistic, donor, eleemosynary, gratis

charlatan-n fraud, cheat, impostor, impersonator, quack, deceiver, hypocrite, pretender, humbug

charm-n fascination, attractiveness, amulet, talisman, incantation, lure, draw, seduce, conjure, hypnotize

chasm-n pit, abyss, gap,

fissure, cleft, hole,
opening, orifice, passage,
channel, gully, mine,
gallery, (closure, blockade,
shut, obstruct)

chaste-*adj* unaffected,
classic, virtuous, undefiled,
simple, virginal, symmetry,
finish, uniform, balanced,
equal, regular, (distortion,
warped, irregular)

cheat-*v* swindle, defraud,
trick, beguile, dupe,
delude, deceive,
deception, falseness,
fraud, delusion, treachery,
(truthful, veracity,
frankness, honesty)

checkered-*adj* varied, plaid,
irregular, alternating,
uneven, barred, checked

cheer-*n* yell, shout, festivity,
hospitality, enliven, inspirit,
approval, sanction,
esteem, praise, applaud,
joyous

cheerless-*adj* dismal,
somber, gloomy,
depressing, sad, dreary,
despondent

cherish-*v* prize, treasure,
nurture, revere, love,
fondness, liking, affection,
feeling, tenderness, (hate,
alienation, coolness)

chew-*v* grind, eat, crunch,
masticate, gulp, gluttony,
feed, devour, swallow,
take, dispatch, munch,
gnaw, (discharge,
secretion, ejection)

chief-*n* first, principal,
foremost, supreme, main,
head, leader, commander,
important, paramount,
significant, (insignificant,
trivial, nothing, trash)

childish-*adj* simple-minded,
infantile, silly, weak,
credulous, puerile,
youthful, young, shallow,
foolish, (wisdom, intellect,
cunning, mature)

chivalrous-*adj* knightly,
brave, courteous, gallant,
war, tenure, courage,
honor, generosity

choke-*v* strangle, suffocate,
congest, clog, stifle,
obstruction, blockage,
closure, bolt, seal, clinch,
(opening, yawning)

chop-*v* cut, hack ,split, hew,
dissection, separation,
division, fracture, rupture,
crack, (attach, fix, affix,
join, union, unite)

chronic-*adj* unceasing,
survive, lasting, inveterate,
constant, eternity,
perpetuity, persistent,
standing, survival,
(transient, passing,
fleeting, flying)

chronicle-*n* registry, annals,
archives, account, epoch,
almanac, calendar, journal,
diary, pendulum,
(anticipation, disregard,
neglect)

cipher-*n* cryptogram, code,
monogram, cryptograph,
naught, zero, numeration,
pagination, recension,
summation, (catalog,
inventory, schedule, index)

circle-*n* globe, ring, orb, disk, circlet, encircle, circumnavigate, gird, circumscribe, surround, compass, inclose

circulate-*v* spread, report, pass, change hands, propagate, revolve, rotation, revolution, gyration, whir, whirl

circumference-*n* periphery, perimeter, circuit, girth, outline, perimeter, ambit, circuit, lines, contour, profile, zone, belt, (verge, brink, brow, side)

circumscription-*n* bound, limit, confinement, case, restriction, enclosure, restraint, envelope, (perimeter, zone, belt, girth, band)

circumstance-*n* situation, condition, environment, surroundings, position, time, place, occurrence, event, quandary, fix, predicament, dilemma

circumvent-*v* thwart, elude, frustrate, outwit, baffle, prevent, preclusion, interruption, hindrance, (assist, help, promotion, patronage)

cite-*v* arraign, summon, allege, quote, adduce, illustrate, bring forward, charge, imputation, accuse, taunt, (vindication, acquittal, apology, gloss, excuse)

civil-*adj* urbane, well-bred, mannerly, respectful, secular, courteous, behavior, breeding, gentility, (discourteous, ungainly manners, rude, insult)

civilize-*v* polish, refine, cultivate, humanize, breeding, good, polite, conform, admissible, (comical, ridiculous, absurdity, ludicrous)

claim-*v* requirement, plea, assert, contend, demand, require, deserve, title, pretense, prerogative, imposition, requisition

claimant-*n* accuser, heir, prosecutor, pretender, petitioner, solicitor, applicant, suitor, beggar, hunter

clamor-*n* outcry, uproar, racket, tumult, din, contention, agitation, cry, shout, roar, scream, cheer, hoot, holler

clamp-*n* fastener, clasp, brace, band, joining, union, connection, unite, attach, affix, (disconnection, disunion, division)

clan-*n* faction, breed, brotherhood, set, sort, family, association, paternity, parent, father, sire, lineage, pedigree

clash-*v* conflict, collide, dispute, contend, impact, collision, concussion, shock, disagreement, discord, dissidence, (concert, conformity, uniformity)

class-n category, division, section, grouping, caste, clique, coterie, order, sort, manner, nature, type, gender, designation

classification-n grouping, sorting, systematization, order, allocation, designate, group, tabulate, index, file, systematize, arrange

cleanness-n pureness, purity, clearness, neatness, immaculateness, purgation, purification, (impurity, dirty, unclean, decay, corruption)

clear-adj bright, unclouded, distinct, intelligible, open, patent, transparent, simpleness, purification, single, sheer, neat

cleft-adj fissure, break, gap, crack, crevice, dissection, forking, branching, divide, split, cloven, halve, (double, renewal, twin)

clever-adj dexterous, adroit, talented, able, gifted, intelligence, capacity, sagacity, discernment, (shallow, imbecility, incapacity)

climax-n zenith, pinnacle, acme, culmination, crest, supremacy, majority, excel, match, culminate, (minority, deficiency, smallness)

clinch-v confirm, close, end, fasten, secure,clench,

rivet, clamp, grapple, combination, mixture, junction, union, (analysis, dissection, decompose)

clique-n coterie, set, group, circle, crowd, party, faction, side, crew, ban, horde, posse, family, clan

clog-n hamper, impede, encumber, obstruct, investment, covering, attire, shoe, pump, boot, sandal, slipper, galoche

cloister-n abbey, convent, hermitage, monastery, restraint, hindrance, repression, confinement, duress, (liberation, emancipation, dismissal)

clown-n jester, rustic, buffoon, fool, boor, humorist, wag, wit, punster, joker, mime, gypsy

club-n stick, cudgel, resort, fraternity, association, rendezvous, party, faction, side, crew, band, horde

clumsy-adj awkward, stupid, unwieldy, bungling, incompetent, unskilled, unfitness, inexpedient, undesirable, inadvisable, (opportunism, graceful, expedient)

clutch-v seize, clench, collar, grip, keep, retain, grasp, hold, secure, retentive, inalienable, (release, abandon, dereliction, dispensation)

coagulate-v thicken, clot, congeal, curdle, density,

solidity, constipation,
cohesion, cake, crystallize,
(sponginess, rarefactive,
expansion)

coarse-*adj* homespun,
rough, uncouth,
unpolished, crude, rude,
vulgar, discord, burr,
jangle, creaking, gruff,
(refined, cultivated, tact,
delicate, good taste,
finesse, discriminate)

coax-*v* entice, cajole,
persuade, wheedle,
motive, intention,
inducement, move, draw,
inspire, (dissuade, against,
warn, indispose)

coerce-*v* make, impel,
force, compel, coaction,
duress, enforcement,
conscription, drive,
constrain, (compelling,
coactive)

cogent-*adj* forcible, strong,
potent, convincing, power,
might, force, energy,
capable, valid, adequate,
almighty, (powerless,
incapable, disabled)

cogitate-*v* muse, ponder,
consider, meditate,
thought, reflection,
consideration, speculation,
consultation, (vacancy,
fatuity, dismiss,
thoughtlessness
unoccupied)

cognizant-*adj* conscious,
sensible, observant,
aware, knowledge, insight,
familiarity, leaning,
reading, doctrine,

(ignorance, blindness)

coherence-*n* adherence,
aggregation, accretion,
congruity, connection,
consistency, harmony,
conformity, viscidity

cold-*adj* chilliness, chill,
coolness, iciness, gelidity,
frigid, biting, piercing,
nipping, raw, wintry,
anguish, arctic

colleague-*n* ally, partner,
associate, companion,
mate, helper, hand, friend,
cooperator, pal,
accomplice, (opponent,
antagonist, adversary)

collect-*v* amass, compile,
demand, exact, meet,
throng, flock, assemble,
ligation, gather,
compilation, conclave,
(dispersion, disjunction,
divergency)

collide-*v* crash, meet,
bump, conflict, clash,
impulse, impetus,
momentum, push, thrust,
shove, throw, explode,
(recoil, rebound, revulsion,
retract)

collision-*n* skirmish,
encounter, conflict,
interference, shock,
impact, discord,
resistance, antagonistic,
oppose, (concur, conspire,
tribute, agree, consent)

colloquial-*adj*
conversational, informal,
chatty, metaphor, figure of
speech, phrase, analogy,
irony, personification

colonize-v establish, settle, found, people, place, situate, locate, localize, make a place for, plantation, camp, (displaced, misplaced, exile, removal)

combination-n aggregation, union, mixture, composite, coadunation, synthesis, inosculation, (disjunction, decomposition)

command-v regulation, order, ordinance, act, bidding, direction, injunction, commandment, ruling, instructions, dispatch, message, (lowness, debasement, depression)

commence-v begin, start, enter upon, outset, inception, genesis, birth, originate, conceive, source, dawn, embarkation, initiate, (end, close, terminate, conclude)

commend-v recommend, praise, acclaim, approve, approbation, applause, clap, esteem, sanction, admiration, appreciate, (dislike, insinuation, ostracism)

comment-n observation, remark, criticism, annotation, interpretation, argument, controversy, debate, reasoning, (mystify, evasion, intuition, instinct)

commission-n warrant, charge, instruction, authorization, mandate, brevet, permit, delegation, consignment, nomination, charter, installation, investiture, accession, (annulment, prohibition)

commit-v perpetrate, consign, intrust, perform, action, doing, performance, exercise, citation, execute, achieve, (inaction, abstinence, passive)

common-adj conventional, usual, prevalent, current, customary, regular, vulgar, ill-bred, general, universal, (special, designate, realize, determine)

commonplace-adj tedious, prosy, monotonous, ordinary, usual, unimportant, worthless, paltry, (important, prominence, significant, concern)

commotion-n disturbance, tumult, turmoil, disorder, agitation, stir, tremor, shake, ripple, jog, jolt, jar, (oscillation, vibration, liberation)

communion-n intercourse, converse, partnership, association, talk, participation, possession, partaking, (possessor, holder, occupant)

compact-n deal, contract, understanding, bargain, engagement, agreement, stipulation, covenant, terse, condensed, thick, constricted, compressed, dense, (contention, disagreement)

companion-*n* partner, chum, colleague, associate, accompany, coexist, attend, synchronize, (alone, isolate, disjoin, one, sole, solitary)

company-*n* association, partnership, group, crowd, cast, syndicate, firm, companionship, assemblage, (dispersion, disjunction, divergence)

compartment-*n* niche, enclosure, division, part, portion, item, segment, fragment, (collectiveness, completeness, bulk, mass)

compassion-*n* condolence, sympathy, tenderness, mercy, pity, commiseration, fellow-feeling, yearning, forbearance, (inclemency, severity, malevolence)

compatible-*adj* harmonious, congruous, suitable, consistent, agreeable, concert, conformity, uniformity, (discord, dissidence, variance, unfitness)

compel-*v* constrain, force, coerce, impel, drive, compulsion, make, press, coactive, oblige, necessitate

compendium-*n* epitome, bulletin, review, brief, analysis, recapitulation, summary, excerpt, note, abstract, digest, (dissertation, theme, discourse)

compensation-*n* repayment, payment, requital, pay, remuneration, reward, honorarium, solatium, mediocrity, generality, compromise

competence-*n* proficiency, ability, capability, sufficiency, means, rich, luxuriant, affluent, wealthy, abundant, (insufficient, meager, shortcoming, small, scarce)

competent-*adj* capable, fit, qualified, efficient

competitor-*n* contestant, rival, entrant, aspirant, claimant, antagonist, adversary, opposition, disputant, enemy, (helper, adjunct, friend, ally, confidant)

compile-*v* arrange, amass, collect, make, write, assemblage, group, cluster, clump, accumulation, heap, pile, (unassembled, dispersed, sparse)

completion-*n* attainment, achievement, execution, fulfillment, performance, accomplishment, conclusion

complex-*adj* complicated, intricate, involved, confused, confusion, disarray, uproar, riot,

rumpus, jumble, huddle,
(orderly, regular, neat, tidy)

complexity-*n*
entanglement, intricacy,
complication, perplexity,
compositeness

compliance-*n* assent,
agree, acquiesce, submit,
obey, conformity, normal,
typical, formal, (abnormal,
unusual, eccentric)

complicity-*n* connivance,
conspiracy, collusion,
confederacy, cooperate,
concur, combine,
understand, unite,
(opposition, antagonism,
counteract, against)

component-*n* integral part,
constituent, ingredient,
member, subdivision,
radical, intrinsic, inherent,
immanent, subsistent,
essential, inwrought,
innate, inbred,
(extraneousness, whole)

compose-*v* make up, form,
construct, fashion,
constitute, assuage, calm,
improvise, create,
reception, (exclusion,
omission, reject)

composed-*adj* serene,
calm, unruffled, tranquil,
collected, unexcitable

composition-*n*
compounding, constitution,
formation, construction,
blend, mixture, texture,
nature

comprehend-*v* conceive,
grasp, understand,
comprise, aware,

cognizant, conscious,
acquainted, (shallow,
unknown, superficial, half-
learned)

comprehensive-*adj*
widespread, synoptic,
inclusive, extensive,
wholesale, full

compress-*v* condense,
reduce, abridge, thicken,
squeeze, compact,
contract, reduction,
lessening, shrinking,
(extension, spread,
obesity)

comprise-*v* embrace,
embody, contain,
comprehend, include,
admission, inclusion,
enclose, receive

compromise-*n* settlement,
arrangement, adjustment,
agreement, composition,
commute, compound,
arrange, imperil, hazard,
jeopardize

compute-*v* reckon, count,
estimate, evaluate, record,
note, memorandum,
archive, scroll, register,
(obliterate, cancel, scratch,
erase, strike out)

concavity-*n* hollow, dip,
depression, cavity, antrum,
trough, furrow, depression,
dip, hollow, (rejection,
swelling, bulge, protrusion)

concealment-*n*
masquerade, secretion,
latency, cover, disguise,
mask, camouflage, screen,
veil, shroud, shelter,
secrecy, privacy, secret

concede-*v* assent, yield, acknowledge, surrender, cede, confess, grant, admittance, ratification, acquiesce, (dissent, discordance, disagreement, discontent)

conceit-*n* egoism, epigram, quip, whim, fancy, pride, vanity, complacency, glorification, airs, self-satisfied, (modesty, humility, blushing, reserve, constraint)

conceive-*v* visualize, fancy, devise, realize, grasp, comprehend, form, produce, become pregnant

concentrate-*v* gather, collect, converge, focus center, fix, assemble, core, nucleus, heart, centralize

concession-*n* permission, acknowledgement, admission, reduction, allowance, grant, gift

conciliate-*v* propitiate, reconcile, satisfy, disarm, placate, mollify, reason, call, inducement, consideration, (dissuade, remonstrate, warn, against, repel)

conciseness-*n* succinctness, brevity, terseness, abridgment, laconicism, condensation, compression

conclude-*v* arrange, finish, settle, terminate, infer, end, deduce, resolve

conclusive - *adj* unanswerable, convincing, indisputable, final, concluding, deduce

concoct-*v* make, hatch, invent, contrive, prepare, falsehood, untruth, lying, perjury, misrepresentation, forgery, (veracity, sincerity, candor, truthful)

concord-*n* accord, symphony, agreement, harmony, consonance, unison, correspondence, amity, congruence, unanimity, alliance, conciliation

concrete-*adj* solid, definite, substantial, hard, exact, specific, adherence, together, aggregation, consolidation, tenacious, (non-adhesion, loose, relaxation)

condescend-*v* descend, deign, vouchsafe, stoop, humility, meek, submission, resignation, (dignified, stately, proud)

condiment-*n* seasoning, sauce, flavoring, relish, salt, mustard, pepper, spice, relish

condition-*n* stipulation, modification, proviso, situation, plight, fitness, assumption, postulate

condolence-*n* pity, sympathy, commiseration, compassion, consolation, comfort

conduct-*v* deportment, guise, behavior, carriage, comportment, demeanor, operate, work, manage, govern, regulate, supervise

confederate-*n* associate,
ally, accomplice,
companion, transient,
passing, evanescent,
fleeting, flying

confer-*v* deliberate, consult,
discuss, converse, bestow,
advise, consul, suggestion,
prompt, recommend

confere-*n* consultation,
interview, meeting, parley

confess-*v* acknowledge,
admit, divulge, reveal,
disclose, assent, accept,
accede, concur, (dissent,
demur, disagree, protest)

confident-*adj* certainty,
trust, self-reliance, spirit,
assurance, expectant,
sure, hopeful, optimistic,
self-sufficient, candid,
open, unsuspecting,
gullible

confine-*v* restrain,
imprison, incarcerate,
cage, bound, enclosure,
limit, inclose, surround,
imprisoned, buried

confirm-*v* endorse, uphold,
corroborate, substantiate,
warrant, vouch, certificate,
facts, record, docket,
(disprove, other side,
oppose)

confiscate-*v* sequestrate,
seize, appropriate, taking,
capture, appropriation,
catch, nab, (return, restore,
redeem)

conflict-*n* battle, combat,
encounter, discord,
dissension, antagonism,

opposition, counteract,
antagonize, (cooperate,
concur, combine)

conformity-*n* agreement,
accord, harmony,
resemblance, congruity,
compliance, observance,
acquiescence, concession,
submission, consent

confound-*v* confuse,
jumble, overthrow, perplex,
bewilder, wonder, marvel,
astonish, admire, (expect,
foreseen, common)

confront-*v* brave, defy,
front, resist, fore, face,
outpost, pioneer, advance,
(rear, guard, stern, behind,
after)

confuse-*v* muddle, disturb,
disconcert, fluster,
bewilder, mistake,
deranged, mislay, disorder,
unsettle, (arrange,
preparation)

confusion-*n*
embarrassment,
discomfiture, tumult,
turmoil, jumble, (dispose,
place, pack, file)

confutation-*n* disproval,
disproof, refutation, refutal,
invalidation, retort, answer,
(demonstrate, prove,
establish)

congeal-*v* thicken, set,
condense, coagulate,
stiffen, harden, density,
solidness, mass, cake,
(thin, fine, tenuous, rarefy)

congenial-*adj* sympathetic,
harmonious, adapted,
compatible, agreement,

accord, adapt, fitness, harmonize, (disagree, hostile, repugnant)

congratulation-n best wishes, felicitation, compliment, gratulation, condolence

congregation-n aggregation, gathering, fold, flock, brethren, assemblage, collection, muster, (dispersed, broadcast, sprinkle)

congress-n parliament, convention, legislature, assembly, council, committee, court, chamber, board, staff

conjecture-n speculation, inference, surmise, supposition, assumption, postulation, condition

conjugate-v coupled, mated, united, bijugate, paronymous, verbal, literal, derivation, root, (corruption, slang, cant)

connect-v attach, unite, link, associate, correlate, relation, reference, correlation, similarity, (disconnection, remote, irrelevant)

conquer-v vanquish, subdue, defeat, overcome, prevail, success, advance, conquest, victory, (fail, repulse, rebuff, defeat, overthrow, slip)

consanguinity-n kindred, relationship, parentage, paternity, connection, propinquity, alliance,

affiliation, affinity

conscientious-adj scrupulous, painstaking, exact, faithful, trusty, upright, duty, obligation, liability, (relaxation, failure, evasion)

conscious-adj understanding, aware, keen, sensible, cognizant, senses, observation, intuition, judgment, (imbecility, brutality, without reason)

conscription-n impressment, compulsory enlistment, draft, compel, force, make, drive, coerce

consecrate-v hallow, devote, dedicate, apply, utilization, work, yield, manipulate, (disuse, abstain, spare, neglect)

consent-v compliance, assent, acquiescence, concurrence, agreement, concession, permission, permit, accession, acknowledgment, (dissent, refusal)

consequence-n proceeding, outcome, result, decision, termination, settlement, prominence, self-importance

consequential-adj sequential, deducible, derivable, inferable, secondary, supercilious, resultant

consider-v regard, notice, heed, believe, adjudge,

deliberate, reflect, ponder, (vacancy, thoughtless, absent)

considerable-*adj* extraordinary, intense, notable, weighty, big, massive, substantial

consideration-*n* regard, observation, notice, kindliness, consequence, inducement, deference, esteem, perquisite

consign-*v* delegate, assign, commit, authorize, send, deliver, dispatch, ship, allotment, assignment, charge, task, apportionment

consistent-*adj* compatible, harmonious,conformable, homogeneous, accordant, agreement, accommodate, conventional, (abnormity, infringement, irregular)

consolation-*n* comfort, solace, assuagement, sympathy, encouragement, relief, softening, alleviation, restorative, (aggravated, exasperation, embitter)

consolidate-*v* incorporate, federate, merge, solidify, compact, coherence, adhere, holdfast, tenacity, (looseness, relaxation, freedom, disjunction)

consonance-*n* accordance, tunefulness, concord, harmony, accord

conspicuous-*adj* prominent, famous, renowned, eminent, notable, obvious, glaring,

salient, (invisible, concealment, obscure)

conspirator-*n* plotter, accomplice, confederate, traitor, combine, scheme, concur, intrigue, plot

constant-*adj* incessant, unflagging, continual, steadfast, stanch, loyal, agree, uniform, level, smooth, (diversify, varied, uneven)

constitute-*v* establish, set up, found, appoint, form, frame, compose, (exclusion, rejection, omission, separate)

constitution-*n* structure, construction, state, condition, code, law, charter, temperament, disposition, nature

constraint-*n* necessity, coercion, repression, unnaturalness, bind, contract, squeeze, compress

construction-*n* formation, structure, build, explanation, translation, erection, creation

consultation-*n* interview, deliberation, conference, council

consume-*v* annihilate, burn, demolish, devour, use up, exhaust, drain, expend, destruction, ruin, downfall, (fabricate, produce, performance, achievement)

consummate-*v* unmitigated, sheer,

perfect, finished, profound, intense, complete, fill, replenish, (deficiency, wanting, defective)

contact-*n* meeting, union, conjunction, adhesion, contiguity, proximity, apposition, abutment, touch, adhere, attach, append, adjoin, (interval, distance)

contagion-*n* pestilence, epidemic, transmission, virus, communication, poisonousness, toxicity

contagious-*adj* transmittable, communicable, catching,

contain-*v* comprise, embody, include, incorporate, hold, portion, segment, fragment, parcel

container-*n* vessel, utensil, vase, jar, bag, bottle

contaminate-*v* pollute, taint, corrupt, foul, defile, uncleanliness, impurity, decay, filth, dregs, (clean, launder, wipe, mop, disinfect)

contemplate-*v* consider, design, ponder, purpose, reflect, muse, view, sight, glimpse, behold, discover, (blindness, undiscerning)

contempt-*n* scorn, disdain, detestation, abhorrence, despise, disrepute, insignificant, immaterial, trivial, (important, prominence, concern, superior)

contemptuous-*adj*

derision, mockery, sneer, spurn, abhor, underestimate (respect, reverence)

contend-*v* hold, maintain, allege, strive, struggle, debate, dispute, reasoning, argument, proposition, (chicane, mystification)

content-*n* real meaning, significance, intent, implication, substance, essence, gist, volume, extent

contention-*n* altercation, struggle, strife, feud, contest, litigation, disagreement, debate, dispute, belligerency

contents-*n* constituents, ingredients, cargo, filling, matter

contingency-*n* prospect, likelihood, situation, case, predicament, incidental, casual, provisional, conditional, accidental

continual-*adj* incessant, repeated, constant, unceasing, perpetuity

continuance-*n* pursuance, maintenance, extension, permanence, duration, perpetuation, stay

contortion-*n* deformation, twist, distortion, crookedness, warp, irregular, unsymmetrical, misshapen, ill-proportioned, stumpy, (symmetrical, shapely, regular, uniform)

contour-*n* form, outline,

shape, figure,
circumference, parameter,
zone, belt

contraband-*n* forbidden,
illegal, smuggled, illicit,
deception, deceit, juggle,
cheat, hoax, decoy, waylay

contract-*n* arrangement,
bargain, compact, promise,
guarantee, promissory,
pledged, (release,
absolute, unconditional)

contradict-*v* deny, dissent,
refute, disprove, gainsay,
(identical, equivalent, the
same)

contrariety-*n* antagonism,
opposition, repugnance,
clashing, disagreement,
antipathy, discrepancy,
inconsistency, contrast

contrary-*adj* opposed,
adverse, opposite,
antagonistic, hostile,
perverse

contrast-*v* dissimilarity,
unlikeness, disparity,
antithesis, foil

contribute-*v* conduce, tend,
advance, subscribe,
donate, giving,
consignment, charity,
generosity, (acquisition,
acceptance, admission)

contrivance-*n* gear, device,
apparatus, scheme, trick,
stratagem

control-*v* dominion, power,
sway, direction, regulation,
might, force, energy,
pressure, strength, ability,
(disability, helplessness)

controversy-*n* dispute,

argument, debate, quarrel,
altercation, contention,
reasoning, discussion,
comment, (evasion,
quibble, pervert, mystify)

conundrum-*n* puzzle,
riddle, enigma, secret,
maze, profound, labyrinth,
paradox, (information,
intelligence, advice, report)

convalesce-*v* recover,
rally, improve, revive,
restoration, renovation,
resume, cure, heal,
remedy, (relapse,
retrogradation, return)

convenient-*adj* serviceable,
suitable, opportune,
advantageous, adaptable,
expedient, eligible, seemly,
becoming, (unfit,
undesirable)

convention-*n* caucus,
meeting, council,
assembly, usage, custom,
practice

conventional-*adj* habitual,
customary, formal, usual,
common, general, familiar,
regular, vernacular,
(infraction, disuse, violate,
infringe)

convergence-*n* confluence,
concurrence,
concentration, concourse,
focalization, meeting,
assemblage

conversion-*n*
transmutation, change,
transformation,
metamorphosis, growth,
regeneration, assimilation

convey-*v* transport, carry,

bear, grant, cede, will,
transfer, deportation,
carriage, delegate, consign

convict-v find guilty, doom,
prisoner, captive, criminal,
rascal, scoundrel, villain,
ruffian, jail-bird, (good
man, hero, angel, saint)

conviction-v view, opinion,
sentence, penalty, belief,
credence, faith, assume,
esteem, (unbelieving,
doubtful, misgiving)

convince-v satisfy, assure,
convert, persuade, belief,
faith, confidence, reliance,
certainty, (doubtful, fallible,
suspicious)

convoke-v collect, muster,
gather, convene, summon,
assemblage, crowd,
throng, mob, hoard,
(disperse, scatter, diffuse)

convoy-v escort, attend,
conduct, guard, watch,
support, accompany,
custody, safety, security,
surety, (insecurity,
jeopardy, risk, hazard)

convulse-v stir, shake,
disturb, rend, wring, pain,
suffering, aching, spasm,
piercing, sharp, (pleasure,
sensual, comfort, luxury)

cool-adj wary, unfriendly,
self-possessed, chilly,
lukewarm, easygoing,
placid, compose, calm,
freeze, chill, harden

cooperation-n combination,
joint operation, union,
participation, concert,
collaboration

coordinate-n organize,
adjust, harmonize,
arrange, preparation,
assortment, allotment,
catalog, tabulate,
(dislocate, disarrange,
break up)

copious-adj plentiful, full,
abundant, profuse, ample,
sufficiency, adequacy,
enough, fullness,
(incompetence, deficiency,
poverty)

copy-n counterpart, effigy,
facsimile, likeness,
similitude, semblance,
imitation, model,
representation, study

cord-n string, twine, rope,
bond, tie, fastening,
shackle, rein, rivet,
padlock, anchor

cordial-adj hearty, friendly,
genial, warm, sincere,
pleasure, sensual, comfort,
luxury, enjoy, (torment,
anguish, agony)

core-n nucleus, kernel,
heart, gist, pith, substance,
center, middle, axis,
concentric

corner-n niche, nook,
monopolize, control, spot,
point, premises, place,
pigeon hole, compartment

corpse-n carcass, dead
body, skeleton, remains,
cadaver, carrion, bones,
relic, mummy, fossil

corpulence-n fleshiness,
portliness, obesity, fatness,
bulk, greatness, expanse,
large, big, ample, (small,

pygmy, minute,
undersized)

correct-*v* reprove, punish,
chastise, remedy, mend,
discipline, rectify, repair,
set right, strict, accurate,
true, perfect, unerring

correlation-*n* reciprocity,
interdependence,
mutuality, correspondence,
comparison, relative,
cognate, (irrelative,
irrespective, arbitrary)

correspondence-*n* letters,
writings, epistle, news,
dispatch, bulletin,
accordance, agreement

corrigible-*adj* tractable,
amenable, submissive,
docile, improvement,
better, increase, ripen,
mature, (worse,
deteriorate, degenerate)

corrode-*v* rust, decay,
wear, waste, deteriorate,
(improve, elaborate,
promote, cultivate,
advance)

corrupt-*adj* base,
dishonest, tainted, rotten,
spoiled, profligate,
dissolute, immoral, infect,
taint, pervert, debase

cosmic-*adj* otherworldly,
heavenly, terrestrial,
universal

cost-*n* expense, charge,
outlay, disbursement,
expenditure, expensive,
dear, high-priced,
(discount, reduction,
allowance, rebate)

council-*n* committee, court,
chapter, chamber, board,
directorate, syndicate,
cabinet, staff, parliament,
(precept, direction, charge)

count-*v* estimate, consider,
figure, reckon, compute,
enumerate, numbering,
calculation, recite

countenance-*n* expression,
aspect, visage, features,
patronage, favor, front,
foreground, advance,
(behind, rear, stern, rum)

counterfeit-*v* fictitious,
bogus, spurious, fake,
imitation, false, copy,
duplication, mirror,
reproduce, (original,
unimitated)

counterpart-*n* duplicate,
complement, facsimile,
replica, match, mate,
similarity, likeness, affinity

counterpoise-*n* balance,
counterweight, equipoise,
counterbalance, ballast,
indemnity, equivalent,
bribe

countersign-*v* watchword,
authentication, seal,
password, identification,
secondary evidence,
corroboration, (unattested,
unauthenticated)

countless-*adj* innumerable,
incalculable, numberless,
illimitable, infinite,
immense, immeasurable

country-*n* nation, state,
power, home, territory,
district, rural regions, field,
meadow, garden,
ornamental

couple-_n_ join, pair, yoke, link, tie, mate, firm, fast, taut, taught, secure, set, intervolved, (sunder, divide, disjoin, dissect, cut up, carve)

courage-_n_ bravery, valor, fearlessness, heart, resoluteness, daring, spirit, boldness, dash, gallantry, heroism, mettle, nerve, grit, fortitude, resolution

courier-_n_ messenger, runner, traveler, envoy, emissary, reporter, informer, correspondent

course-_n_ procedure, path, behavior, succession, channel, drift, trend, progress, flight, routine, (await, loom, predestine, doom)

court-_n_ palace, castle, staff, retinue, train, bar, session, bench, make love, woo, cajole, invite, solicit, praise, (forbearance, refraining, avoidance, evasion, elusion)

courtesy-_n_ politeness, refinement, cultivation, gentility, urbanity, culture, elegance, civility, polish, (discourtesy, repulsive, disrespect, impudent)

courtship-_n_ suit, courting, wooing, flirtation, endearment, caress, fondling, embrace, salute, kiss, amorous, (glum, morose, frumpish, surly)

cove-_n_ inlet, bay, harbor, lagoon, gulf, concavity, depression, dip, hollow, indentation, cavity, dent, pit, basin, (convexity, prominence, projection, swelling)

covenant-_n_ agreement, pact, compact, bargain, agree, stipulate, undertake, observe, comply, perform, (fail, neglect, omit, elude, evade, ignore, infringe)

covering-_n_ screen, shield, shelter, protection, carapace, concealment, seclusion, hide, mystification, (uncover, inform, enlighten, open)

covet-_v_ want, crave, envy, long for, desire, wish, greedy, hunger, hanker, solicitude, anxiety, yearning, aspiration, (cold, frigid, lukewarm, careless, listless)

cowardice-_n_ graveness, pusillanimity, timidity, timorousness, baseness, effeminacy, abject fear, faintheartedness

cower-_v_ shrink, crouch, quail, fawn, grovel, fear, timidity, diffidence, apprehensive, solicitude, anxiety, misgiving, (trust, confidence, reliance, faith)

coy-_adj_ demure, retiring, shrinking, shy, tremble, shake, shudder, nervous, restless, despondent, (hope, trust, aggressive, outspoken, forward)

crabbed-_adj_ tempered,

surly, cross, perverse,
peevish, illegible, intricate,
squeezed

crack-v burst, break split,
seam, rut, cleft, rip, fissure,
sunder, divide, separate,
disjoin, isolate, abscind,
(attach, fix, join, unite,
connect, hold, bind)

craft-n handicraft, trade,
artfulness, trickery, deceit,
vessel, boat, expertness,
art, skill, dexterity,
adroitness, competence,
(quackery, folly, stupidity,
indiscretion)

cram-v crowd, jam, stuff,
choke, guzzle, gorge,
assemble, muster, group,
cluster, pack, bunch,
(disperse, disjunction,
scatter, sow, spread)

cramp-n hamper, restrain,
handicap, paralyze,
cripple, incapacitate,
contract, reduce, diminish,
(expand, extend, augment,
develop, swell)

crass-adj stupid, raw, elude,
gross, ignorant,
incomprehension,
simplicity, shallow,
superficial, green,
(instructed, learned,
educated, enlightened)

crave-v yearn for, long for,
beseech, ask, beg, pray,
desire, petition, ravening,
hungry, famished, desirous

crawl-v grovel, fawn, cower,
drag, lag, lumber, creep,
saunter, plod, trudge,
moderate, slow, (speed,

scuttle, gallop, rush,
velocity)

crazy-adj mad, lunatic, sick,
crack-brained, shaky,
fanaticism, oddity,
eccentricity, twist, insane,
crazed, frantic, raving,
(sanity, soundness,
rationality, lucidity)

create-v make, originate,
form, bring into being,
occasion, devise,
conceive, invent, breed,
propagate, envisage

creation-n invention,
conception, causation,
origination, formation,
constitution, cosmos,
universe

creator-n originator, maker,
author, producer, god,
supreme being

creature-n lower animal,
beast, individual, mortal,
dependent, slave, being,
thing, something, matter,
substantial, (nonentity,
shadow, phantom, nothing,
naught)

credence-n reliance, trust,
assurance, acceptance,
acknowledgment, credit,
faith, dependence,
(uncertain, doubtful,
incredulous)

credibility-n belief,
believable, trustworthiness,
honesty, faith, trust,
confidence, reliance,
repute, honor, merit,
esteem, prestige

credulity-n gullibility,
infatuation, self delusion,

self deception, naivete,
silly, stupid, infatuated,
simple, (incredulous,
skeptical, suspicious,
distrustful)

creed-*n* dogma, faith,
doctrine, belief, firm,
implicit, persuasion,
articles, canons,
catechism, (doubt, distrust,
disputable, unworthy)

crest-*n* culmination, tip,
height, top, plume, seal,
device, ridge, summit,
vertex, apex, zenith,
pinnacle, (base, bottom,
nadir, foot, fundamental)

crew-*n* mob, company,
gang, throng, sailors,
squad, crowd, horde, body,
tribe, party, clan,
brotherhood, (adrift, stray,
dishelvelled, streaming,
scatter)

cringe-*v* flinch, shrink,
wince, fawn, grovel,
submit, yield, non-
resistance, obedience,
surrender, succumb,
parasite, bow, stoop,
servile, supple, (bully,
dictate)

cripple-*n* disable, hurt,
incapacitate, enfeeble,
helpless, prostration,
paralysis, palsy, apoplexy,
exhaustion, (potent,
capable, virtue,
qualification)

crisis-*n* emergency, trial,
extremity, exigency, crux,
full of incident, eventful,
stirring, bustling, (loom,

await, eventually,
forthcoming)

criterion-*n* standard, norm,
measure, test, rule,
conformation, support,
ratification, corroboration,
authentication, (oppose,
unauthenticated, non-
conformity)

critical-*adj* disparaging,
faultfinding, judicious,
analytical, crucial, turning
point, reprove, flay,
censure, examine,
analyze, judge

crooked-*adj* deceptive,
fraudulent, sneaking,
warped, awry, twisted,
askew, distorted,
(symmetrical, shapely,
finished, beautiful)

cross-*n* intersection,
traversing, decussation,
hybridization, passage,
entwine, weave, twist,
wreathe, dovetail

crouch-*v* bend, stoop,
fawn, cower, cringe, low,
neap, debased, underlie,
slouch, wallow, grovel,
depress, (tower, pillar,
dome, height, elevate)

crown-*n* diadem, coronet,
crest, top, reward, garland,
prize, accredit, empower,
commission, represent,
(dismiss, cancel, repeal)

crucial-*adj* decisive, final,
determining, supreme,
demonstrate, prove,
establish, show, verify,
(refute, disprove, expose,
rebut)

crude-*adj* unfinished, vulgar, raw, rude, uncouth, unprepared, unwrought, incomplete

cruel-*adj* savage, inhuman, unkind, barbarous, brutal, merciless, ruthless

crumble-*v* perish, break up, fall to pieces, decay, degenerate, deteriorate

crush-*v* press, squeeze, suppress, overwhelm, disconcert, shame, bruise

crust-*n* coating, coat, hull, shell, rind, cover, canopy, bandage, veneer, inunction, incrustation , conceal, (uncover, expose)

cry-*v* clamor, shout, outcry, ejaculation, utterance, vociferation, call, shriek, howl, scream, screech, sob, weeping, lamentation, plaint, whimper

cue-*n* password, catchword, hint, intimation, inform, acquaint, communicate, present, specification, (disguise, screen, mystify, seclusion)

culprit-*n* offender, victim, criminal, felon, evildoer, rough, rowdy, ruffian, bully, hangman, incendiary, criminal, (model, paragon, hero, demigod, innocent, benefactor)

cultivate-*v* develop, work, foster, till, advance, farm, gardening, husbandry, agriculture

cultivation-*n* refinement, breeding, civilization, learning, education, tillage, agriculture, husbandry, improvement

cumbersome-*adj* ponderous, burdensome, unwieldy, oppressive, clumsy, awkward, lumbering, bulky, unmanageable, (expedient, convenient, suitable)

cunning-*adj* subtlety, deceit, craftiness, chicanery, circumvention, guile, knavery, maneuvering, skill, dexterity

cup-*n* glass, mug, goblet, hollow, excavation, chalice tumbler, tankard, jug

curb-*n* restrain, control, check, repress, slacken, retard, confine, duress, custody, restrict, (liberate, free, unfetter, untie, loosen, relax)

curiosity-*n* research, inquisitiveness, thirst for knowledge, inquiring mind, interest, (uninterested, indifferent, impassive)

current-*adj* common, instant, prevalent, circulating, flow, stream, draft, existing, present, actual, present time, (any time, sometime)

curse-*n* denounce, damn, swear, blaspheme, bane, imprecation, anathema, hurtful, sting, painful, bane, scourge, (remedy, help, redress, sedative)

curt-*adj* blunt, brusque, rude, abrupt, brief, short, succinct, concise, brevity, abbreviate, compress, compact, (lengthy, endlong, interminable)

curtail-*v* lessen, reduce, abridge, abbreviate, cut, retrench, mutilate, amputate, abscind, thin, prune, (add, annex, reinforce, supplement)

curtain-*n* veil, screen, hanging, blind, drapery, conceal, hide, masquerade, hiding place, reserve, (mention, acquaint, informant, outpouring)

custody-*n* imprisonment, care, bondage, charge, protection, keeping, confinement, durance, duress, arrest, (liberate, free, redemption, acquittal)

custom-*n* rule, fashion, precedent, practice, patronage, trade, usage, regular, usual, habitual, normal

cut-*v* divide, split, sever, shape, reap, gather, separate, part, detach, divorce, rupture, (attach, fix, firm, fast, join, unite)

cynical-*adj* sardonic, surly, satirical, contemptuous, misanthropic, disdainful

D

dabble-*v* trifle, potter, moisten, paddle, splash, dilute, immerse, wash, sprinkle, drench

dagger-*n* stiletto, knife, poniard, sword, weapon, armament, saber, resentment, displeasure, animosity, wrath

dainty-*adj* exquisite, pretty, delicate, particular, meticulous, delicious, appetizing, tasty, attractive, lovely, (annoying, nuisance, infestation, molestation)

dally-*v* philander, flirt, dawdle, prolong, idle, protract, delay, suspend, waive, retard, postpone, procrastinate, (prompt, immediate, haste, sudden)

damage-*n* injure, impair, harm, mutilate, hurt, deteriorate, wane, degenerate, decay, injury, loss, (fructify, ripen, mature, promote)

damp-*adj* humid, moist, foggy, watery, moisture, wet, dank, infiltrate, muggy, drench, dewy, (dry, arid, drought)

dance-*v* prance, glide, move, flutter, perform, party, ball, cotillion, hop, jump, oscillate, agitate, pulsate, effervescence

danger-*n* jeopardy, hazard, peril, risk, insecurity, precariousness, venture, instability, exposure, (safe, secure, impregnability, invulnerability)

dangle-*v* wave, hang,

swing, be suspended,
droop, sling, pendulum,
depend, pensive, loose,
flowing, (support, aid, prop,
stand, anvil, stay)

dare-v challenge, venture,
brave, face, defiance,
threat, defy, bluster,
(agree, accord,
sympathize)

darkness-n blackness,
murk, swarthiness,
obscurity, duskiness,
gloominess, dimness,
dinginess, lightless,
opacity, tenebrous

dart-n throw, hurl, direct,
spurt, shoot, scud, propel,
project, fling, cast, pitch,
chuck, toss, (pull, haul,
draw, lug, rake, drag, tow,
trail, train)

dash-v break, crush,
shatter, depress,
discourage, frustrate,
imbue, blend, speed, rush,
sprint, mark, stroke, line,
trace, hint, tinge, grain

daunt-v frighten, alarm,
cow, discourage, fear,
timid, anxiety, solicitude,
care, apprehension,
(courage, bravery, valor,
spirit)

daze-v bewilder, dazzle,
stupefy, blind, spark, flash,
blaze, scintillation, shine,
glow, glitter, twinkle,
brighten, (dark, obscurity,
gloom, dusk, extinction)

dazzle-v impress,
confound, bedazzle, awe,
refraction, distortion,

illusion, false light

dead-adj lifeless, deceased,
defunct, departed, late,
inanimate, extinct, fatal,
mortal, destructive,
murderous

deaden-v incapacitate,
muffle, paralyze, numb,
subdue, invalid,
prostration, exhaustion,
impotent, (potency, ability,
elasticity, magnetism)

deal-v allot, distribute,
dispense, inflict, give,
deliver, administer,
arrange, allotment, sort,
classify, (derangement,
disorder, disorganize)

dearness-n expensiveness,
high price, costliness,
overcharge, extravagance,
sumptuous, valuable,
(cheapness, dislike, hate,
loathe)

debar-v hinder, forbid,
check, obstruct, exclude,
deny, prohibit, bar, stile,
barrier, restraint, prevent,
impediment, obstacle, (aid,
assistance, promote,
reinforce)

debase-v deprave, degrade,
depreciate, lower,
dishonor, disgrace,
deterioration, degradation,
corruption, adulteration

debate-v discussion,
argument, controversy,
contention, conversation,
oral communication,
reasoning, comment,
(answer, response, reply,
replication)

debt-n liability, debit, obligation, claim, due, deferred payment, deficit, insolvency, (credit, trustworthiness, reliability, reputation)

decay-v putrefy, crumble, rot, wither, fall to pieces, decompose, pare, reduce, attenuate, scrape, render smaller, (expand, spread, extend, overgrown)

decease-v demise, dying, departure, passing, death, dissolution, release, rest, extinction, bereavement, (respiration, vitality, animation, subsist)

deceit-n falsehood, sham, fraud, treachery, trickery, double dealing, perversion, hollowness, quackery, prevarication, (truthful, veracious, scrupulous)

decent-adj ordinary, clean, virtuous, passable, modest, pure, indifferent, middling, mediocre, average, tolerable, (unparalleled, superhuman)

deception-n insidiousness, duplicity, deceit, wiliness, sophistry, cunning, dissimulation, falsehood, imposition, misrepresentation, bluff, chicanery, treachery, (veracity, frankness, truth, honesty, sincerity)

decide-v resolve, settle, determine, choose, decree, arbitrate, fix upon,

judge, result, conclusion, valuation, (misjudge, bias, warped, partiality)

decipher-v translate, decode, discover, explain, make out, interpret, definition, explanation, solution, answer, (misrepresent, misinterpret, distort)

decision-n resolve, decree, verdict, firmness, will, purpose, judgment, result, conclusion, deduction

declaration-n proclamation, avowal, announcement, bulletin, assertion, notice, profess, acknowledge, state

decline-v waste, age, die, decay, refuse, repel, shun, spurn, slope, declivity, descent

decomposition-n dissolution, break-up, disjunction, disintegration, cariosity, putrefaction, putridity (cleanliness, combination)

decoration-n embellishment, trimming, adornment, ribbon, laurel, medal, ornament, wreath, festoon, (simplicity, plain, homely, unaffected, chaste)

decoy-n lure, inveigle, entice, entrap, ensnare, deception, falseness, untruth, fraud, deceit, guile

decrease-v diminution, lessening, mitigation, reduction, abatement,

shrinkage, contraction,
shorten, abbreviate,
(increase, augmentation,
addition, accumulation)

decree-*n* ordinance, edict,
mandate, verdict, decision,
regulation, command,
order

decrement-*n* diminution,
decrease, deduction,
attenuation, abatement,
waste, loss, (addition,
adjunct)

decry-*v* disparage, slander,
belittle, underestimate,
censure, degrade,
depreciation, undervaluing,
modesty, (overestimating,
exaggeration, vanity)

dedicate-*v* devote, offer,
consecrate, inscribe, mark,
name, figure, repute,
enthrone, celebrate,
glorify, (disrepute,
discredit, disgrace, stain)

deduction-*n* curtailment,
subtraction, removal,
excision, abstraction,
consequence, implication,
derivation, corollary,
discount, allowance,
(addition, attach, join,
interpose, append)

deed-*n* feat, exploit, action,
performance, document,
evidence, confirmation,
warrant, credential,
admission, (vindication,
counter-protest, oppose,
rebut, countervail)

deep-*adj* bottomless,
profound, unfathomable,
abstruse, astute,

designing, cunning,
concavity, submerged,
(shallow, superficial)

deface-*v* mutilate, distort,
injure, disfigure, mar,
blemish, deteriorate,
shapeless, formless,
deform, (conformation,
formation, build, trim,
fashion)

defame-*v* slander, abuse,
disparage, revile, taint,
smirch, sully, disrepute,
discredit, shame, disgrace,
(regard, respect, dignity,
splendor)

defeat-*v* vanquish, subdue,
conquer, refute, rebut,
silence, overcome, failure,
abortion, inefficacy,
ineffectual, (success,
advancement, good
fortune, prosperity)

defect-*n* flaw, fault, lack,
deficiency, imperfection,
weakness, shortcoming,
error, failing, blemish,
deficient, unsound

defense-*n* security, guard,
protection, preservation,
resistance, vindication,
support, advocacy, plea,
espousal, fortification,
entrenchment, palisade,
(attack, aggression,
encroachment, offense,
onslaught, assail)

defenseless-*adj*
unshielded, powerless,
unarmed, helpless,
exposed, (strength,
adamant, resistless,
invincible)

defensible-adj impregnable, invulnerable, supportable, maintainable, excusable, justifiable

defer-v retard, postpone, delay, procrastinate, adjourn, yield, comply, give in, capitulate

defiance-n challenge, threat, provocation, opposition, disobedience, insurgency, rebellion, insubordination, revolt, (obedience, submission)

deficient-adj lacking, short, wanting, insufficient, inadequate, shortcoming, inferior, minority, small, subordinate, (superior, supreme, great, advantageous)

define-v construe, expound, explain, bound, limit, circumscribe, description, meaning, distinct

definite-adj clear, plain, positive, specific, particular, limited, precise, concrete, certain, surety, (doubtful, uncertain, vague, fallibility)

deflect-v curve, bend, turn, swerve, diverge, deviation, stray, introvert, divert, digress, departure, (set, undeviating, straight, directly)

deformity-n misproportion, disfigurement, ugliness, crookedness, malformation, distortion, (symmetrical, shapely, beautiful, parallel, uniform)

defraud-v swindle, hoax, trick, dupe, cheat, deceive, untruth, fraud, guile, misrepresentation, chicane, (truthful, frankness, sincerity, honesty)

defray - v settle, meet, liquidate, discharge, pay, acknowledgment, release, receipt, repayment, satisfaction, reimbursement, (non-payment, default, repudiation)

defy-v face, confront, brave, oppose, challenge, threaten, dare, defiance, disobey

degrade-v shame, disgrace, humiliate, dishonor, fall, abasement, deteriorate, despicable, unbecoming, scandalous, (dignity, stateliness, splendor, noble)

degree-n gradation, grade, step, extent, measure, point, amount, mark, rate, standard, height, range, scope, intensity, strength,(quantity, instantaneity)

deify-v idolize, venerate, canonize, immortalize, exalt, repute, distinction, dedication, consecration, enthronement, celebration, (dishonor, shameful, stain, disgrace)

deity-n omnipotence, god, omniscience, providence, supreme being, creator, almighty, hold, preserve, atone, redeem

dejection-*n* despondency, melancholy, depression, pessimism, despair, sorrow, sadness, grief, dolefulness, distress, weariness, (cheerfulness, happy, geniality, gaiety)

delay-*v* retard, obstruct, linger, defer, impede, postpone, procrastinate, put off, adjourn, late, tardy, belated, (immediately, briefly, shortly, quickly)

delectable-*adj* pleasant, delightful, tasty, delicious, pleasurable, savory, relish, delicacy, appetizing, zestful, (acrid, repulsive, nasty, sickening, nauseous)

delegate-*v* substitute, envoy, agent, proxy, assign, consign, entrust, authorize, empower, commission, assignment, deputation, (annulment, nullification, cancel)

delete-*v* cancel, expunge, erase, obliterate, efface, (record, note, register, endorse, memo)

deliberate-*v* meditate, reflect, reason, ponder, well-considered, gradual, voluntary, leisurely

deliberation-*n* coolness, caution, prudence, deliberateness, slowness, discretion, prudence, calculation, foresight, (impetuous, levity,

imprudence, presumption, audacity)

delicacy-*n* daintiness, luxury, elegance, tidbit, discrimination, tact, culture, sensitiveness, frailty, infirmity, savoury, palatable, ambrosia

delicious-*adj* delectable, dainty, pleasing, luscious, palatable, tasty, relish, good, ambrosia, zest, appetizing, sweet, nectarous, (offensive, repulsive, nasty, nauseous)

delight-*n* please, gratify, charm, enchant, enjoy, pleasure, fruition, satisfaction, happiness, rapture, ecstasy, (annoyance, irritation, worry, plague)

delineate-*v* block, depict, sketch, portray, set forth, illustrate, represent, imitate, sculpture, engrave, design, draft, trace, (distort, exaggerate, daub, scratch)

delinquent-*adj* derelict, remiss, neglectful, rough, rowdy, ruffian, bully, incendiary, thief, murderer, criminal, (model, paragon, hero, innocent, benefactor)

delirious-*adj* crazed, raving, mad, insane, light-headed, lunacy, eccentricity, maniacal, reasonless, demented, (sanity, soundness, rationality, sobriety, lucidity)

deliverance-*n* liberation, release, rescue, reprieve, extrication, emancipation, redemption, salvation, (restraint, retention)

delude-*v* dupe, bluff, trick, fool, hoodwink, deceive, false impression, deception, hallucination, fault, blunder, (fact, reality, accuracy, delicacy, rigor)

deluge-*v* downpour, flood, inundation, rainstorm, supersaturate, excessive, superabundant, overflowing, (insufficient, meager, paltry, empty)

delusion-*n* illusion, magic, fallacy, misconception, hallucination, conjuring, infatuation, oddity, (sane, rational, reasonable)

demand-*v* order, impose, ask, exact, question, require, claim, requisition, request, market, ultimatum

demolish-*v* devastate, ruin, overthrow, wreck, crush, explode, invalidate, defeat, (establish, prove, make good, verify)

demonic-*adj* devilish, hellish, possessed, fiendish, vampire, ghoul, fiend, supernatural, weird, unearthly, haunted

demonstration-*n* verification, proof, substantiation, conclusiveness, testimony, exhibition, mass-meeting, (confutation, refute)

demoralize-*v* incapacitate, unnerve, undermine, corrupt, deprave, pervert, render-powerless, disqualify, (powerful, puissant, potent, capable)

demur-*v* protest, cavil, object, wrangle, scruple, remonstrance, disbelieve, dissent, unwilling, hesitate, (determination, resolve, vigor, resoluteness)

demure-*v* precise, priggish, solemn, sad, sedate, shy, bashful, retiring, modesty, reserve, constraint, blushing, (vain, pretentious, conceit, selfishness)

den-*n* sanctum, cave, lair, study, retreat, cell, abode, dwelling, lodging, domicile, residence, habitation

denial-*n* repudiation, negation, contradiction, disallowance, disbelief, disavowal, protest, recusancy, (affirmance, declaration, oath, assurance)

denomination-*n* persuasion, designation, name, side, specification, kind, sect, class, division, category, province, domain

denote-*v* betoken, signify, represent, express, imply, convey, designate, specify, indication, feature, type, characteristic

denounce-*v* arraign, charge, censure, rebuke, blame, curse, damn, accuse, reprehend, chide,

admonish, disapprove,
(approval, approbation,
advocacy, esteem)

density-n solidness, body,
compactness, thickness,
impenetrability,
impermeability, coherence,
ignorance, crassness,
ineptitude, opacity,
dullness, obtuseness,
(intelligence, rarity)

dent-n depression, hollow,
indentation, cavity,
concavity, dip, cavernous,
excavate, burrow, tunnel,
(convex, project, swelling,
bilge, bulge, protrusion)

denunciation-n defiance,
condemnation, curse,
arraignment, imprecation

deny-v differ, protest,
contradict, reject, doubt,
discredit, dissent,
discontent, disagreement,
non-conformity, (assent,
acquiescence, admission,
unanimity)

department-n jurisdiction,
bureau, office, division,
part, function, capacity,
sphere, orb, field, line,
walk, routine

departure-n embarkation,
start, exit, leaving, egress,
parting, withdraw, adieu,
farewell, removal, (return,
remigration, arrive)

depend-v trust, credit, rely,
hang, be contingent,
uncertain, casual, doubtful,
dubious, vague, hesitant,
(positive, absolute,
definite, decisive, without

question)

depict-v delineate, portray,
represent, picture,
describe, mimic,
illustrative, imitate,
figurative, (distort,
exaggerate, misrepresent,
daub)

deplore-v bewail, lament,
regret, mourn, complain,
grievous, sad, pitiable,
repine, (content,
satisfaction, ease,
cheerfulness)

deport-v banish, transport,
exile, remove, send,
transit, displace, drift,
bring, fetch, transpose

deposit-v installment,
pledge, payment, alluvium,
place, situate, locate,
settlement, establish,
(displace, eject, removal,
unload)

deposition-n sworn
evidence, affidavit,
allegation, dethronement,
expulsion, archive, docket,
certificate, (efface,
obliterate, erase, cancel)

depository-n warehouse,
storehouse, vault, store,
repository, conservatory,
closet, reservoir, cistern

depravity-n badness,
corruption, perversion,
degeneracy, wickedness,
impairment, injury,
damage, loss, wrong,
aggrieve, annoyance,
(improvement,
amendment, reform,
revision)

deprecation-n remonstrance, disapprobation, protest, disapproval, mediation, expostulation, intercession

depreciate-v lessen, fall, drop, slight, undervalue, underrate, disparage, slander, affront

depression-n sinking, cavity, hollow, dip, diminution, humiliation, abasement, subversion, melancholy, dispiritedness, gloom, despondency, sadness, (cheerfulness, elevation)

deprive-v bereave, strip, dispossess, despoil, rob, clutch, capture, distress, divestment, extortion, eviction, (restitution, replevin, redemption, atonement)

depth-n profoundness, extent, profundity, intensity, completeness, abundance, (shallowness, veneer, superficiality)

deputy-n substitute, proxy, surrogate, delegate, agent, representative, alternate

derangement-n discomposure, disorder, confusion, embarrassment, mess, tangle, inversion, mania, insanity, madness, (sanity, arrangement)

dereliction-n abandonment, relinquishment, neglect, omission, desertion, failure, fault, evasion, (duty, respect, homage)

deride-v disdain, scorn, jeer, mock, ridicule, irruption, snigger, satirize, parody, travesty

derive-v secure, get, gain, account for, deduce, infer, etymologize, trace, estimation, valuation, appreciation, assessment, (discover, find, determine, evolve)

derogatory-adj scandalous, unbefitting, ignoble, discreditable, disrepute, degrade, dishonor, expel, disgrace, (distinct, repute, dignity, rank, standing)

descend-v dismount, slide, go down, tumble, detail, special, particular, specific, proper

descent-n drop, plunge, fall, declination, comedown, gravitate, decline, sink, spring, issue, (ascent, ascension, rising, originate, upgrowth)

description-n statement, account, record, report, summary, outline, depiction, representation

desert-n waste, wilderness, forsake, abandon, leave, run away, worth, due, recompense, meed

deserter-n fugitive, truant, runaway, apostate, changeful, reactionary, apostatize, (arbitrary, dogmatic, positive, uninfluenced)

design-v arrangement, make-up, depiction,

drawing, aim, intent, project, pattern, model

designate-v show, specify, indicate, name, call, particularize, individualize, special, proper, detail, definite, (general, prevail, generic, collective, broad)

desire-v inclination, fancy, wish, whim, propensity, fondness, need, want, exigency, urgency, hunger, necessity, passion, (dislike, indifference, satiety)

desist-v halt, discontinue, stop, quit, cease, abstain, interrupt, pause, rest, suspend, (continue, persistence, sustain)

desolate-adj uninhabited, deserted, waste, forlorn, miserable, forsaken, lonely, seclusion, solitude, isolation, (sociality, visit, welcome, hospitality)

despair-n dejection, misery, despondency, wretchedness, anguish, hopelessness, desperate, relinquish, (hope, trust, confidence, reliance, faith)

desperate-adj wild, frantic, frenzied, raging, reckless, despairing, incurable, impossible, impervious, impassible, (practical, feasible, compatible)

despise-v scorn, condemn, disdain, disregard, hate, disgust, contempt, derisive, withering, pitiful, despicable

despond-v lament, mourn, despair, falter, sink, melancholy, sad, dejected, depressed, heaviness, dismal, demure, gravity, (cheerful, geniality, gaiety, liveliness)

despotism-n imperialism, tyranny, autocracy, oppression, authority, influence, patronage, power, prerogative, jurisdiction, (anarchy, relaxation, remission, abdication)

destination-n port, goal, halting place, point, mark, end, close, termination, conclusion, finale, consummation, (beginning, commencement, opening, outset)

destiny-n fortune, fate, lot, fatalism, prospect, decree, expectation, impending, future, (eventuality, incident, proceeding, advent)

destitute-adj poor, penniless, lacking, bereft, needy, deficiency, inadequate, emptiness, poorness, depletion, (sufficient, adequate, enough, luxury)

destruction-n demolition, ruination, dissolution, devastation, cataclysm, perdition, extermination, annihilation, extirpation, (preservation, production)

desultory-adj disconnected, digressive, rambling, fitful,

aimless, erratic, broken,
spasmodic

detach-v disconnect, sever,
unfasten, loosen,
separation, segregation,
portion, division, squad,
detail, (unite, join, together,
connect)

detail-n item, particular,
feature, party, patrol,
description, account,
statement, report,
summary, specification,
delineation, representation

detain-v withhold, delay,
retard, secure, retention,
retain, detain, keep,
custody, tenacity, grasp,
gripe

detect-v discern, reveal,
expose, unearth, perceive,
discover, find, determine,
evolve, fix upon,
determine, (result,
conclusion, upshot,
deduction)

deter-v discourage, hinder,
restrain, hold back,
dissuade, deprecation,
dampen, deport, against,
remonstrate, disincline,
(induce, entice, allure,
bewitch)

deterioration-n impairment,
detriment, injury, harm,
debasement, damage,
loss, degeneration,
vitiation, dilapidation,
disrepair (improvement,
betterment, amendment)

determination-n firmness,
resolution, resolve,
judgment, decree, result,

conclusion, evaluate,
assess, estimate,
(misjudge, positive,
intolerant, impracticable)

determine-v impel, insure,
influence, ascertain,
conclude, define, decree,
designate, specify

detest-v loathe, abhor,
abominate, despise,
dislike, disgust,
disagreeable, disincline,
repel, sicken, nauseous,
(desire, wish, fancy,
fantasy, want, need,
inclined)

detraction-n derogation,
disparagement, scandal,
defamation, calumny,
contempt, disapprobation,
(approbation, flattery)

devastate-v ravage, sack,
pillage, lay waste, ruin,
destructive, subversive,
ruinous, incendiary,
extinguish, (produce,
create, construct, erect,
fabricate)

develop-v promote, build,
evolve, grow, enlarge,
produce, perform, flower,
generate, impregnate,
prolific, induce,
(destruction, dissolution,
ruin, annihilate, abolish)

development-n
consequence, outgrowth,
growth, expansion,
evolution, effect,
eventuality, resulting from,
emanate, (cause, origin,
source, element, principle)

deviation-n divagation,

digression, aberration,
variation, alteration,
diversion, declination,
swerve, warp, drift,
(continuance, direction,
straightness)

device-*n* stratagem, trick,
design, contrivance,
appliance, emblem, type,
figure, representation,
characteristic, diagnostic

devious-*adj* circuitous,
erring, rambling, indirect,
diversion, digression,
refraction, departure,
aberration, (course,
aligned, direct, straight)

devise-*v* create, contrive,
scheme, originate, will,
bequeath, plan, scheme,
design, project,
suggestion, resolution

devoid-*adj* destitute, void,
lacking, wanting, absent,
not present, empty, truant,
vacant, elsewhere,
inexistent, (present, fill,
pervade, permeate,
occupy, moored)

devote-*v* destine, preordain,
addict, consecrate,
dedicate, apply, utilize,
resolve, determination,
desperation, vigor, (fickle,
levity, weakness, waver,
hesitate)

devotee-*n* zealot, fanatic,
fan, enthusiast, believer,
religionist, inclination,
desire, magnet, attraction,
aspirant, solicitant,
(reluctance, lackadaisical,
half-hearted)

devotion-*n* loyalty, passion,
fidelity, worship, homage,
yearning, gallantry,
benevolence, attachment,
rapture, adoration, (hate,
detest, abominate, abhor)

devour-*v* consume,
annihilate, swallow,
masticate, rumination,
gulp, eat, edible,
succulent, potable,
bibulous, (eject, emission,
egestion, evacuation)

devout-*adj* sincere,
reverent, pious, religious,
holy, beatification,
regeneration, conversion,
veneration, (irreverence,
hypocrisy, bigot, impiety,
sacrilege, blasphemy)

dexterous-*adj* clever,
adroit, expert, proficient,
handy, skillful, dexterity,
competence, facility,
mastery, cleverness,
(bungle, unskillful,
thoughtless)

diabolic-*adj* impious,
infernal, devilish, satanic,
fiendish, hurtful, injurious,
deleterious, malignity,
malevolence, (goodness,
excellence, beneficial,
proficient)

dialect-*n* tongue, speech,
brogue, cant, idiom,
vernacular, colloquialism,
slang, expression,
provincialism

dictate-*v* suggest,
prescribe, direct, order,
charge, compose, draw up,
advice, council, instruction,

enforce, recommend

dictatorial-*adj* domineering, overbearing, autocratic, peremptory, superiority, insolence, arrogance, overbearance, (servile, obsequious, supple, cringe)

die-*v* fade, expire, perish, depart, to be killed, mold, seal, punch, matrix, death, dissolution, departure, (life, vitality, respire, vivification, animation)

dietetic-*adj* alimental, dietary, nutritious, treatment, help, remedy, medicine, antiseptic, corrective, restorative, sedative, (bane, curse, rust, leaven, poison)

difference-*n* unlikeness, dissimilarity, variety, diversity, heterogeneity, dissonance, disparity, contradiction, contrast, incongruousness, dispute, contend, bicker, (identity, similarity)

differentiate-*v* separate, discriminate, adapt, distinguish, set apart, sever, estimate, refinement, diagnosis, (uncertain, unmeasured, overlook)

difficulty-*n* arduousness, impracticability, hardness, impossibility, tough, scrape, entanglement, (smooth, facilitate, ease, unclog)

diffuseness-*n* verbosity, amplification, wordiness, verbiage, loquacity, looseness, exuberance

digest-*v* classify, settle, arrange, summarize, assimilate, transform, endure, think out, reflect, cogitate, consider, (vacant, unoccupied, inconsiderate)

dignity-*n* honor, nobility, distinction, stateliness, august, lofty, majestic, haughtiness, vainglory, supercilious, (humble, disgrace, service, submissive)

digress-*v* diverge, swerve, ramble, wander, deviate, stray, straggle, sidle, rove, dodge, meander, veer, (straight, aligned, undeviating, course)

dilapidated-*adj* crumbling, decayed, ruined, worn out, deterioration, debasement, recession, retrogradation, (improvement, melioration, betterment, amendment)

dilate-*v* amplify, stretch, expatiate, enlarge, expand, increase, develop, rarefaction, germination, growth, (contraction, reduction, diminution, decrease)

dilemma-*n* perplexity, mess, difficulty, strait, difficulty, impractical, embarrassment, impossibility, tough, hard, (manageable, wieldy, submissive, yielding)

dilute-*v* thin, reduce,

weaken, water, declension, delicacy, invalidation, decrepitude, asthenia, fragile, unsubstantial, (strength, power, energy, stamina)

dim-*adj* obscure, dull, hazy, vague, cloudy, faint, blackness, darkness, obscurity, gloom, pale, fade, lack luster, (shine, glow, glitter, shimmer, glimmer)

dimension-*n* extent, area, measurement, expanse, size, proportions, amplitude, mass, capacity, enormity, (intangible, impalpable, inappreciable, infinitesimal)

diminish-*v* curtail, abase, reduce, decrease, weaken, small, slight, little

dip-*v* slope, declivity, decline, inclination, slant, lean, include, distort, oblique, depression, hollow, indentation, cavity, (convexity, prominence, projection, swell)

diplomacy-*n* tact, skill, negotiation, address, politics, chicanery, maneuver, concealment, guile, strategy, (artlessness, simplicity, innocence, candor)

dire-*adj* dreadful, shocking, horrible, calamitous, deplorable, fearful, ominous, bad, annoyance, molestation, abuse, (valuable, advantageous, profitable, edifying)

dirty-*adj* soiled, sullied, filthy, stormy, murky, threatening, leaden, contamination, unclean, impure, defilement, (clean, pure, lavation, disinfection)

disable-*v* impair, cripple, incapacitate, maim, helpless, prostration, paralysis, collapse, invalidity, ineptitude, (powerful, mighty, ability, ableness, competence)

disadvantage-*n* hindrance, drawback, detriment, harm, injury, inferior, minority, subordinative, shortcoming, deficiency, (superiority, supremacy, great, exceed)

disagreement-*n* difference, dissonance, discrepancy, inequality, variance, dissent, controversy, inaptitude, impropriety, unsuitability, opposition

disappearance-*n* vanishing, evanescence, dissolution, fading, occultation, eclipse, exit, departure, dissolve, (appearance, visible, show, manifest)

disappointment-*n* frustration, chagrin, bafflement, discontent, failure, disconcerted, miscalculation, (expectation, breathless, anticipation, contemplation)

disapprobation-*n* disapproval, displeasure,

disfavor, denunciation, condemnation, rebuke, admonition, reprimand, castigation, objurgation, reprobation

disarrange-v disorganize, disturb, disorder, derange, mislay, jumble, shuffle, muddle, dislocate, confuse, (arrange, analysis, digest, classify)

disaster-n affliction, cataclysm, calamity, adversity, accident, blow, failure, misfortune, catastrophe, downfall, (prosper, welfare, affluence, success)

disbelieve-v discredit, doubt, challenge, lack faith, infidelity, misbelief, dissent, incredulous, suspicious, septic, (credulity, gullible, simple, confident, believing)

discard-v abolish, reject, repudiate, cancel, nullify, oversight, absent, abstracted, perplex, bewilder, trash, (observe, scrutinize, study, revise)

discern-v appreciate, comprehend, perceive, experience, detect, distinguish, discriminate

discharge-v release, exude, absolve, abolish, discard, perform, settle, transact, dismiss, oust, disband, demobilize

disciple-n follower, pupil, adherent, student, scholar, apprentice, beginner, recruit, novice, neophyte, apostle, (teacher, trainer, instructor, institutor, master)

discipline-n orderliness, subordination, control, obedience, correction, chastisement, development

disclaim-v repudiate, deny, disown, renounce, disavowal, contradiction, recusancy, protest, prohibition, (affirmation, allegation, assertion, declaration)

disclosure-n divulgence, vent, utterance, exposure, revelation, admission, declaration, confession, avowal, (concealment, ambush)

discomfort-n suffering, discontent, soreness, painfulness, disquiet, displeasure, annoyance, (happiness, cheerfulness, refreshment, enchantment)

disconcert-v upset, abash, trouble, frustrate, bewilder, perplex, balk, disrepute, discredit, tarnish, degrade, beggar, stigmatize, (dignity, stateliness, solemnity, grandeur)

disconnection-n separation, interruption, cleavage, break, dissociation, irrelation, deviation, sunder, divide, dissect, anatomize, sever, (join, unite, associate, suture, stitch)

disconsolate-*adj* sorrowful,
melancholy, hopeless,
forlorn, desolate, dejection,
depression, prostration,
(liveliness, life, vivacity,
jocularity, mirth)

discontent-*n* uneasiness,
dissatisfaction, regret,
disappointment, soreness,
mortification,
repining, (content,
serenity, gratification,
happiness)

discontinuity-*n* disunion,
fracture, disconnection,
cessation, disruption,
(continuity, succession,
sequence)

discord -*n* dissidence,
clash, dissension,
disagreement, difference,
variance, division, schism,
faction, (concord,
harmony, agreement)

discount-*v* concession,
abatement, allowance,
qualification, poundage,
rebate, depreciation

discourage-*v* depress,
deter, dishearten, daunt,
divert, dissuade, deport,
remonstrate, warn,
disincline, (stimulate,
excite, inspirit, persuade)

discourse-*n* discuss,
declaim, talk, lecture,
expatiate, explain,
exercise, task, curriculum,
course, elementary, teach,
(bewilder, uncertain,
mystify, conceal)

discourtesy-*n* incivility,
rudeness, impoliteness,

tactlessness, rusticity,
unmannerly, disrespect,
impudence, barbarism,
(courtesy, politeness,
gentility, refinement)

discovery-*n* ascertainment,
detection, exposure,
finding, revelation,
contrivance, unearthing,
invention, device, design,
(concealment, veil, cover,
camouflage, screen)

discredit-*v* shame, debase,
disbelieve, disgrace,
disrepute, dishonor,
tarnish, defile, pollute,
humiliate, reproach,
(distinguish, elevate,
dedicate, ascent,
exaltation)

discretion-*n* prudence,
option, volition, freedom,
wariness, caution, wary,
judicious, choice, elect,
preference, choose,
(indifference, indecision,
neutrality)

discrimination-*n*
distinction, differentiation,
diagnosis, estimation,
discernment, acuteness,
clearness, acumen, insight

discuss-*v* examine,
analyze, reason, argue,
debate, consider, study,
controversy, inquire,
question, investigate,
(answer, retort, discover,
rationale)

disdain-*v* derision, scorn,
haughtiness, arrogance,
airs, contempt, insolence,
indifference, unconcern,

careless, (anxiety,
impetuosity, propensity,
willingness)

disengage-*v* disentangle,
disconnect, sever, free,
extricate, clear, liberate,
release, emancipation,
dismissal, (confine, duress,
restraint, repress)

disfigure-*v* deface, impair,
mutilate, mangle, mar,
ugly, deformity,
inelegance, blemish,
squalor, eyesore, gaunt,
(beauty, elegance, grace,
form, gloss)

disgrace-*n* dishonor,
shame, degrade, discredit,
humiliate, corrupt,
recreant, venal, insidious,
perfidious, arrant, (upright,
honest, equitable,
impartial)

disguise-*n* camouflage,
mask, concealment, blind,
cloak, pretense, hide,
mystify, secrecy, reserve,
cover, screen, (enlighten,
acquaint, knowledge,
publicity)

disgust-*v* repugnance,
loathing, aversion,
repletion, dislike, gall,
abomination, sicken,
repel, (desire, passion,
crave, care for, affect)

dishonest-*adj* fraudulent,
false, crooked,
dishonorable, deceptive,
untruth, guile,
misrepresentation,
distortion, (veracity,
honesty, frankness,

truthful, true)

disinfect-*v* purify, cleanse,
fumigate, sanitize,
ventilate, immaculate,
clear, clarify, deodorize,
refine, (dirt, filth, soot,
contaminate)

disinherit-*v* oust, disown,
deprive, cut off, transfer,
alienate, assign, limit

disintegrate-*v* break up,
crumble, disband,
disperse, decompose,
powdery, pulverulent

disjunction-*n* disunion,
disconnection, parting,
partition, break,
disengagement

dislike-*v* disinclination,
displeasure, disfavor,
reluctance, repugnance,
abomination, antipathy,
abhorrence, hatred

dislocate-*v* disarrange,
displace, disjoin, disunite,
derange, separate,
disjunctive, asunder,
distinct, unconnected

dismal-*adj* gloomy, somber,
depressing, funereal,
sorrowful, mournful,
annoyance, grievance,
nuisance, vexation,
(gratify, delight, gladden,
captivate)

dismantle-*v* destroy,
undress, strip, disrobe,
worthless, inadequate,
waste, cripple, lame,
useless, (utility,
usefulness, conducive,
remunerative)

dismiss-*v* send away,

banish, discharge, let go,
disband, eject, relinquish,
abandon, dispense,
riddance, (retain, keep,
detain, custody, tenacity)
disobedience-n unruliness,
insubordination, mutiny,
intractableness, revolt,
obstinacy, noncompliance
disorder-n disarrangement,
confusion, untidiness,
disarray, derangement,
anomaly, disunion,
anarchy, chaos, clutter
disown-v repudiate, deny,
renounce, disclaim, reject,
retract, dispute, ignore,
rebut, disavow, protest,
(affirmation, declare,
positive, emphatic)
disparage-v belittle, decry,
discredit, underrate,
abuse, scoff at,
underestimate, depreciate,
modesty, minimize,
(oversensitive, exaggerate,
vanity, magnify)
dispatch-v dismiss, slay,
alacrity, expedition,
promptness, urgency
dispense-v allot, portion,
distribute, bestow,
administer, apportion,
disperse, diffuse, shed,
spread, dissemination,
(assemble, collect, gather,
muster, compilation)
dispersion-n distribution,
scattering, propagation,
dissipation, dissemination,
allocation, apportionment
displacement-n transfer,
dislocation, replacement,

disturbance, eject,
expulsion, dismissal
displease-v vex, disturb,
annoy, offend, maltreat,
sicken, repel, disenchant,
disagreeable, distasteful,
(pleasant, agreeable,
amuse, delectable)
disposition-n emotion,
temperament, passion,
predisposition, tendency,
inclination, propensity
disprove-v refute, rebut,
defeat, confute, negative,
expose, invalidation,
conviction, clincher,
(categorical, decisive)
dispute-v clash, wrangle,
bicker, confute, argue,
debate, challenge, quarrel,
disqualify-v incapacitate,
disfranchise, unfit, disable,
helpless, exhaust, invalid,
inefficiency, collapse,
(attribute, quality, qualify)
disquiet-v turbulence,
uneasiness, commotion,
anxiety, restlessness,
changeable, versatility,
mobility, vacillation,
(stability, vitality, solidity)
disregard-v affront, slight,
insult, overlook, underrate,
belittle, inconsiderate,
escape one's attention,
(attention, consideration,
reflection, regard)
disrepute-n dishonor,
discredit, disfavor,
disesteem, derogation,
abasement, degradation,
ignominy, disgrace
dissatisfy-v offend, vex,

provoke, annoy, anger,
displease, chafe, anxiety,
concern, grief, bitterness,
tribulation, (happiness,
felicity, comfort, delight)

dissemble-v feign, hide,
disguise, mask, simulate,
deception, untruth, guile,
misrepresentation,
pretense, sham, (veracity,
truthfulness, frankness,
sincerity)

dissent-v nonagreement,
nonconsent, difference,
variance, discordance,
schism, disaffection,
secession

dissertation-n treatise,
theme, thesis, essay,
discourse, investigation,
commentary, lecture,
sermon

dissimilarity-n unlikeness,
divergence, variation,
difference, novelty,
originality, diversity,
disparity, (similarity,
resemblance, similitude,
semblance)

dissolve-v end, destroy,
abolish, disintegrate,
vanish, evaporate, fade,
liquefy, decompose,
disappear, (visible,
perceptible, perceivable,
discernible)

dissonance-n controversy,
incongruity, dissension,
discordance, harshness,
disagreement, discretion,
(agreement, accord,
unison, harmony)

dissuasion-n expostulation,

diversion, remonstrance,
deprecation, constraint,
check, control

distance-n remoteness,
span, space, interval,
coldness, frigidity,
reservation, aloofness, out
skirts, (nearness,
proximity, propinquity)

distasteful-adj unsavory,
unpalatable, bitter,
disagreeable, uninviting,
unsatisfactory, painful,
irritating, grievance,
(pleasure, attraction,
loveliness)

distinct-adj apart, explicit,
separate, characterize,
clear-cut, distinguishable,
disconnected, disjoined,
divide, sever, (attach,
entangle, twine, cohere,
incorporate)

distinguished-adj famous,
celebrated, noted,
illustrious, eminent,
superior, supreme,
majority, (inferior, smaller,
subordinative, deficient)

distortion-n deformation,
contortion, twisting,
perversion, irregular,
misrepresentation,
misunderstanding,
exaggeration, (interpret,
decipher, understand,
explanatory)

distress-n sorrow, agony,
affliction, anguish, grief,
misery, misfortune, pain,
concern, unhappiness,
infelicity, (enjoyment,
gratification, fruition, relish)

district-n tract, section, neighborhood, division, commune, county, state, region, sphere, ground, circuit, territory, (space, expanse, range, latitude)

distrust-n qualm, doubt, suspicion, apprehension, disbelief, mistrust, discredit, infidelity, dissent, doubtful, (believe, credit, faithful, dependence)

disturb-v upset, muddle, shake, stir, misplace, worry, trouble, disquiet, tumult, disorder, perturbation, derangement, agitation

disuse-n desuetude, non-use, abandonment, neglect, relinquishment, discontinuance

divergence-n ramification, furcation, branching, divarication, separation, detachment, dispersion, deviation, disagreement

diversion-n recreation, pastime, variation, break, sport, festivity, gala, rejoicing, (weariness, irksome, monotonous)

divert-v delight, deflect, entertain, switch, turn inequality, multiformity, divergence, variation, dissimilitude

divestment-n unstrapping, unclothing, excoriation, desquamation, excavation, uncover, strip, bare, denude, dishabille, (invest, cover, vesture, array)

divide-v assign, separate, distribute, allot, sunder, cleave, part, detach, sever, dissect, mangle, disconnect, (pin, nail, secure, set, firm, fast, close)

divine-adj superhuman, godlike, celestial, holy, religious, perfection, indefectibility, paragon, summit, (imperfect, inadequate, deficient, fault)

division-n rupture, breach, split, schism, parting, share, portion, section, apportionment, system, discord, disjunction

dizzy-adj vertiginous, giddy, light-headed, confused, absent, abstracted, inattentive, muddle, disregard, (attentive, observant, reflective, regardful)

docile-adj submissive, gentle, tractable, obedient, aptitude, edification, willing, inclined, geniality, volunteering, (unwilling, disinclination, volition)

doctrine-n maxim, theory, creed, dogma, principle, record, note, register, testimonial, commemorate, (obliterate, cancel, delete, erase)

dogmatic-adj arrogant, dictatorial, bigoted, opinionated, certainty, necessity, surety, reliability, gospel, (uncertain, hesitating, suspenseful, perplexity)

domain-*n* sphere, realm, territory, dominions, estate, lands, property, possession, right, title, claim, possess, chattel

domestic-*adj* broken, tame, inland, home, family, inhabitant, resident dweller, occupier, native,

doom-*n* judgment, sentence, fate, fortune, ruin, lot, destiny, future, impend, destined, threaten, loom, forthcoming, (eventual, proceed, circumstance, casualty)

door-*n* gate, entrance, portal, obstacle, outlet, inlet, barrier, beginning, inception, introduction, source, (end, close, termination, conclusion)

doubt-*v* question, mistrust, disbelieve, distrust, incredulity, disbelief skepticism, agnosticism,

downfall-*n* overthrow, fall, misfortune, wreck, crash, destruction, breaking up, disorganization, desolation, (productive, flowering, erection, perform)

downright-*adj* plainly, bluntly, completely, absolutely, utterly, simply, innocence, candor, sincere, honestly, (cunning, craftiness, artificial, maneuvering)

downy-*adj* lanate, woolly,

flocculent, soft, fluffy, pliable, mollify, mellow, relax, mash, knead, yielding, (hard, rigid, inflexible, stiff, starched)

draft-*n* sketch, drawing, breeze, air, select, enlist, impress, conscript, commandeer

drag-*v* creep, trail, lag, crawl, elapse, pull, tug, traction, rake, tow, wrench, jerk, haul, (propel, project, throw, fling, cast, pitch, toss)

drain-*v* flow out, leak, discharge, empty, exhaust, egestion, evacuation, vomit, emission, effusion, expulsion, (reception, admission, importation, ingestion)

draw-*v* lure, attract, fabricate, describe, sketch, portray, drag, pull, haul, design, picture, draft, (misrepresent, distort, exaggerate, caricature, daub)

dreadful-*adj* horrible, frightful, tremendous, shocking, formidable, depressing, dejected, heaviness, sadness, (cheerful, genial, gay, good humor)

dream-*n* vision, reverie, fantasy, fancy, shadow, inattentive, absent, bemused, preoccupied

dreary-*adj* somber, gloomy, depressing, monotonous, humdrum, dull, solitude,

seclusion, isolation, lonely,
(happy, content, coexist)

dregs-*n* settlings, lees,
sediment, residue, trash,
refuse, riffraff, common,
low, beggarly, uncivilized,
(aristocrat, noble,
gentlemen, distinctive)

dress-*n* attire, clothe, drape,
deck, berate, scold, adorn,
embellish, garments,
raiment, apparel, vesture,
garb

drink-*v* sip, quaff, tipple,
carouse, imbibe, absorb,
toast, pledge, libation,
potation, draft, gulp,
swallow, (eject, emission,
emit, evacuate)

drive-*v* impel, oblige, force,
urge, steer, manage,
control, ride, travel, thrust,
aim, compel, enforce

driver-*n* coachman, whip,
charioteer, teamster,
chauffeur, director,
manager, master,
taskmaster

droop-*v* despond, decline,
sink, wither, fade, hang,
lean, drop, decay,
retrograde, go down,
downhill, (improve,
meliorate, betterment,
mend)

drop-*v* slide, sink, fall,
discontinue, collapse, faint,
discard, give up, drip,
trickle, descent

dross-*n* rubbish, garbage,
trash, waste, leavings,
sediment, grounds,
unimportant, insignificant,

trivial, (important,
prominence, consideration,
material)

drought-*n* parched,
aridness, thirst, lack,
dearth, scarcity,
insufficient, inadequate,
scantiness, famine,
(sufficient, enough,
adequate, fullness)

drown-*v* suffocate, drench,
submerge, overpower,
overwhelm, deaden,
victimize, choke, stifle

drunkenness-*n* inebriety,
intemperance, drinking,
inebriation, insobriety,
intoxication, libations,
bacchanalia

dryness-*n* aridity, aridness,
drought, parched,
desiccation, dehydration,
evaporation

duality-*n* twofold, double,
biform, duplicity, polarity,
two, deuce, couple, pair,
twins

dubious-*adj* questionable,
doubtful, suspicious,
uncertain, hesitation,
perplexity, embarrassment,
dilemma, (certainty,
gospel, reliable, infallible)

ductile-*adj* pliable, pliant,
flexible, malleable, tactile,
manageable, compliant,
docile, tractable

duel-*n* affair of honor, single
combat, fight, competition,
rivalry, contest, opposition,
satisfaction, (peace,
harmony, tranquil,
concord)

dullness-*n* stupidity,
  slowness, stagnation,
  dimness, sluggishness,
  apathy, obscurity,
  uninteresting, insipid,
  unimaginative
dumb-*adj* voiceless,
  silence, taciturnity, slow-
  witted, stupid, inarticulate,
  suppress, mute, (voice,
  sound, utter, articulate)
dupe-*n* victim, sucker, easy
  mark, fool, puppet,
  deceive, trick, fool,
  delusion, deception, false
duplication-*n* doubling,
  iteration, renewal,
  facsimile, copy, imitate,
  mirror, reflect, reproduce,
  repeat, (original,
  unmatched, unique)
durability-*n* permanence,
  continuance, persistence,
  immutability, stability,
  unchangeable, constant,
  (erratic, vagrant,
  alternating, mobile)
duty-*n* respect, deference,
  homage, reverence,
  obligation, service,
  responsibility, task,
  commission, charge, trust
dwarf-*n* midget, pygmy,
  Lilliputian, little, urchin, elf,
  puppet, shrimp, runt,
  minute, (mammoth,
  elephant, hippopotamus,
  colossus)
dwelling-*n* domicile, abode,
  house, residence,
  habitation, housing, home,
  berth, throne, tenement,
  barn, mansion, villa,

hermitage
dwindle-*v* contract, lessen,
  shrink, diminish, decline,
  decrease, abate,
  depreciate, deteriorate,
  shorten, (increase,
  enlarge, expand, augment,
  raise)
dynamic-*adj* magnetic,
  power, impelling, driving,
  energetic, impulse,
  forcible, active, strong

E

each-*adj* apiece, seriatim,
  respectively, severally,
  individual, special,
  particular, separate,
  (generally, generic,
  universal)
eager-*adj* zealous, ardent,
  earnest, fervent, intent,
  willing, voluntary, inclined,
  favorable, ready, forward,
  (unwilling, renitency,
  reluctance, indifference)
earliness-*n* promptitude,
  punctuality, readiness,
  quickness, haste, speed,
  swiftness, alacrity,
  prematureness, precocity,
  anticipation, hastiness,
  (lateness, tardiness, delay,
  deferring)
earnest-*adj* fervent,
  zealous, ardent, grave,
  eager, solemn, weighty,
  serious, determined
ease-*n* enjoyment,
  readiness, contentment,
  expertness, cheerfulness,
  comfort, resignation,

satisfaction, (discontent,
grief, disappointment,
mortification)
easy-*adj* unconcerned,
smooth, untroubled,
unconstrained, gentle,
facile, simple, tractable,
manageable, compliant
eat-*v* devour, consume,
fare, rust, corrode, erode,
masticate, consume,
nourishment, subsistence,
provision, (excrete,
discharge, secrete)
ebb-*v* waste, decay,
decline, recede, withdraw,
return, reflux, recoil,
regress, fall, deteriorate,
resilience, (progress,
advance, proceed)
eccentric-*adj* irregular,
peculiar, odd, deviating,
erratic, unsettled,
demented, possessed,
maddened, moonstruck
ecclesiastical-*adj* religious,
priestly, clerical,
sacerdotal, scriptural,
biblical, prophetic,
apostolic, canonical
echo-*n* repercussion,
repeat, reverberation,
reproduce, resound, ring,
reflex, hollow, sepulchral,
chime, (dead sound,
dampen, muffled, thud)
economy-*n* frugality,
thriftiness, savings,
prevention of waste,
parsimony, retrenchment,
careful, saving, sparing,
(liberality, generosity,
munificent, freely,

bountifulness)
edible-*adj* digestible, eating,
epulation, masticate,
nourishment, sustenance,
nurture, subsistence, feed,
swallow, gulp, munch,
nibble, culinary, nutritive,
succulent, potable,
bibulous, (discharge,
excretion, exude, secrete,
emanate, extrude)
edification-*n* performance,
achievement, flower,
fructify, evolution,
development, growth,
genesis, bring forth,
(destruction, dissolution,
consumption, run,
breakdown, abolish,
annihilation)
educate-*v* instruct, tutor,
direction, guidance,
preparation, discipline,
practice, study, lecture,
inoculation, impregnate,
enlighten, inform, coach,
disseminate, (bewilder,
perversion, misinformation,
deceive, mislead,
unedifying)
effect-*n* consequence,
result, outgrowth,
development, derivative,
(cause, origin, source,
foundation, groundwork)
efficient-*adj* skillful,
capable, clever,
knowledgeable, adroit,
masterful, accomplished,
ingenuity, endowed,
competent, (unskilled,
blunder, inability, stupidity,
failure, fumble, disqualify)

ego-_n_ vanity, conceit, self-esteem, admiration, gaudery, assurance, complacency, praise, glorification, laudation, (modesty, timidity, humility, reserve, demureness, sheepish)

either-_adj_ choice, option, alternative, selection, prefer, to set apart, preference, elect, discretion, decision, (neutrality, indifference, waive, abstain, refrain, indecision, neither)

elaborate-_adj_ improve, betterment, melioration, amend, elevate, increase, promote, reform, revise, refine, cultivate, enhance, polish, refresh, bolster, revamp, (recede, retrograde, decrease, degrade, deter, impair, deteriorate, degenerate, decline)

elate-_v_ cheerfulness, gaiety, geniality, good humor, glee, merriment, hilarity, laughter, rejoice, liveliness, jocularity, mirth, exhilaration, joviality, vivacity, (dejected, depressed, weariness, melancholy, sadness, dismal, despondent, solemnity, sorrowful)

elect-_v_ choice, option, discretion, alternative, decision, poll, ballot, vote, selection, pick, choose, cull, separate, prefer,

excerpt, (neutral, indifference, waive, abstain, refrain, reject)

elementary-_adj_ simple, homogeneity, sheer, neat, unsophisticated, basic, (combined, complicated, developed, complex)

elevation-_n_ height, altitude, pitch, loftiness, stature, prominence, mount, tower, soar, surmount, lofty, rise, mountainous, upper, gigantic, picture, drawing, sketch, (lowness, depression, lowlands, underlie, crouch, slouch, grovel, at a low ebb)

eliminate-_v_ deduction, retrenchment, removal, mutilation, amputation, curtailment, withdraw, diminish, abscind, prune, subtract, decrease, (addition, annexation, adjection, increase, supplement, inclusive, reinforce)

elude-_v_ refraining, forbearance, avoidance, abstain, eschew, shun, keep away from, shirk, dodge, recede, evade, aloof, (pursuit, chase, hunt, follow, leap, seek, engage, quest, prosecute)

emanate-_v_ egress, exit, emersiongence, evacuation, distillation, pouring, discharge, drain, emerge, move, pass, evacuate, escape, outlet, export, expatriation,

remigration, departure,
(ingress, entrance,
introgression, influx,
intrusion, invasion, import,
infiltration)

embark-v departure, port-
of-embarcation, outset,
start, removal, adieu,
farewell, starting point, set
out, quit, vacate,
(admission, insertion,
immigration, insinuation,
penetrate)

embarrass-v difficulty,
dilemma, perplexity,
entanglement,
awkwardness, quagmire,
unwieldy, restriction,
hindrance, impediment,
restraint, (support, uplift,
advance, furtherance,
promotion, favor,
patronage, advocacy)

embellish-v ornament,
decoration, architecture,
lace, fringe, border,
edging, wreath festoon
garland, pattern, improve,
(disfigure, deformity,
delete, blemish, flaw, scar)

embitter-v aggravate,
render worse,
exasperation,
exacerbation,
overestimation,
exaggeration, acerbate,
heightening, (relief,
deliverance, refreshment,
easement, softening,
alleviation, mitigation,
soothing)

emblazon-v bright, vivid,
intense, deep, rich, gay,

gaudy, showy, flashy,
glaring, flaring,
inharmonious,
ostentatious, pomposity,
splendor, (pale, neutral,
monochrome, colorless,
hueless, faint, dull, muddy,
discolored, achromatic)

embolism-n interference,
intervention, dovetailing,
infiltration, parenthesis,
obtrusion, interpenetrate,
obtrusion, (surround,
beset, encompass,
environ, encircle, embrace,
circumvent)

embrace-v contain, hold,
embody, involve, implicate,
inclusion, admission,
comprehension, reception,
intimate, cordial, devoted,
sincere, affection,
(alienation, dislike,
animosity, hostility,
exclusion, rejection, exile,
separation, elimination,
repudiation)

embroil-v derange,
unsettle, disturb, confuse,
muddle, fumble,
perturbation inversion,
complicate, disorder,
involve, convulse,
disconsert, dissension,
division, rupture,
(harmony, agreement,
sympathy, unison, accord,
reunion, conciliation)

embryo-n beginning,
commencement, opening,
inception, initial, onset,
genesis, birth, start,
originate, conceive, initiate,

groundwork, foundation, pivot, hinge, (creation, harvest, result, end, termination, conclusion, finale, consummation, death, finality, finish, close, expiration)

emergency-*n* critical situation, crisis, pinch, quandary, full of incident, circumstance, adventure, contingency, phenomenon,eventuality, concern (ease, feasibility, flexibility, smooth, lighten, manageable, submissive, disburden)

emigrate-*v* migrate, traverse, wander, travel, journey, egress, exit, evacuation, emersion, export, emerge, emanate, evacuate, (ingress, entrance, entry, influx, incursion, invasion, import, infiltration, immigration, admission)

eminence-*n* high, eminent, exalted, lofty, tall, gigantic, Patagonian, towering, elevated, dignity, importance, primacy, elevation, dedication, glorification, enshrinement, consecration, (disrepute, discredit, tarnish, taint, defilement, degradation)

emit-*v* ejection, emission, effusion, rejection, extrusion, discharge, expulsion, eviction, excrete, secrete, shed, void, effuse, spend, pour

forth, (reception, admission admittance, importation, introduction, absorption, insertion)

emotion-*n* feeling, affection, suffering, endurance, tolerance, supportance, experience, response, sympathy, sensation, pathos, passion, eagerness, enthusiasm, excitation, (insensitivity, indifference, peacefulness, impassive)

empire-*n* property, realty, land, acres, ground, command, sway, rule dominion, sovereignty, government, jurisdiction, (laxity, toleration, anarchy, relaxation, deposition, abdicate, depose, dethrone)

employ-*v* occupation, function, capacity, place, post, vocation, calling, occupy, undertake, transact, task, engagement, profession, commission, subjection, dependence, subordination, bondage, servitude, (freedom, independence, play, free, franchise, liberal, dismissal)

empower-*v* permission, allow, liberty, indulge, authorize, admission, accordance, might, power, potency, ability, able, qualify, (impotence, disability, incapacity,

invalidity, incompetence,
helplessness, collapse,
exhaust, disqualification)

empty-*adj* void, clear,
vacate, depart, eject, exit,
evict, emission, expulsion,
extrusion, deport, exhaust,
spend, use, consume,
impoverish, drain,
disperse, squander,
(provide, supply, fill,
furnish, replenish, recruit,
provide, admit, ingest,
absorb, gulp)

emulate-*v* excellence,
goodness, merit, virtue,
worth, superiority,
perfection, prime, exude,
imitate, copy, simulation,
follow, model after,
assimilation, (originality,
unparalleled, mistreat,
injurious, detrimental,
mischievous, nocuous)

enact-*v* perform,
movement, evolution,
perpetration, execution,
deed, proceeding,
participate, put-in-motion,
achieve, rule, regulation,
ordinance, statute,
(unlawfulness, inactivity,
idle, refrain, incomplete,
non-performance,
incomplete, neglect)

enamel-*n* polish, varnish,
gilding, embellish, lacquer,
paint, veneer, (blemish,
disfigure, deform, injure,
tarnish)

enchanting-*adj* elegant,
beauty, grace, polish,
radiance, splendor,
gorgeous, dazzling,
refined, idolatrous,
adoration, (repugnant,
shudder, irritating,
revolting, annoying,
provoking, obnoxious,
repulsive, offensive)

enclosure-*n* domain,
territory, district, zone,
compartment, place, spot,
document, envelope, den,
cell, dungeon, (liberate,
free, extricate, open,
spacious, boundless,
uncircumscribed)

encounter-*v* event,
occurrence, incident, affair,
phenomenon,
circumstance, accident,
adventure, crisis,
emergency, experience,
arrive, (depart, exodus,
await, future, impending,
destiny)

encourage-*v* induce,
persuade, lure, bribe,
prompt, inspire, beckon,
stimulate, tempt, seduce,
coax, tantalize, fascinate,
cajole, support, promote,
accommodate, help,
contribute, expedite,
bolster, uphold, (prevent,
obstruct, stop, interrupt,
impede, restrict, restrain,
block, inhibit, discourage,
hamper)

encroach-*v* trespass,
infringe, extravagate,
surpass, overstep, exceed,
invalidate, unlawful,
unauthorized, forfeited,
improper,

disfranchisement,
(sanction, warranty,
immunity, franchise,
vested-interest, deserve,
merit, substantiate)

encumber-v difficulty,
impracticability, tough,
dilemma, perplexity,
entanglement,
awkwardness, delicate,
vexed, impossible,
hindrance, restriction,
obstruction, stumbling-
block, (ease, flexibility,
feasible, smooth,
disencumber)

encyclopedia-n book,
volume, manual,
publication, knowledge,
possess knowledge,
learning, instructed,
educational, enlightened,
informed, bookish,
scholastic, profound,
(uninformed, uncultivated,
ignorant, simplistic,
unexplored)

end-n terminate, close,
finish, final, conclusion,
expire, result, discontinue,
(beginning, start, open,
commence, initial,
inaugurate, genesis)

endeavor-v pursuit,
enterprise, pursuance,
adventure, quest, exert,
labor, resolution, intention,
purpose, determined,
ambition, aim,
(indiscriminate,
promiscuous, incidental,
repose, without purpose)

endorse-v confirmation,

corroboration, support,
ratification, authentication,
admission, indication,
attest, document, refer,
substantiate, verify,
acknowledge, concur,
cooperate, agree, affirm,
consent, recognize, avow,
(dissent, discordance,
protest, contradict,
disagree, conflicting,
disavow, object)

endowment-n cleverness,
talent, ability, ingenuity,
capacity, forte, gift,
intelligence, capability,
expertness, dexterity,
adroitness, proficiency,
competence, excellence,
qualification, bestowal,
donation, investiture,
award, (grant, acceptance,
incompetence, inability,
disqualification, unfit,
inexperienced, awkward)

endure-v durable,
persistent, lasting,
continuing, permanence,
survive, longevity,
prolongation, protraction,
remain, continue, abide,
lingering, eternal,
everlasting, perpetual,
stable, established,
unchanged, subsist, (alter,
change, modify, deviate,
transformation, revolution,
short-lived, perishable,
impermanent)

energy-n power, might,
force, control, ascendancy,
authority, strength,
competency, pressure,

voltaism,
electromagnetism,
influence, enablement,
efficiency, endowment,
susceptibility, friction,
potential, intensity, vigor,
elasticity, (inertness,
dullness, inactivity,
languor, quiescence,
latency, passive, torpid,
sluggish, slow, tame,
lifeless, uninfluential,
incapacity, inefficacy)

enforce-v persuade, prevail,
enlist, engage, animate,
incite, provoke, instigate,
actuate, encourage,
dictate, press, compel,
force, compulsory,
constraint, necessitate,
oblige, stringent, duress,
coercion, (loss of right,
discourage, encroach,
breach, violate, forfeit,
unsanctioned)

engage-v motive, reason,
intention,inducement,
attraction, enticement,
allurement, fascination,
influence, bribe, lure,
campaign, crusade,
expedition, mobilization,
tactics, strategy, battle,
combative, militant,
appoint, commission,
assign, commit, authorize,
(annul, cancel, revoke,
dismiss, abolish, retract,
rescind, reverse, disclaim,
dissolve, null)

engrave-v memory,
remembrance, retention,
reminiscence, recognition,

keepsake, figure, emblem,
motto, put an indication,
label, imprint, Hallmark,
inscribe, (forgotten,
unremembered,
obliteration, mindless,
oblivious)

engulf-v dive, plunge,
submerge, sink,
importation, admission,
ingestion, absorption,
inhalation, suction,
interjection, import,
engorge, inhale, ingest,
(ejection, emission,
epulation, spew, disgorge,
dislodge, expectorate,
eviscerate, deport)

enigmatic-adj uncertain,
doubt, dubiety, hesitation,
perplexity, dilemma,
bewilderment, timid,
vacillation, vagueness,
obscurity, precarious,
casual, random,
hypothetical, paradoxical,
occasional, provisional,
(assurance, reliability,
infallible, unerring, positive,
dogmatic, explicit,
expressive, clear, lucid,
precise)

enjoy-v pleasure, sensual,
gratification, titillation,
comfort, luxury, relish,
revel, bask, cordial,
palatable, fruition,
satisfaction, delight,
refresh, happiness,
rapture, overjoyed,
captivated, ecstasies,
entranced, (suffer, pain,
ache, displeasure,

discomfort, weariness,
irritation, worry, infliction,
vexation, sorrow,
unhappiness)

enlarge-*v* increase,
augment, extend, develop,
grow, spread, gain,
intensify, enhance,
magnify, exaggerate, add,
expand, swell, inflate,
germinate, larger, amplify,
bulbous, (decrease,
subtract, reduce,
decrease, shrink, diminish,
contract, shrivel)

enlighten-*v* inform,
acquaint, knowledge,
communicate, announce,
instruct, outpour, report,
expound, explain, detect,
illuminate, reflect,
refraction, shine, glow,
glitter, twinkle, gleam,
glimmer, sparkle, radiate,
(darken, gloom, obscure,
shade, dim, eclipse,
extinguish, dingy, conceal,
disguise, ignore, suppress)

enough-*adj* sufficient,
adequate, full, abundance,
copious, profuse, galore,
outpouring, abound,
exuberate, inexhaustible,
ample, commensurate,
(insufficient, inadequate,
want, lack, require,
deplete, empty)

enrapture-*v* pleasurable,
delectability, amusing,
inviting, charm, fascinate,
enchanting, amiability,
seduction, amenity,
loveliness, goodness,

flatter, refresh, enliven,
attractive, alluring,
delightful, felicitous,
(annoying, grievance,
burden, bother, hurt,
displease, disturbing,
enraging, disgusting,
enrage)

entangle-*v* attach, affix,
bind, clinch, twine, encase,
gird, tether, fasten, secure,
twist, pinion, string, leash,
couple, intervolved,
embroil, unsettle, disturb,
complicate, ravel, dishevel,
tangle, wrangle, breach,
(discontinuity, separation,
dismemberment, sunder,
divide, abscind, rupture,
split, disentangle, unleash)

enterprise-*n* undertaking,
engagement, venture,
speculate, negotiate,
commerce, interchange,
quest, pursue, follow,
pursuit, course, (abstain,
refrain, escape, retreat,
reject, disengage, elude,
elusive, evasive)

entertain-*v* observance,
attention, application,
diligent, recognize,
mindful, regardful,
examine, scrutinize,
consider, social gathering,
joviality, hospitality,
welcome, festive,
fraternize, visit, consort,
reception, party,
(seclusion, exclusion,
privacy, reclusion,
isolation, desertion,
solitary)

enthusiasm-n emotion,
sensation, cordiality,
eagerness, zeal,
excitation, lively,
experience, warm, quick,
feverish, flamboyant,
fanatical, hysterical,
impetuous, impressed,
moved, touched, affected,
penetrating, (distract,
inactive, indifferent,
preoccupation, disregard,
disconcerted, inattentive)

entrance-n inlet, orifice,
mouth, porch, portal,
portico, door, gate,
threshold, vestibule, origin,
source, begin, commence,
enter, debut, inaugurate,
ingress, entry, influx,
immigration, (egress, exit,
evacuation, emerge.
discharge, conclude)

entrap-v snare, trap,
ambush, misinform,
deceptive, cunning,
deceitful, elusive,
insidious, risk, danger,
peril, insecurity, jeopardy,
precariousness, instability,
vulnerability, endanger,
(safety, security, protect,
invulnerable, defensible,
tenable, secure)

entrust-v commission,
delegate, assign, procure,
errand, appoint, nominate,
return, install, employ,
empower, represent,
bestow, give, present,
consign, dispense, endow,
award, gift, donation,
grant, benefaction,

(acquire, receive, accept,
assign, beneficiary, admit,
cancel, repeal, dismiss,
abolish)

enunciate-v pronounce,
accentuate, aspirate,
deliver, vocal, phonetic,
articulate, distinct, remark,
emphatic, assert, affirm,
report, express, state,
communicate, present,
(retract, repudiate, rebut,
silence, mute, suppress,
muffle, raucous, husky,
dry)

envoy-n messenger,
emissary, ambassador,
marshal, crier, trumpeter,
courier, representative,
functionary, diplomat,
delegate, commissioner

equal-adj sameness,
symmetry, balance,
evenness, monotony,
level, equivalent, match,
capability, capacity,
quality, attribute,
endowment, virtue, gift,
qualification, susceptibility,
(helplessness, inability,
incompetence, inept,
unevenness, inequality,
partial)

eradicate-v extract, remove,
eliminate, extricate,
exterminate, eject,
eviscerate(insert, implant,
inject, import, introduce,
infuse)

erect-v form, fabricate,
produce, create, construct,
manufacture, build,
organize, establish,

achieve, complete,
perform, forge, carve,
chisel, constitute, institute,
accomplish, evolve,
(destroy, destruct,
dissolve, break, disrupt,
ruin, smash, annihilate,
demolish)

erratic-adj inconstant,
versatile, changeable,
unstable, vacillate,
fluctuate, vicissitude, alter,
shifting, unstable, vary,
fickle, restless, spasmodic,
divert, deviate, wandering,
(stable, unchangeable,
constant, immobile, sound,
stiff, solid, established,
permanent, firm, settled)

eruption-n violent,
vehement, impetuous,
boisterous, effervescent,
turbulent, severe,
ferocious, raging,
exacerbate, malign,
forceful, spastic, explode,
volcanic, rampage, riotous,
(moderate, temperate,
relaxed, gentle, sober,
quiet, calm, tranquil,
pacify, sedative, balmy,
smooth)

escape-v release,
disengage, liberate,
discharge, emancipate,
dismiss, deliverance,
absolve, extricate, acquit,
free, dismantle, untie,
violate, transgress,
derelict, neglect, evade,
(responsible, accountable,
conscientious, restrain,
hinder, coerce, repress,

custody, arrest,
incarcerate, unrestricted)

essential-adj inherent,
important, intrinsic,
quintessence, incarnate,
backbone, principle, main,
major, chief, consummate,
prominent, necessary,
required, indispensable,
urgent, exact,
(insignificant, meaningless,
immaterial, minuscule,
diminutive, minor,
infinitesimal, paltry)

establish-v found, settle,
permanent, vested,
produce, create, construct,
form, fabricate,
manufacture, produce,
institute, evolve, develop,
generate, genesis,
contrive, build, accomplish,
(ruin, smash, crash,
destroy, abolish, suppress,
overthrow, demolish,
ravage, devastate, wreck,
consume)

esteem-v credit, assurance,
faith, trust, confidence,
presumption, dependence
on, reliance, conviction,
implicit, unshaken, dogma,
credence, credulous,
confident, assured,
sanctioned, advocacy,
approved, (dislike,
denunciation,
condemnation,
scandalous, discredit,
suspicious, doubtful,
skeptical)

et cetera-adj add, annex,
increase, increment,

supplement, affix, append,
furthermore, along with,
insert, and-so-forth,
access, include, upward,
(none, naught, deduction,
removal, abstraction,
curtailment, decrease.
abscind, decimate)

eternity-*n* perpetuity, ever,
immortality, everlasting,
perpetuation, forever,
endless, eternal,
ceaseless, evergreen,
imperishable, always,
lasting, continual, lingering,
permanent, (temporary,
perishable, briefly,
transient, sudden, quick,
short)

ether-*n* buoyancy, lightness,
volatility, levity, gossamer,
float, airy, weightless,
sublimated, inflation,
sponginess, absence of
solid, thin, tenuous, hollow,
(density, solid, compact,
thick, weight, gravity,
heaviness, pressure)

etiquette-*n* rule, standing
order, precedent, routine,
mode, vogue, conformity,
practice, custom, habit,
manners, breeding,
demeanor, gentility,
decorum, propriety,
carriage, (vulgar, bad
taste, awkward, tactless,
ill-bred, coarseness, rough,
slovenly, ungenteel,
gaudy, horrid, obtrusive)

evade-*v* conceal, secrecy,
hide, stealth, mask,
disguise, ensconce, muffle,
whisper, suppress, veil,
evasive, deceive, forge,
distort, avoid, escape,
retreat, reject, shun,
(pursue, chase,
scrupulous, frank, open,
candid, straightforward,
outspoken, undisguised)

event-*n* occurrence,
incident, affair, transaction,
proceeding, phenomenon,
circumstance, adventure,
consequence, happening,
encounter, undergo,
contest, competition,
engagement, tussle,
conflict, (uneventful, idle,
without incident)

evergreen-*adj* continuous,
progressive, successive,
unbroken, uninterrupted,
perennial, constant, entire,
linear, lasting, persistent,
perpetual, (temporary,
transient, fleeting, short-
lived, impermanent,
spasmodic, unsuccessful)

evil-*adj* harm, hurt, mischief,
nuisance, ill, tragedy,
badness, bane, outrage,
wrong, injure, grievance,
oppress, persecute, abuse,
overburden, victimize,
molest, (goodness,
excellence, merit, virtue,
value, worth, beneficial,
right, commendable)

evoke-*v* request, motion,
apply, canvass, address,
appeal, solicit, invite,
petition, beseech, plead,
implore, invoke, urge,
beset, ask, beg, crave,

pray, (protest, effect,
consequence, ignore)
evolution-*n* pullulate, bring
forth, create, beget, get,
generate, hatch, develop,
produce, form, make, ,
progress, journey, flow,
move, mobilize, (rest, still,
immobile, hold, halt,
remain, stop, stagnate)
exacerbate-*v* exalt,
strengthen, intensify,
enhance, magnify,
aggravate, exaggerate,
increase, growth, advance,
ascend, sprout,
exasperation, impetuosity,
effervescence, turbulence,
confusion, hysterical,
(moderate, relax,
remission, mitigation,
tranquil, pacify, soften,
decrease, moderate)
exact-*adj* similar,
semblance, parallelism,
likeness, match, accurate,
precise, gospel, authentic,
true, accurate, actual,
definite, right, correct,
punctual, constant,
unerring, (erroneous,
untrue, false, wrong,
unsubstantial, inaccurate,
different, incorrect)
exalt-*v* raise, intensify,
enhance, magnify,
exaggerate, increase,
enlarge, develop, spread,
lift, sublimate, erect,
elevate, heighten,
(depress, lower, reduce,
over-throw, decrease,
diminish, lessen, weaken,

depreciate)
examine-*v* scan, scrutinize,
inspect, review, glance,
consider, account,
indicate, observe, inquire,
request, investigate, seek,
search, explore, ransack,
rummage, (answer,
respond, retort,
acknowledge, escape,
unobservant, thoughtless,
careless, inattentive)
example-*n* prototype,
original, model, pattern,
precedent, standard, type,
copy, conform, instance,
sample, illustration,
specimen, rule,
agreement, observance,
exemplification, (original
duplicate, imitation,
irregularity, eccentricity,
abnormal, oddity, curiosity,
hybrid, unconventional,
infraction)
exception-*n* abnormal,
irregular, peculiar, unusual,
unexpected,
unconventional,
remarkable, queer,
exceptional, informal,
unaccustomed, exclusive,
(typical, normal, formal,
orthodox, sound, rigid,
positive, ordinary,
common, conventional)
excite-*v* energy, intensify,
vigor, strength, pressure,
poignancy, severity,
agitation, effervescence,
stir, stimulate, kindle,
exert, inflame, (inert, dull,
inactivity, languor, passive,

slow, lifeless, dormant)
exclusive-*adj* special,
particular, specify,
characteristic,
individualize, custom,
unusual, rare, singular,
curious, odd,
extraordinary, strange,
remarkable, noteworthy,
eccentric, peculiar,
abnormal, (conventional,
ordinary, conformity,
symmetry, conventional,
regular, usual)
excuse-*v* forgive, pardon,
condonation, remission,
absolution, amnesty,
reprieve, exoneration,
release, indemnity, forget,
acquit, vindicate, apology,
justify, warrant, advocate,
defend, contend, (accuse,
charge, impute, reproach,
denounce, inexcusable,
vicious)
exercise-*n* task, curriculum,
study, lesson, lecture,
sermon, apologue,
parable, action,
performance, perpetration,
movement, operation,
work, labor, execution,
procedure, deed, act,
proceeding, enact,
(passiveness, nothing,
inactivity, unintelligent,
misinformation)
exert-*v* hold, grasp, grip,
reach, command, use,
employ, exercise,
application, consume,
resort, wield, handle,
manipulate, avail,

(abstinence, relinquish,
discard, dismiss, waive,
neglect)
exhaust-*v* disarm,
incapacitate, disqualify,
unfit, invalidate, deaden,
cramp, muzzle, paralyze,
fatigue, weariness,
collapse, prostration,
(refresh, restoration,
revival, repair, refection,
recover, electricity, power,
energy, magnetism)
exile-*n* remove, eject,
unload, displaced,
homeless, seclusion,
privacy, reclusion, recess,
solitude, isolation,
loneliness, estrangement,
exclude, repel, expatriate,
outlaw, ostracize,
(companion, community,
welcome, reception,
gather, visiting, social,
conviviality, fellowship)
exit-*n* depart, embarkation,
removal, exodus,
valediction, adieu, farewell,
flight, egress, evacuation,
emerge, emanate, export,
(ingress, entrance, influx,
import, invasion,
admission, insertion)
exonerate-*v* disencumber,
disengage, disentangle,
extricate, unravel, untie,
unload, emancipate,
manage, accomplish,
absolve, dispense,
release, (prohibit, exclude,
embargo, forbid,
restrictive, difficult, hard,
tough, dilemma)

expand-*v* increase,
enlarge, extend, dilate,
develop, augment, gain,
ascend, exalt, intensify,
enhance, magnify, add,
develop, spread,
increment, (contraction,
consume, lessen, shrink,
collapse, emaciate,
atrophy, lose, reduce,
decrease, limit)

expedient-*adj* desirable,
suit, fitness, agreeable,
propriety, opportunism,
befit, conform, acceptable,
convenient, worthwhile,
applicable, useful,
(impropriety, unfit,
undesirable, objectionable,
unsatisfactory, improper)

expel-*v* ejaculate, eject,
discharge, push, fling,
throw, toss, projectile,
propel, project, send,
shoot, launch, deport, emit,
reject, banish, extradite,
exit, drain, evacuate,
(reception, admission,
admit, entrance, ingest,
absorb, receive, inhale)

F

fable-*n* fallacy,
misconception, error,
laxity, mistake, blunder,
misprint, delusion,
hallucination, deception,
mislead, deceive,
erroneous, untrue,
fallacious, unreal,
unauthenticated, (real,
actual, veritable, true,

exact, accurate, definite,
precise, defined)

fabulous-*adj* great,
abundant, intense, strong,
immense, enormous, vast,
extreme, excessive,
extravagant, exorbitant,
outrageous, preposterous,
unconscionable,
monstrous, stupendous,
astonishing, incredible,
marvelous, (small, little,
diminutive, minute, paltry,
faint, slender, light, slight,
scanty, meager, sparing,
few, moderate)

face-*n* exterior, surface,
outside, skin, superficial,
frontal, confront,
encounter, clash, contend,
confront, brave, dare,
summon, meet, stand-up,
valiant, resolute, stout,
determined, (cowardly,
shy, timed, soft, spiritless,
skittish, fearful, cower,
skulk, flinch, interior, inner,
within)

factor-*n* number, symbol,
figure, cipher, formula,
function, sum, multiplicand,
multiple, dividend, prime,
director, manager,
moderator, taskmaster,
delegate, consignee,
envoy, merchant, trader,
complimentary, positive,
negative, formula

fade-*v* vacant, empty,
blank, hollow, vanish,
evaporate, dissolve,
disappear, without,
dreamy, shadowy,

ethereal, immaterial,
nominal, nothing, luminary,
(substantial, exist, full,
tangible, essential,
material, reappear)
fail-*v* feeble, impotent,
relaxed, powerless, weak,
soft, fragile, flimsy,
unsubstantial, rickety,
cranky, drooping, lame,
withered, shattered,
decrepit, languid, spent,
decayed, worn, (strong
mighty, vigorous, forcible,
hard, adamantine, stout,
robust)
faint-*adj* small, atom,
particle, molecule, granule,
minimum, diminutive,
minute, paltry, slight,
scanty, meager, sparing,
weak, feeble, debilitate,
frail, fragile, languid,
decayed, rotten, wasted,
(strong, mighty, stamina,
muscle, virile, vigor, great,
immense, enormous,
abundant, considerable)
fair-*adj* colorless,
monochrome, pale, blanch,
hueless, pallid, dull,
muddy, sallow, dingy,
ghastly, lusterless,
moderate, ordinary,
average, indifferent,
(unparalleled, ripen,
mature, shiny, dark, tone)
faith-*n* belief, credence,
credit, assurance, trust,
confidence, certainty,
conviction, hopeful,
optimism, aspire,
expectation, confidence,

reliance, (hopelessness,
despair, despondency,
pessimism, forlorn, doubt,
misbelief, infidelity,
dissent)
fallacy-*n* false, illogical,
unsound, invalid,
deceptive, evasive,
irrelevant, vague,
unwarranted,
inconsequential,
inconsistent, fallacious,
(logical, correct,
reasonable, rational,
controversial, debatable,
relevant)
false-*adj* error, fallacy,
misconception, mistake,
fault, blunder, delusive,
deceptive, heresy, untrue,
incorrect, lie, guile, perjury,
forgery, invention,
fabrication, distortion,
evade, sham, (truthful,
scrupulous, sincere, frank,
honest, sober, exact, real,
authentic, precise, actual,
certain)
falter-*v* slow, slack, tardy,
leisurely, deliberate,
gradual, languid,
moderate, slouch, shuffle,
totter, stagger, mince,
lumber, linger, loiter,
saunter, plod, trudge,
dawdle, (gallop, canter,
trot, hasten, run, race,
whisk, fast, hurry, fly,
eloquent)
familiar-*adj* aware,
cognizant, acquaint,
inform, versed, instructed,
learned, lettered,

educated, enlighten,
bookish, accomplished,
profound, recognized,
occurrence, habitual,
usual, ordinary, (unusual,
unconformable, ignorant,
uninformed, shallow,
empty, illiterate)
family-*n* kin, relation,
fraternity, paternal,
maternal, ancestral, linear,
patriarchal, party, alliance,
linked, banded, united
fancy-*n* prefer, persuade,
option, select, pick, whim,
humor, drollery,
pleasantry, brilliant, desire,
wish, solicitous, overjoyed,
entranced, enchanted,
ravished, fascinated,
captivated, (afflicted,
worried, displeased,
aching, griped, grieve,
lament)
fantasy-*n* desire, wish,
fancy, want, need,
inclination, propensity,
liking, fain, anxious,
curious, craving, thirst,
(indifference, neutrality,
coldness, unconcern,
apathy, disdain)
far-*adv* distance, space,
remote, elongation,
remove, span, away,
inaccessible, out-of-reach,
unapproachable, asunder,
unconnected, (close, tight,
taut, firm, inseparable,
near, proximity, vicinity,
confines, alongside)
farce-*n* absurd, imbecility,
nonsense, paradox,

inconsistency, blunder,
muddle, preposterous,
senseless, inconsistent,
ridiculous, foolish, witty,
quick, nimble-witted,
jocular, waggish,
whimsical, playful,
pleasant, sparkling, (dull,
dry, commonplace,
pointless, flat, stale)
farewell-*n* depart, goodbye,
outward, exit, embark,
decampment, forfeiture,
loss, bereavement,
deprivation, lose, bereft,
(recover, regain, retrieve,
inherit, arrival, advent,
land, welcome)
fascinate-*v* influence,
prompting, dictate,
impulse, instigate,
encouragement, incentive,
incendiary, provoke,
arouse, stimulate, induce,
move, persuade, prevail,
wonder, astonish, amaze,
awe, (expect, common,
ordinary, dissuasion,
disincline, averse,
discourage)
fast-*adj* firm, close, tight,
taut, secure, set,
intervolved, inseparable,
indissoluble, fickle, erratic,
afloat, alternating, speed,
hasten, scamper, run,
swift, nimble, agile,
expeditious, galloping,
quick, (gradual, slow,
leisurely, tardy, gentle,
easy, deliberate, relax,
stagger, plod, trudge,vary,
vacillate)

fat-*n* large, big, great,
considerable, bulky,
voluminous, ample,
massive, capacious,
comprehensive, spacious,
might, towering, corpulent,
stout, portly, full, plump,
whopping, thundering,
fleshy, burly, vast, (little,
small, dwarf, pygmy,
midget, minute, diminutive,
microscopic, petty, wee,
undersized, short,
infinitesimal)

fathom-*n* length, line, bar,
rule, furlong, examine,
study, consider, calculate,
dip, dive, delve, probe,
sound, conclusion,
ascertain, deduce, derive,
gather, collect, (answer,
response, reply, rebut,
retort, rejoin, explain,
discover)

fault-*n* interruption,
disjunction, anacoluthon,
break, fracture, flaw, crack,
cut, gap, mistake, blunder,
oversight, misprint,
botchery, error, fallacy, fail,
unsuccessful, unfortunate,
(success, fortunate,
triumphant, definite,
precise, continuous,
consecutive, progressive,
unbroken, entire)

favorite-*n* pleasurable,
pleasing, agreeable,
acceptable, welcome,
satisfactory, luscious,
luxurious, sensual,
attractive, engaging,
captivating, alluring,

enticing, appetizing,
charming, delightful,
ravishing, beloved, loving,
adore, enamored, (hate,
alienation, estrangement,
coolness, enmity,
animosity, spiteful,
malicious, insulting,
irritating, provoking,
displeasing, annoy, cross,
harass)

fearful-*adj* displease,
annoy, disturb, perplex,
sadden, painful, sicken,
disgust, revolt, nauseate,
disenchant, repel, offend,
shock, skulk, slick, flinch,
cower, sneak, timid,
skittish, spiritless,
(courage, bravery, valor,
resolute, boldness, gallant,
contempt, confident,
achieve, fortitude, valiant)

feather-*n* plumage, plume,
crest, tuft, fringe, toupee,
nap, pile, floss, fur, down,
light, subtle, airy,
weightless, ethereal,
sublimated,
uncompressed, volatile,
buoyant, floating, (gravity,
heaviness, pressure,
ponderous, smooth, polish,
level, glossy, silken)

feature-*n* principle,
characteristic, fixed,
incurable, ineradicable,
fixed, invariable, form,
figure, shape,
conformation, construction,
cut, set, build, lineament,
posture, attitude,
(disfigure, deface, mutilate,

derange, shapeless,
unfashioned, intrinsic,
subjective)
felicitous-*adj* agreeing,
suiting, accordant, unison,
harmonize, congenial,
becoming, reconcilable,
accordance, consistent,
elegant, polished,
classical, graceful, easy,
readable, fluent, flowing,
unaffected, (graceless,
harsh, abrupt, dry, stiff,
cramped, formal, forced,
labored, artificial)
fence-*n* forgery, perjury,
false, untruth,
misrepresentation, lying,
invention, fabrication,
subreption, enclosure,
refuge, sanctuary, retreat,
shelter, screen, hiding
place, (truthful, true,
veracious, pure, sincere,
candor, honesty, fidelity)
ferment-*v* disorder,
derangement, irregularity,
untidiness, turmoil,
disturbance, convulsion,
tumult, uproar, inert,
inactive, passive, torpid,
sluggish, dull, heavy, flat,
slack, dead, uninfluential,
latent, dormant,
smoldering, (activity,
agitation, effervescence,
perturbation, orderly,
regular, proper, uniform,
methodical, symmetrical,
systematic)
fertile-*adj* productive,
prolific, teeming, fruitful,
luxuriant, pregnant,

generate, propagate,
sufficient, ample,
abundant, enough,
adequate, copious,
abounding,
commensurate,
satisfactory, valid, tangible,
(deficient, inadequate,
imperfect, scantiness,
scarce, poverty, famine,
drought)
festoon-*n* curved, linear,
lineal, bowed, vaulted,
hooked, semicircular,
crescentic, luniular, fig-
shaped, bow-legged,
oblique, circular,
ornamented, beautified,
gilt, tessellated, (simple,
plain, ordinary, homely,
eyesore, straight, direct)
fetch-*v* bring, worth, rate,
value, appraisement, cost,
figure, demand, fare,
(reduce, discount,
abatement)
feverish-*adj* haste, urgency,
acceleration, spurt, rush,
forced, march, dash,
flutter, flurry, hurried,
impetuous, excite, affect,
touch, move, (leisurely,
slow, deliberate, quiet,
calm, undisturbed, ease)
fidelity-*n* veracity,
truthfulness, frankness,
sincerity, candor, honesty,
scrupulous, frank, open,
trustworthy, unaffected,
honorable, faithful, loyal,
(violate, lawless,
transgressive, elusive,
evasive, false, deceitful,

fraudulent, dishonest,
unfaithful)
field-n spacious, roomy,
expansive, capacious,
ample, wide, vast,
uncircumscribed,
boundless, arena, zone,
meridian, territorial,
parochial, provincial,
patch, plot, region, realm,
domain, tract, court,
(niche, nook,
compartment, precinct)
fiery-adj violent, vehement,
warm, acute, sharp, rough,
rude, ungentle, bluff,
boisterous, wild, brusque,
abrupt, impetuous,
rampant, turbulent,
disorderly blustery, raging,
uproarious, frenzied,
(moderate, lenient, gentle,
mild, cool, sober,
temperate, reasonable,
measured, calm, quiet,
tranquil, still, slow)
fight-v contention, strife,
contest, struggle,
belligerency, controversy,
war, litigation, sparring,
competition, rivalry,
opposition, combative,
contending, embattled,
militant, (tranquil, pacific,
peaceable, untroubled,
harmony, quiet, neutrality,
conciliatory, composing,
amnesty, arrangement)
file-v arrange, distribute,
sort, prepare, dispose,
organize, analyze, classify,
digest, divide, catalog,
tabulate, index,

systematize, methodize,
regulate, register,
consecutive, continuous,
progressive, successive,
linear, (broken, interrupted,
unconnected, gap, litter,
scatter, disarrange,
disorganize)
fill-v complete, entire,
replenish, totally,
brimming, plenary, occupy,
inhabit, moored, domiciled,
populous, attend, dwell,
reside, lodge, nestle, roost,
permeate, (absent, away,
gone, missing, lost,
omitted, nonexistent,
empty, void, vacant,
devoid)
final-adj end, close,
terminate, dissonance,
conclude, finale, period,
term, consummation,
finish, expire, last,
complete, accomplished,
culmination, result,
exhaust, (beginning,
commencement, opening,
outset, inception
introduction, inauguration,
embarkation, initial, first,
incipient, leading)
find-v discover, detect,
hunt, determine, evolve,
decision, deduction, gain,
acquire, obtain, purchase,
remunerative, lucrative,
(lose, mislay, forfeit,
deprived)
fine-adj thin, narrow,
slender, close, taper, slim,
scant, spare, delicate,
incapacious, contracted,

lean, emaciated, meager,
gaunt, lanky, weedy,
flimsy, slight, (thick, broad,
dense, widen, ample,
extend, spread)

finesse-*n* clever, talent,
ability, ingenuity, capacity,
endowed, skillful,
dexterous, adroit, expert,
apt, handy, quick, deft,
ready, gain, smart, ready,
proficient, masterful,
thorough, accomplished,
able, ingenious, (bungling,
awkward, clumsy,
unskillful, slovenly, gawky,
inept, incompetent, stupid,
unfit)

fire-*n* heat, warmth, hot,
torrid, smoking, burning,
alight, afire, ablaze,
unquenched, smoldering,
flow, sweat, sultry, hellish,
inferno, (heavenly,
celestial, cold, cool, frigid,
fresh, keen, bleak,
shivering, bitter, chill,
inclement, biting, icy,
glacial, frosty, freezing)

first-*adj* initial, beginning,
commence, opening,
outset, inception,
introduction, inaugurate,
manifest, apparent,
entrance, inlet, dawn,
genesis, birth, origin, start,
front, (end, last,
consummation, finish,
terminate, conclude,
expire, definitive)

fish-*n* chase, hunt, sport,
pursuit, prosecution, quest,
scramble, inquire,

investigate, unearth, ferret
out, seek, search, track,
trail, feel out, (answer,
respond, reply,
acknowledge, discover,
explain, refrain, spare,
abstain, unsought, avoid,
neutral, evasive)

fit-*v* conform, consistent,
adapt, adjust, graduate,
assimilate, match, suit,
harmony, unison,
appropriate, deft, apply,
meet, dovetail, (unfit,
unsuited, inconsistent,
mismatch, intrusive,
uneven)

fix-*v* join, unite, attach,
affix, fasten, bind, secure,
clinch, twist, tie, string,
strap, sew, lace, stitch,
tack, knit, button, buckle,
hitch, lash, truss, bandage,
braid, (sunder, divide,
disjoin, sever, abscind, cut,
saw, snip, nip, cleave,
split, chip, crack, carve)

flagrant-*adj* immoral,
impropriety, scandal,
looseness, demoralization,
corruption, atrocity,
infirmity, weakness, frailty,
(virtuous, merit, worth,
excellence, credit, self-
control, self, denial,
fulfillment)

flat-*adj* inert, dull, torpor,
languor, quiescence,
inaction, sloth, obstinacy,
passive, sluggish, slack,
tame, slow, blunt, lifeless,
uninfluential, latent,
dormant, low, neap,

debase, nether, crouched,
subjacent, squat, prostrate,
(high, elevated, eminent,
exalted, lofty, tall, gigantic,
towering, soaring)

flatter-v cunning, crafty,
artful, skillful, subtle, feline,
profound, designing,
contriving, intriguing,
strategic, diplomatic,
artificial, sly, insidious,
stealthy, charming,
fascinating, enchanting,
humor, amuse, gratify,
(hurtful, bitter, displease,
annoy, trouble, disturb,
cross, perplex, molest,
tease, tire, irk, bother,
pester, harass, harry,
badger, beset, persecute,
heckle)

flaw-n discontinue, pause,
interrupt, intervene, break,
interpose, disconnect,
separation, gap, opening,
hole, chasm, crack, slit,
fissure, rift, breach, gash,
cut, leak, dike, fault,
erroneous, untrue,
unsound, illogical,
inaccurate, incorrect,
(exact, accurate, definite,
precise, well defined, just,
right, correct, strict, close,
liberal, rigid)

fleece-v tegument, skin,
pellicle, fell, fur, leather,
hide, pelt, cover, theft,
steal, thievery, robbery,
depredation, plunder,
pillage, black-mail,
burglary, buccaneer, strip,
abduct, confiscate,

sequester

fling-v propel, project,
throw, cast, pitch, chuck,
toss, jerk, heave, hurl, flirt,
fillip, dart, lance, tilt, sling,
send, discharge, shoot,
bolt, (draw, pull, haul, lug,
drag, tug, tow, trail,
wrench, jerk, tactile)

float-v navigate, sail,
nautical, naval, coasting,
afloat, transport, tender,
whaler, slaver, coaster,
yacht, launch, buoyant,
ascend, rise, (descent,
drop, fall, gravitate, sink,
droop, settle, decline,
dismount)

flock-n crowd, horde, body,
tribe, crew, gang, band,
party, company, troop,
army, regiment, assemble,
dense, muster, together,
collect, convene,
congregate, accumulate,
(disperse, adrift, stray,
disheveled, dissemination,
dissipation, scatter,
disband, disembody,
dispel)

floor-n ground, base,
foundation, substructure,
pavement, deck, footing,
basis, bottom, nadir, foot,
fundamental, horizontal,
level, even, plan, flat,
smooth, succeed, flushed,
victorious, unbeaten,
(unsuccessful, highest,
top, crest, apex, zenith,
upper most)

flounder-v inconstancy,
versatile, unstable,

vacillate, changing, ever
changing, fluctuating,
restless, agitating,
variable, erratic, fickle,
irresolute, capricious,
spasmodic, (fixed,
steadfast, firm, steady,
balanced, valid,
immovable, riveted,
tethered, anchored,
moored, established)

flourish-v prosperity,
welfare, well-being,
affluence, success, wealth,
thriving, fortunate, lucky,
flushed, felicitous,
effective, flower, (abortive,
addle, fruitless, bootless,
inefficient, inefficacious,
lame, insufficient,
unavailing, useless,
swamp)

flow-v elapse, lapse, run,
proceed, advance, pass,
roll, slide, glide, progress,
loose, dependent, stream,
flux, run, course, move,
shifting, restless, nomadic,
(still, fixed, stationary,
sedentary, quiet, calm,
anchor, still, restful)

flower-n produce, create,
construct, form, fabricate,
manufacture, build, erect,
edify, organize, establish,
achieve, evolve, develop,
grow, genesis, bear,
generate, impregnate,
(destroy, destruct, waste,
dissolve, consume, ruin,
crash, smash, extinction,
subversive, suicidal,
squash, squelch)

fluctuate-v change,
inconstancy, versatility,
mobility, instability,
vacillate, alter,
restlessness, fidget,
disquiet, agitate, variable,
waver, shift, shuffle, flitter,
totter, tremble, oscillate,
alternate, (tethered, fixed,
steadfast, firm, balanced,
permanent, constant,
unchanged, undeviating,
durable, perennial)

flush-v flat, plane, flounder,
jet, spurt, squirt, spout,
splash, rush, gush, deluge,
inundation, stream, flux.
flow, brook, torrent, (gust,
blast, breeze, squall, gale,
storm, tempest)

fly-v flit, elapse, lapse, flow,
run, proceed, advance,
slide, glide, pass, transient,
fleeting, shifting,
spasmodic, wild, abrupt,
impetuous, turbulent,
disorderly, (moderate,
gentle, lenient, still, slow,
smooth, tame, peaceful,
standing, perpetual)

fold-v halve, divide, split,
cleave, bisect, enclose,
envelope, (circumvent,
skirt, twine)

follow-v succeed, next,
ensue, conform, observe,
obey, comply, supervene,
consecutive, continue,
sequel, behind, attend,
pursue, beset, tread,
example, (precede,
forerun, lead, advance,
prior, former, foregoing,

before, advance, start,
preliminary)
fool-*n* deceive, false, fraud,
guile, delusion, circumvent,
overreach, maneuver,
cunning, deceptive,
counterfeit, pseudo,
pretend, feign, tricky,
adulterate, rotten, disguise,
simulate, disrespect,
aweless, irreverent,
disparaging, insulting,
rude, derisive, sarcastic,
(respect, regard,
consideration courtesy,
reverence, honor, esteem
estimation, veneration,
admiration, approbation)
foot-*n* bottom, nadir, sole,
toe, hoof, fundamental,
founded, based, ground,
broad, support,
foundation, base, basis,
bearing, hold, landing, aid,
prop, stand, shore, truss,
beam, rafter, (suspend,
hang, pendulum, swing,
dangle, swag, flap, loose,
flowing)
forbear-*v* refrain, abstain,
inaction, neutrality,
avoidance, evasion,
elusion, seclusion, flight,
escape, recoil, reject,
unsought, shun, spare,
shirk, dodge, parry,
fugitive, (pursuit, pursue,
enterprise, adventure,
scramble, chase, hunt,
prosecute)
forbid-*v* prohibit, disallow,
bar, forefend, withhold,
limit, circumscribe, restrict,

taboo, interdict, exclude,
dissent, negative,
unconsenting, unavowed,
discontented, (assent,
admission, agreement,
affirm, recognition,
acknowledge, permit,
indulgent, allow)
force-*v* power, potency,
might, energy, ascend,
control, authority, ability,
ableness, competency,
efficiency, enablement,
influence, capability,
almighty, adequate,
efficacious, valid, able,
(powerless, impotent,
unable, incapable,
incompetent, harmless,
weaponless, null, void,
nugatory, ineffectual,
failing, inadequate)
forecast-*v* foresight,
deliberation, prevision,
longsightedness,
anticipation, providence,
surmise, foregone
conclusion, prudence,
foreknowledge,
precognition, prediction,
announcement,
premonition, warning,
prognosis, prophecy,
horoscope, preparation,
rehearsal, provision,
arrange, array,
(unnurtured, uneducated,
premature, undigested,
improvidence)
forefathers-*n* paternal,
parental, maternal, family,
ancestral, linear,
patriarchal, descendant,

heir, generation, (succeed,
ensue, alternate, after,
latter, follow)
foreign-*adj* irrelative,
irrespective, unrelated,
arbitrary, independence,
adrift, isolated, insular,
extraneous, strange, alien,
outlandish, exotic, intrude,
emigrant, outsider,
inadmissible, (implicate,
integral, member, merge,
constitute, relative,
cognate, referable, akin,
family, allied, affiliated,
fraternal)
foremost-*adj* superior,
supreme, greater,
advantage,
preponderance,
advantageous, prevalence,
nobility, preeminence,
culmination,
transcendence, excess,
major, higher, exceeding,
distinguished, vaulting,
important, (inferior,
minority, smaller, minor,
less, deficient,
subordinate, secondary,
least, under, lower,
diminish)
forestall-*v* subsequently,
afterwards, later,
thereafter, thereupon,
since, beforehand,
anticipate, prior, previous,
precede, posthumous,
premature, before long,
unexpected, postpone,
(adjournment, succeed,
supervene, posterior,
following, after, later,

postliminium, postdate)
forfeit-*v* fail, evasion,
unobservance, omission,
neglect, informality,
infringement, infraction,
violation, transgression,
break, retraction,
repudiation, nullification,
protest, lapse, deprivation,
loss, (fulfillment,
satisfaction, faithful, profit,
earnings, proceeds,
acquire, advantageous,
gainful, remunerative,
paying, lucrative)
forlorn-*adj* dejected,
depression, prostration,
lowness, oppression,
heaviness, gloom,
weariness, melancholy,
sadness, dismal,
despondent, blank,
discourage, dispirit, frown,
spiritless, grieve, affliction,
(cheerful, happy, smiling,
blithe, bright, airy, jaunty,
sprightly, vivacious,
sparking, winsome, frisky,
playful, jocular)
form-*n* copy, facsimile,
counterpart, effigy,
likeness, similitude,
semblance, cast, imitation,
model, representation,
orderly, regular, correct,
methodical, uniform,
symmetrical, unconfused,
arranged, systematic,
(disorderly, promiscuous,
indiscriminate, chaotic,
complex, intricate,
complicated, perplexed,
knotted, tangled,

dislocated)

formula-_n_ rule, routine, uniformity, constancy, standard, model, precedent, conformity, principle, steady, legal process, law, code, statute, canon, ordinance, decree, numeral, divisible, prime, fractional, (irregular, diversified, indiscriminate, desultory, difference, illegal, prohibited, unlawful, illicit, uncharted, unauthorized, unofficial)

fortuitous-_adj_ casual, accidental, adventitious, causeless, incidental, contingent, undetermined, possible, unintentional, haphazardly, random, speculation, venture, chance, undesigned, unpremeditated, indiscriminate, promiscuous, undirected, without purpose, (intended, advised, determined, prepense, undertaking, design, ambition)

fortune-_n_ chance, indetermination, accident, hazard, haphazard, random, fate, lottery, casually, happen, destiny, foredoom, predestined, fatalism, wealthy, rich, affluent, opulent, moneyed, capital, afford, (poor, indigent, poverty, needy, necessary, distressed, bereft, bereaved, reduced)

forward-_adj_ early, prime,

timely, punctual, prompt, summary, discourteous, disrespect, impudent, ill-breed, vulgar, unpolished, rude, saucy, harsh, austere, sarcastic, biting, caustic, snarling, surly, (courteous, polite, civil, mannerly, urbane, well-behaved, polished, cultivated, refined, gallant, late, tardy, slow, behind, behind, backward)

foundation-_n_ stability, constancy, immobile, sound, vital, stable, established, fixture, tower, pillar, fixed, durable, tethered, anchored, moored, (unstable, fluctuation, movable, vicissitude, shake, totter, flitter, flutter, flounder, mobile, transient)

fracas-_n_ disorder, derangement, irregular, anomaly, confusion, disarray, muddle, hodgepodge, chaos, medley, scramble, embroilment, whirlwind, unsymmetrical, untidy, (order, uniformity, symmetry, series, routine, method, disposition, arrangement, discipline)

fracture-_n_ separation, parting, detachment, segregation, divorce, supposition, divide, sunder, sever, cut, saw, carve, dissect, mangle, gash, hash, slice, whittle,

disperse, apportion,
(attach, fix, join, unite,
embody, affix, fasten, bind,
secure, tie, pinion, string,
strap, link, marry)
frail-*adj* weak, relax,
languor, impotence,
infirmity, fragile,
declination, loss, dull,
spent, weatherbeaten,
decayed, rotten worn,
seedy, wasted,
defenseless, feeble,
debilitate, unnerved,
powerless, flaccid,
nervous, soft, womanly,
unsubstantial, (strong,
mighty, vigorous, forcible,
hard, adamantine, stout,
robust, sturdy, hardy,
powerful, potent, valid,
resistless, impregnable,
sovereign, athletic)
frame-*v* support, aid, prop,
stand, anvil, shore, skid,
rib, truss, bandage, stirrup,
stilt, scaffold, skeleton,
beam, rafter, backbone,
set, fit, mold, tone, tenor,
turn, trim, guise, fashion,
light, style, character,
structural, organic, model,
formal, (dangle, swag, flap,
trail, flow, suspend, hand,
sling, append, pensive,
depend, swing, loose,
flowing)
free-*adj* sunder, divide,
sever, abscind, splinter,
chip crack, divorce, part,
detach, separate, cutoff,
adrift, loose, disentangle,
isolate, liberate, apart,

rupture, breach, split,
divulge, section, rift,
incision, fission, (attach,
fix, affix, fasten, pinion,
string, gird, tether, moor,
harness, chain, fetter, join,
twine, twist, incorporate,
close, secure, leash,
couple, nail, bolt)
frequent-*adj* repeat, again,
often, anew, over again,
once more, ditto, many,
iterate, harping,
recurrence, succession,
monotony, rhythm, imitate,
incessant, perpetual,
continual, constant,
habitual, commonly,
(seldom, rarely, scarcely,
hardly, infrequently, few,
never, inconstant)
fresh-*adj* new, novelty,
recent, immaturity, youth,
innovation, renovation,
modern, mushroom,
renew, green, evergreen,
raw, virgin, neoteric,
newborn, (old, antiquity,
maturity, decline, decay,
senility, seniority,
archaism, ancient,
venerable, prime,
obsolete)
fret-*v* suffer, pain, dolor,
ache, twinge, twitch, gripe,
headache, hurt, cut, sore,
discomfort, malaise,
spasm, cramp, nightmare,
throb, agitate,
sharp,piercing, throbbing,
gnawing, anguish,
experience, writhe, (enjoy,
luxurious, sensual,

comfortable, cozy, snug,
agreeable, grateful,
refreshing, cordial, genial,
palatable, fragrant,
melodious, lovely,
beautiful)

fringe-*n* closure,
obstruction, plug, block,
stop, button, shut, bar,
bolt, stop, seal, plumb,
choke, border, (vent,
vomiter, orifice, mouth,
throat, portal)

frivolous-*adj* foolish,
imbecility, stolidity, dull,
incompetence, frivolity,
irrationality, trifling,
giddiness, eccentricity,
extravagant, absurdity,
shallow, weak, stupid,
idiotic, vacant, bewildered,
bovine, silly, senseless,
nonsensical, inept, giddy,
idle, (sober, prudent,
cautious, staid, solid,
considerate, wise,
watchful, provident,
intelligent, acute, rational,
sound, clever, shrewd,
discerning, penetrating)

front-*n* cover, guise, outfit,
envelop, involve, sheathe,
foreground, face, advance,
outpost, countenance,
pioneer, insolence, (rear,
back, posteriority, guard,
nape, stern, rump, breech,
dorsal, after, aft, astern,
behind, divest, bare,
dishabille)

frugal-*adj* economical,
saving, thriftiness,
retrenchment, prevention,
sparing, careful,
parsimony, abstinence,
moderation, temperance,
forbearance, self-denial,
restraint, (pleasurable,
indulgence, self-
indulgence, effeminacy,
excess, dissipation,
generous, bountiful, liberal,
free, unsparing, carte
blanche)

frustrate-*v* thwart,
disconcert, balk, foil, baffle,
snub, override, circumvent,
defeat, spoil, mar, cripple,
extinguish, dishearten
dissuade, undermine,
meddle, encumber, choke,
bar, block, barricade,
prevent, oppose, (assist,
help, lift, advance, favor,
advocate, sustain,
reinforce, support, uphold,
bolster, nurture)

fuel-*n* firing, combustible,
coal, anthracite, coke,
carbon, charcoal, turf,
peat, firewood, bobbing,
match, light, incense,
brand, torch, fuse, (non-
combustible, non-
flammable)

fugitive-*n* temporarily,
awhile, short, briefly,
transient, evanescence,
impermanence, fly, **gallop,**
vanish, evaporate,
refugee, emigrant,
vagabond, nomad,
wanderer, adventurer,
rover, straggler, rambler,
(durable, lasting,
permanent, survive, **long-**

standing, persistent,
perpetual)

full-*adj* much, great, might,
importance, considerable,
fair, huge, big, abundant,
intense, strong, sound,
heavy, plenary, complete,
entirety, perfection,
altogether, effectual,
wholly, totally, (incomplete,
imperfect, fault, short,
meager, lame, sketchy,
small, minimum, little,
diminutive, minute)

fumble-*v* jumble, muddle,
toss, hustle, derange,
misarrange, misplace,
mislay, decompose,
disorder, disorganize,
embroil, unsettle, disturb,
touch, feel, handle, thumb,
paw, grope, grabble,
twiddle, (arrange,
distribute, sort, assort,
allotment, apportionment,
analyze, classify, digest)

fumigate-*v* vaporize,
gasify, evaporate, exhale,
volatile, smoke, transpire,
emit, clean, purify,
defecate, purge, launder,
(rot, fester, putrefy, reek,
stink, mold, dirty, filthy,
grimy, soiled, contaminate,
taint, corrupt, liquefied)

function-*n* numeral,
symbol, divisible, prime,
fractional, decimal,
arithmetic, analysis,
algebra, integral, calculus,
useful, serviceable,
subservient, conducive,
efficient, effective,

applicable, advantageous,
expedient, (uselessness,
inefficacy, futility,
inadequate, inefficient,
unskillful)

fundamental-*adj* essential,
quintessence, incarnation,
intrinsic, inherence,
normal, implanted, natural,
radical, hereditary,
congenital, support, base,
basis, bearing, footing,
hold, (dependency,
suspension, hanging,
swing, dangle, append,
extrinsically, extraneous,
incidental, accidental)

fungus-*n* growth, carbuncle,
wart, polypous, fungous,
blister, boil, poison, leaven,
virus, venom, arsenic,
antimony, mildew, dry-rot,
cancer, canker, rust,
(remedial, restorative,
nutritious, peptic, curable,
cellular, spongy,
infundibular)

furbish-*v* improve,
betterment, melioration,
mend, amend, advance,
elevate, increase, reform,
correct, refine, prepare,
provide, forthcoming,
adornment, embellishment,
japanning, varnish,
cosmetic, (pitted,
discolored, imperfect,
impairment, injury,
damage, loss, detriment,
decline, decay,
dilapidation, atrophy,
collapse)

furnish-*v* provide, purvey,

reinforce, supply, find,
cater, victual, forage,
replenish, elaborate,
mature, ripen, mellow,
season, temper, anneal,
commissariat, reserve,
(shiftless, wasteful, spend,
squander, drain,
consume, expend,
exhaust, disperse)

fury-*n* violence, inclemency,
vehemence, might,
impetuosity,
boisterousness,
effervescence, turbulence,
bluster, uproar, riot,
severe, exacerbation,
orgasm, force, outrage,
shock, trepidation,
perturbation, ruffle, hurry,
fuss, flurry, fluster, (cool,
passiveness, calmness,
composure, tranquil,
serenity, quiet, staidness,
restraint, submissive)

fuse-*v* join, junction,
attachment, ligation,
corporate, unite, fix, affix,
fasten, bind, secure,
clinch, twist, knit, braid,
splice, gird, tithe, molten
(separate, disjoin,
discontinue, leave,
asunder, adrift, insular, rift,
unconnected, apart)

G

gag-*n* render mute,
constrained, imprisoned,
pent up, stiff, control
repress, smother,
suppress, rein, hold,

enchain, shackle, bridle,
muzzle, pinion, handcuff,
secure, (liberate,
disengage, release,
emancipate, discharge,
dismiss, deliver, acquittal)

gage-*n* measure, weigh,
survey, appraise, assess,
estimate, reckon, gauging,
standard, rule, caliper,
meter, rod, check,
compass, rate

gain-*v* benefit,
improvement, advantage,
interest, service, behalf,
satisfactory, commend,
useful, good, blessing,
fortune, treasure,
happiness, profit, earnings,
income, proceeds, fruition,
harvest, (lose, forfeit,
lapse, privation,
bereavement, deprivation,
riddance, incur, mislay,
minus)

galaxy-*n* assemblage,
collection, location,
ligation, compilation, levy,
gathering, muster, flux,
verge, meeting, group,
cluster, myriad, multitude,
numerousness, profusion,
multiple, heavenly bodies,
stars, asteroids, nebulae,
milky, way, galactic circle,
(few, scant, thin, rare,
scatter, scarce, infrequent,
handful, minority)

gall-*n* torment, torture, rack,
discomfort, malaise,
twinge, twitch, pained,
ache, unsavory,
unpalatable, bitter, acrid,

rough, offensive, repulsive,
nauseous, loath,
unpleasant, (palatable,
nice, dainty, delectable,
gusty, appetizing,
exquisite, luscious,
pleasurable, gratification)

gamble-v chance, accident,
fortune, hazard, attribute,
imputation, ascription,
attribution, rationale,
speculation, venture,
stake, betting, adventurer,
(intentional, knowingly,
advisedly, designedly,
purposely, studiously,
deliberately, attribute)

game-n beast, brute,
animal, fleshy, zoological,
pursuit, enterprise,
undertaking, adventure,
quest, business, hobby,
chase, hunt, sporting,
follow, prosecute, fun,
frolic, amusement,
entertain, diversion,
relaxation, solace,
pastime, pleasure,
merriment, laughter,
regatta, (weary, disgusting,
tiresome, irksome,
uninteresting, dry,
monotonous, dull, arid,
humdrum)

gang-n assemblage,
gathering, collection,
compilation, levy, muster,
crown, throng, flood, rush,
deluge, horde, body, tribe,
crew, band, squad, party,
go, moving, mobile,
mercurial, restless,
shifting, nomadic, unquiet,

erratic, (quiet, tranquility,
calm, repose, peace,
stagnate, unassembled,
disperse, sparse, sporadic,
adrift, disheveled,
streaming)

garble-v mutilate, amputate,
abscind, excise, pare, thin,
prune, decimate, abrade,
scrape, file, geld, diminish,
curtail, shorten,
disseminate, exclude, bar,
leave, reject, repudiate,
blackball, relegate,
segregate, banish,
separate, omit, week,
winnow, (containing,
constituting, inclusion,
admission,
comprehension, reception,
addition, annexation,
addition, affix, subjoin)

garland-n circle, circlet,
ring, areola, hoop,
bracelet, armlet, round,
annular, orbicular, oval,
ovate, elliptic, spherical,
wreath, fascia, crown,
corona, coronet, chaplet,
festoon, embroidery,
ornamented, embellish,
beautified, adorn, (simple,
plain, homely, ordinary,
unaffected, chaste, severe,
bald, flat, dull, convoluted)

garrison-n occupied,
indigenous, native,
domestic, domiciled,
naturalized, vernacular,
domesticated, domiciliary,
safe, utility, efficacy,
serviceable, adequate,
efficient, prolific, shelter,

concealment, fortification,
munition, ditch,
entrenchment, barrier,
fence, (aggressive,
attacking, offensive,
obsidianus, incursion,
invasion, encampment,
bivouac)

gasp-*v* blow, sneeze,
sternutation, hiccup,
cough, waft, respire, puff,
wheeze, snuff, fan,
ventilate, tempestuous,
droop, broken-winded,
fatigue, weariness,
yawning, lassitude,
exhaustion, (refreshed,
recuperative, respire,
breathe, reinvigorate, flow,
profluent, effluence)

gather-*v* assemble, collect,
locate, compile, lever,
muster, concourse, verge,
hoard, meet, flock,
cumulative, populous,
gainful, profitable, acquire,
remunerative, lucrative,
(loss, forfeit, privation,
riddance, bereaved,
dispossessed, quit,
deprivation)

gay-*adj* colorful, hue, tint,
dye, shade, pigment,
chromatic, bright, vivid,
intense, deep, fresh,
unfaded, rich, gorgeous,
gaudy, florid, showy,
flaunting, flashy, glaring,
flaring, discordant,
(mellow, harmonious,
sweet, delicate, tender,
refined, dismal, somber,
melancholy, dark, gloomy,

dreadful)

gazette-*n* publication,
current, notorious, flagrant,
circulated, propagation,
edition, newspaper,
journal, imprinted, edition,
diary, log, book, record,
note, almanac, ledger,
archive, scroll, chronicle,
portfolio, (obliterate,
erasure, cancel, out of
print, unregistered,
unwritten, efface)

gear-*n* clothes, things,
array, attire, vesture, garb,
apparel, wardrobe, outfit,
equipment, uniform,
regimentals, livery,
accouterment, toggery,
handle, shaft, shank,
blade, tiller, helm, pulley,
crank, winch, lever,
(divested, nude, exposed,
thread-bare, bareness,
exfoliation, disrobe,
dismantle, dishabille)

gem-*adj* super-excellence,
superiority, perfection,
prime, flower, cream,
goodness, merit, worth,
beneficial, edifying,
satisfactory, jewelry,
bijouterie, trinket, locket,
necklace, bracelet, anklet,
precious, brilliant, (pitted,
injured, deformed,
defective, flow, stain,
tarnished, disfigured,
hurtful, noxious,
detrimental, mischievous,
malignant)

general-*adj* universal,
miscellany, catholic, every,

all, generic, common,
ecumenical,
transcendental, prevalent,
prevailing, always,
prescription, usage, rule,
standing order, precedent,
routine, rut, groove,
habitual, conformable,
military authority, marshal,
potentate, sovereign,
tyrant, (servant, subject,
retainer, squire, vassal,
slave, unusual,
uncommon, special,
disusage, unconformity,
unaccustomed)

genial-*adj* warm, mild,
ardent, aglow, productive,
bringing forth, birth,
evolution, development,
growth, genesis, perform,
operate, flow, formative,
sensual, voluptuous,
agreeable, cordial, sweet,
melodious, (painful,
aching, sore, gripe, gnaw,
torture, torment, agonize,
crucify, tingle, writher,
rack, fall, destroy,
dissolution, consumption,
subversive, ruinous,
incendiary, deleterious)

genius-*n* intellect,
understanding, reason,
mental, rational,
subjective, faculties,
senses, consciousness,
observation, percipience,
instinct, conception,
capacity, wit, ability,
skillful, dexterous, adroit,
expert, proficient, masterly,
clever, (foolish, inept,

inexperienced,
incompetent, stupid,
unqualified, vacant,
thoughtless, diverted,
narrow-minded, dull,
thoughtless)

gentle-*adj* moderate,
temperate, sober,
calmness, relaxed,
tranquil, mitigate, pacify,
sedative, lessen, slow,
smooth, unexciting,
hypnotic, soft, bland,
lenient, reasonable,
peaceful, mild, demure,
imperturbable, enduring,
(vehement, demonstrative,
violent, wild, furious, fierce,
fiery, hot-headed, madcap,
over-zealous, enthusiastic,
impetuous, passionate,
fanatical)

genuflection-*n* bowing,
courtesy, curtsy,
obeisance, depress, drop,
sink, fall, debase, abase,
reduce, prostration,
subversion, precipitation,
kneel, surrender, kowtow,
homage, (disrespectful,
aweless, irreverent,
disparaging, insulting,
rude, sarcastic, elevate,
raise, erection, upheaval)

gestation-*n* production,
creation, construction,
formation, fabrication,
manufacture, building,
erection, flowering, fructify,
birth, delivery,
confinement, travail, labor,
midwife, obstetrics,
gender, propagation,

impregnation, (destroy, waste, disruption, consumption, ruin, smash, sacrifice, demolish, dispel, smash, quell, shatter)

ghastly-*adj* pale, uncolored, achromatic, hueless, pallid, faint, dull, muddy, dead, dingy, ashy, cadaverous, ashen, misshapen, plain, homely, ugly, deformed, disfigurement, distorted, graceless, uncouth, rugged, rough, gross, rude, awkward, (beautiful, elegant, graceful, adorned, brilliant, radiance, splendor, gorgeous, magnificent, pretty, handsome, dapper, jaunty, shiny)

giant-*n* gargantuan, monster, mammoth, whale, behemoth, leviathan, colossus, whopper, great, ample, large, corpulent, stout, fat, huge, immense, enormous, mighty, stupendous, infinite, brawny, lumpish, strong, mighty, robust, powerful, potent, valid, resistless, (frail, fragile, shatter, flimsy, unsubstantial, rickety, little, dwarf, pygmy, scant, minute diminutive, puny, infinitesimal, atomic)

giddy-*adj* inattentive, absent, abstracted, distrait, lost, preoccupied, disconcerted, napping, dreamy, thoughtless, scatter-brained, wild,

careless, disregard, heedless, neglectful, fickle, unsettled, vacillation, timid, (self-controlled, determined, decisive, resolute, vigor, zeal, devotion, self-possessed, definitive, peremptory, flinching, shrinking, firm, relentless)

gild-*v* cover, canopy, bandage, cutaneous, armor-plated, iron-clad, sheath, wrap, veneer, face, coating, paint, anoint, incrustation, whitewash,envelop, deceive, falseness, untruth, fraud, deceit, guild, misrepresent, trick, cheat, juggle, collusion, (line, stuff, incrust, wad, pad, truth, open)

gird-*v* bind, firm, fast, close, tight, taut, secure, set, nail, bolt, hasp, clasp, rivet, solder, wedge, miter, attach, affix, secure, engage, strengthen, vigor, force, might, robust, sturdy, hardy, powerful, potent, dynamic, (weak, feeble, debilitate, impotent, relaxed, unnerved, unstrung, flaccid, soft, effeminate, frail, flimsy)

glad-*adj* gratification, pleasure, enjoyment, fruition, relish, satisfaction, happiness, felicity, bliss, beatitude, joy, gladness, delight, glee, cheer, **comfort, overjoyed,**

enchanted, raptured,
ravished, fascinated,
captivated, pleasing,
(suffer, painful, ache,
smart, grieve, mourn,
yearn, repine, droop,
languish, despair,
displeasure, annoyance,
irritation, infliction, anxiety,
grief, sorrow)

glance-v view, look, espial,
ken, glimpse, peep, gaze,
stare, leer, contemplation,
visual, ocular, behold,
perceive, ophthalmic,
sight, examine cursorily,
skim, watchful, (inattentive,
unobservant, blind, close,
dismiss, discard,
discharge, oversight,
disregard, heedlessness,
overlook)

glare-v garish, blazing,
ablaze, rutilant, meteoric,
phosphorescent, aglow,
shining, luminous, bright,
vivid, splendent, lustrous,
flash, sparkle, scintillate,
coruscate, reflection,
refraction, dispersion,
gleam, twinkle, shimmer,
radiate, (dark, dim, dull,
dingy, fade, grimey, shade,
obscure, eclipse, gloom,
extinguish)

glass-n transparent,
pellucid, lucid, diaphanous,
limpid, clear, serene,
crystalline, vitreous,
hyaline, smooth, polish,
gloss, even, flat, sleek,
brittle, fragile, break, frail,
lacerate, (tenacious, tough,

strong, opaque, film, thick,
cloudy, hazy smoky,
murky, dirty, rough,
rugged)

glide-v motion, movement,
move, going, flow, flux, run
course, stir, evolution,
kinematics, step, rate,
pace, tread, stride, gait,
port, cadence, carriage,
transitional, motive,
shifting, mobile, mercurial,
unquiet, (still, fixed,
stationary, sedentary, stay,
pause, lull, tranquil,
deliberate, slow, gradual)

glimmer-n light, ray, beam
stream, gleam, streak,
moon, glow, flush, halo,
glory, luminous, lucid,
bright, vivid, lustrous,
shimmer, sparkle,
scintillate, radiate, (dark,
obscurity, gloom, eclipse,
shade, sunless, somber,
dim, dingy, gloomy,
overcast)

glorify-v dedication,
consecration,
enthronement,
canonization, celebration,
enshrinement, hero,
worthy, notability, rank,
great, eminence,
importance, elevation,
ascent, super, exaltation,
dignify, aggrandizement,
(discredit, disrepute, bad,
disapprobation, dishonor,
disgrace, shame,
humiliation, tarnish, taint,
defilement, pollute)

gloss-n smooth, lubricity,

velvet, silk, satin, slide, glass, ice, plane, file, mow, shave, level, roll, macadamize, polish, glabrous, slippery, lubricious, oily, soft, (render rough, uneven, knotted, aspergillus, crisp, gnarled, unpolished, rough-hewed, gnarled, crumble, corrugate)

glut-*v* satiety, satisfaction, saturation, repletion, surfeit, weariness, spoiled, child, cloy, quench, slake, pall, gorge, surfeit, swallow, enough, bolt, devour, gobble up, gulp, raven, greedy, adequacy, omnivorous, over-fed, (fast, starve, clam, famish, perish, unfed, hungry)

go-*v* motion, movement, transit, going, evolution, wander, gone, lost, departed, defunct, negative, elapse, lapse, flow, run, duration, proceed, advance, pass, expire, progress, (stop, admit, absorb, swallow, enter, introduce, receive, import, insert)

Godspeed-*n* depart, go, move, begone, farewell, adieu, good-bye, withdraw, vacate, leave, evacuate, abandon, remove, exit, embarkation, exodus, flight, (arrive, reach, attain, overtake, disembark, welcome, fetch, destined, reception)

good-*adj* savory, well-tasted, tasty, palatable, nice, dainty, delectable, gusty, appetizing, delicate, delicious, exquisite, rich, luscious, ambrosial, relish, zest, virtue, virtuousness, moral, ethic, merit, worth, (scandal, laxity, looseness, demoralizing, depravity, pollution, profligacy, atrocity, infirmity, error, defect, deficiency)

gorge-*v* ravine, break, gap, opening, hole, chasm, cleft, mesh, crevice, creek, cranny, crack, slit, fissure, crevasse, abyss, gulf, inlet, frith, strait, gully, pass, furrow, satiety, satisfaction, saturation, repletion, glut, surfeit, weariness, quench, slake, fatigue, (fastidiousness, nicety, epicure, gourmet, dainty, join, adjoin, touch, meet, osculate, coincide, coexist, adhere)

gorgeous-*adj* beauty, form, elegance, grace, unadorned, symmetry, comeliness, fairness, polish, gloss, good looks, bloom, brilliancy, radiance, splendor, magnificence, handsome, pretty, lovely, refined, shapely, colored, bright, vivid, (achromatic, hueless, pale ,ugly, plain, homely, ordinary, unsightly, deformed, eyesore, frightful, ghastly, graceless, gross)

gospel-*n* certainty,
necessary, certitude,
surety, assurance, moral,
infallibleness, reliability,
scripture, positive,
dogmatism, sure, solid,
absolute, positive,
unerring, authentic, official,
evident, (uncertain,
dubious, hesitation,
suspense, perplexity,
dilemma, bewilderment,
vagueness, confused)

grace-*n* style, elegance,
purity, ease, readiness,
polished, classical correct,
artistic, chaste, pure,
academical, easy, fluent,
flowing, tripping,
unaffected, natural,
unlabored, mellifluous,
(stiffness, barbaric,
euphuism, graceless,
harsh, abrupt, dry,
cramped, formal, forced,
artificial, mannered)

gradation-*n* degree, extent,
measure, amount, ratio,
stint, standard, height,
pitch, reach, amplitude,
range, scope, caliber,
shade, tenor, compass,
station, rank, order,
uniformity, correct,
methodical, systematic,
(confusion, disorder,
jumble, huddle, wrong,
fortuitous, perplexed,
quantitative, some, more,
less, any)

gram-*n* essence, small,
little, tenuity, paucity, few,
insignificance, mediocre,

moderate, atom, particle,
molecule, diminutive,
minute, paltry, faint,
slender, slight, scanty,
meager, sparing, modest,
mere, low, infinitesimal,
stark, bare, (vast,
immense, enormous,
extreme, excessive,
extravagant, exorbitant,
outrageous, preposterous)

grammar-*n* punctuate,
syntax, parts of speech,
language, conjugation,
case, declination,
rudiments, elements,
outlines, alphabet, begin,
commence, rise, arise,
originate, conceive, initiate,
open, (end, final, terminal,
consummate, finish,
conclude, solecism, bad,
false, slipslop,
ungrammatical, incorrect)

grand-*adj* important,
momentous, serious,
earnest, noble, solemn,
impressive, commanding,
imposing, urgent, pressing,
critical, prominent, grave,
superior, instant, essential,
vital, absorbing,
considerable, significant,
telling, (poor, paltry, trifling,
trivial, slight, slender, light,
flimsy, frothy, idle, foolish,
powerless, petty, pitiful)

grant-*v* admit,
acknowledge, avowal,
reveal, divulge, allow,
concede, confess,
disclose, transpire,
permission, empower,

license, authorize, absolve,
entrust, sanction, license,
privilege, favor, (prohibit,
forbid, disallow, hinder,
restrict, exclude, withhold,
bar, veto, limit, ambush,
conceal, stalk, cover,
recess)

graphic-*adj* intelligent,
clear, explicit, lucid,
perspicuity, legibility,
precise, simplify,
understand, comprehend,
distinct, positive,
illustrative, expressive,
recognizable, obvious,
(riddle, paradox,
unaccountable, illegible,
vague, loose, ambiguous,
obscure, perplexed,
negative, nebulous)

grasp-*v* comprehend,
understand, catch, follow,
collect, master, lucid,
luminous, transparent,
plain, distinct, explicit,
positive, definite, take hold,
retain, detain, detention,
custody, tenacity, firm
hold, grip, secure,
(relinquish, abandon,
renounce, derelict,
surrender, dispense,
resign, eliminate)

gratuitous-*adj* intuitive,
instinctive, impulsive,
independent, unconnected,
inconsistent, fallible,
groundless, unproved,
evasive, irrelevant, cheap,
low, moderate, reasonable,
depreciated, unsalable,
gratis, without charge,
(expensive, extravagant,
exorbitant, extortionate,
premium, priceless,
precious, overcharged,
rationalistic,
argumentative,
controversial)

gravity-*n* force, power,
pressure, elasticity,
electricity, magnetism,
galvanism, capability,
voltaism, attraction,
dynamic, energy, friction,
suction, capacity, weight,
heaviness, ponderous,
load, burden, (levity,
lightness, buoyancy,
leaven, subtle, airy,
weightless, floating,
portable, powerless,
impotent, valid, effective,
influential, productive)

grease-*n* lubricate,
smoothly, anoint, oil,
glycerine, lather, wax,
payment, settle, discharge,
quit, acquit, liquidate,
retribution, remit,
installment, (disgorge,
repay, refund, reimburse,
insolvent, bankrupt,
gazetted, protest,
dishonor, rub, scratch,
scrape, rasp, scrub, grind,
friction)

greed-*n* desire, avidity,
covetous, ravenous,
craving, voracity, gluttony,
hunger, longing,
hankering, solicitude,
impatient, impetuous, over-
anxiety, gorge,
gormandize, devour,

gobble-up, gulp, raven,
guzzle, cram, fill, (fast,
starve, perish, Lenten,
unfed, famish, indifferent,
cold, neutrality, unconcern)

gregarious-*adj* social,
companion, comradeship,
conviviality, good
fellowship, festivity,
hospitality, heartiness,
cheer, welcome, greetings,
receptive, fraternize,
(seclusion, exclusion,
privacy, retirement,
reclusion, recess, solitude,
isolation, loneliness,
estrangement, voluntary
exile)

grieve-*v* mourn, anxiety,
concern, grief, sorrow,
distress, affliction, woe,
bitterness, heartache,
heaving, aching, bleeding,
misery, tribulation,
wretchedness, desolation,
despair, prostration,
(happiness, felicity, bliss,
beatitude, enchantment,
transport, rapture,
ravishment, ecstasy,
paradise, Elysium)

grind-*v* reduce, contract,
decrease, lessen, shrink,
collapse, emaciation,
consumption, atrophy,
condensation,
compression, compact,
smaller, squeeze, lessen,
narrow, constrict, crush,
dwarf, (expand, increase,
enlarge, extend, augment,
amplify, spread, increment,
growth, develop)

grip-*n* power, retention,
retain, detention, custody,
tenacity, firm hold, grasp,
forfeit, secure, clutch,
swoop, wrench, take,
catch, hook, nab, (return,
restore, reparation,
release, replevin,
redemption, recovery,
recuperate, surrender,
yield, forego, renounce,
abandon, expropriate)

gross-*adj* great, magnitude,
size, multitude, immensity,
enormity, infinity, fullness,
great quantity, volume,
monstrous, incredible,
whole, total, aggregate,
amount, sum-total,
command, hold, grasp,
reach, clutch, regime,
monarchy, (fractional,
fragmentary, sectional,
divided, partial,
compartment, portion,
section, piece)

grotto-*n* alcove, hermitage,
greenhouse, portico, lobby,
court, porch, veranda,
arbor, depression, dip,
hollow, depressed,
concave, cavernous, cave,
cove, (cupola, dome, arch,
balcony, eaves, pilaster)

ground-*n* land, earth,
ground, dry land,
continent, mainland,
peninsula, delta, coast,
shore, soil, clay, loam,
acres, real estate, cause,
origin, source, principle,
element, reason, rationale,
occasion derivation,

(consequently, necessarily, eventually, derivative, sea, ocean, water, waves, billows)

grow-*v* increase, enlarge, extension, accession, augment, gain, strengthen, intensify, enhance, magnify, redouble, dilate, exaggerate, expansibility, germination, growth, swollen, develop, amplify, widen, (reduce, scrape, compress, lessen, shrink, collapse, emaciate, atrophy)

guard-*v* protect, preserve, custody, chaperone, watch, warden, preserve, shelter, shroud, flank, secure, trust, defend, garrison, driver, coachman, whip, fireman, (danger, peril, insecure, jeopardy, risk, precariousness, exposure, vulnerability, instability)

gypsy-*n* vagabond, nomad, Bohemian, wanderer, pilgrim, emigrant, fugitive, refugee, runner, courier, comet, pedestrian, tourist, passenger, excursionist, explorer, adventurer, rover, rambler, straggler, gad-about, (dupe, dull, credulous)

H

habit-*n* essence, temper, spirit,humor, capacity, constitution, character,

type, quality, garment, garb, palliative, apparel, wardrobe, wearing apparel, clothes, array, outfit, morning dress, uniform, (divestment, nudity, bareness, undress, uncover, denude, disrobe, extraneousness, accident, derived from without)

hack-*v* cut, sunder, divide, subdivide, sever, abscind, saw, snip, nib, nip, cleave, rend, slit, split, splinter, carve, cut up, dissect, disintegrate, disperse, separate, discrete, ass, donkey, jackass, mule, horse, (join, attach, unite, fasten, bind, fix, affix, buckle, gird, close)

hackneyed-*adj* dictum, saying, adage, proverb, sentence, perception, enlightenment, glimpse, inkling, trite, reflection, conclusion, golden rule, motto, axiom, maxim, aphorism, (blunder, muddle, absurd, imbecility, farce, rhapsody, sell, pun, ignorance, blindness)

haggard-*adj* fatigue, weariness, yawning, drowsiness, lassitude, tiredness, exhaustion, faintness, collapse, prostration, (refreshed, recover, revival, repair, refection, renew)

hail-*n* welcome, arrive, advent, landing, hither, good day, reach, advent, reception, home, goal, port, haven, sleet, ice, snow, flake, crystal, drift, frost, icicle, (heat, caloric, fire, spark, flash, flame, blaze, bonfire, fireworks, depart, decampment, leave, outward, whence, hence, farewell, adieu, good bye)

half-_n_ bisect, halving, divide, split, cut in two, cleave, dimidiate, separate, fork, bifurcate, cleft, bipartite, fork, prong, gradual, degree, retard, relax, slacken, moderate, rein, curb, leisurely, at half speed, slow, (hurry, accelerate, quicken, haste, rapid, scuttle, scud, gallop, amble, troll, hasten, duplicate, twice, once more, over again, renewal, double)

halt-_v_ cease, discontinue, desist, stay, break, leave, hold, stop, stick, interrupt, suspend, enough, truce, weak, debility, stony, loss, drop, crumble, totter, tremble, shake, limp, fade, languish, decline, flag, (strength, power, energy, vigor, force, physical, spring, elasticity, tone, tension, continue, persist, go, sustain, uphold, keep, perpetuate, maintain, preserve)

hammer-_n_ repeat, iterate, reiterate, recurrence, succession, monotony, rhythm, recur, revert, reappear, often, blow, dint, stroke, sledge, mall, maul, mallet, flail, batter, pile-driving, punch, bat, axe, (recoil, react, spring, revulsion, rebound, reflex, reverberate, rebuff, repulse, return)

hand-_n_ organ of touch, touch, feel, handle, finger, thumb, feel, palpation, tingle, tangible, dextral, right-handed, ambidextrous, right and left, flank, quarter, (numb, intangible, impalpable, insensibility to touch)

handbook-_n_ information, enlightenment, acquaintance, knowledge, publication, guide, manual, map, plan, chart, gazetteer, work, volume, tract, pamphlet, circular, portfolio, (conceal, hide, cloak, secrete, cover, screen, cloak, veil, shroud, masquerade)

handsome-_adj_ liberal, free, beautiful, pretty, lovely, graceful, elegant, delicate, dainty, refined, fair, personable, comely, good-looking, dapper, jaunty, natty, quaint, (ugly, deformed, inelegance, disfigurement, squalor, monster)

handy-_adj_ near, proximity, propinquity, vicinity, nigh, nearby, elongation, background, spread,

neighboring, adjacent,
adjoining, proximate,
intimate, (distant, remote,
far, extend, stretch, away,
apart, asunder)
hang-*v* dependent,
suspending, swing, dangle,
swag, draggle, flap, trail,
flow, sling, hook up, hitch,
fasten, append, strangle,
garrote, throttle, choke,
stifle, suffocate, smother,
asphyxiate, (support, bear,
carry, sustain, bolster,
hold, shoulder)
hapless-*adj* unfortunate,
mishap, unblest, unhappy,
unlucky, decayed, poor,
adverse, disastrous,
calamitous, ruinous, dire,
deplorable, anxiety,
solicitude, trouble,
concern, grief, sorrow,
distress, (prosperous,
thrive, flourish, smooth,
well-being, affluent,
success, blessing, lucky)
hard-*adj* strong, strength,
power, vigor, force, brute
force, mighty, adamantine,
stout, robust, sturdy,
powerful, potent, puissant,
valid, reinforce, stamina,
nerve, muscle, sinew,
steel, energy, grip, bone,
dynamite, rigid, renitency,
inflexible, stubborn, stiff,
firm, (soft, pliable, flexible,
plasticity, tender, supple,
lithe, limber, limp, frail,
fragile, flimsy,
unsubstantial, rickety,
drooping, withered,

shattered)
hardly-*adv* scarcely, slight,
scanty, limited, sparing,
few, low, below, moderate,
modest, inappreciable,
infinitesimal, mere, simple,
sheer, stark, bare, little,
diminutive, nothing,
morsel, thimble, trifle,
unimportant, insignificant,
trivial, paltry, indifference,
nonentity, (important,
consequence, prominence,
considerable, significant,
concern, emphasis, great,
vast, immense, enormous,
extreme, goodly,
unsurpassed)
hark-*v* hear, audible,
acoustic, listen, catch a
sound, attentive, mindful,
observant, alive,
awakened, behold,
breathless, heed,
cognizant, recognize,
(absent, abstract,
disregard, heedless,
indifference)
harm-*n* evil, ill, hurt,
mischief, nuisance,
disaster, accident,
casualty, mishap,
adversity, tragedy, ruin,
destroy, catastrophe,
calamity, bale, bad,
painful, grievance,
injurious, detrimental,
noxious, mischievous,
nocuous, vile, foul, rotten,
(good, excellent, better,
superior, above par, nice,
fine, genuine, favorable,
fair, benefit, advantage,

improvement, interest,
well, right, satisfactory)
harness-*v* fasten, attach,
fix, affix, bind, secure,
clinch, twist, tie, pinion,
string, strap, sew, lace,
stitch, tack, knit, button,
buckle, hitch, last, truss,
bandage, braid, splice,
swathe, gird, tether, moor,
picket, chain, fetter, yoke,
collar, halter, muzzle, gag,
bit, brake, curb, snaffle,
bridle, rein, (sunder, divide,
subdivide, sever, dissever,
abscind, saw, snip, nib,
nip, cleave, rend, slit, split,
carve)
hatch-*v* produce, create,
construct, formation,
fabricate, manufacture,
build, architect, erect,
edification, establish,
workmanship, perform,
achieve, complete, flower,
fructify, bring forth, birth,
deliver, evolve, develop,
grow, enclosure, barrier,
barricade, gate, door,
hatch, (destroy, waste,
dissolve, disrupt, consume,
nullify, annul, demolish,
deteriorate, perish, fall)
hateful-*adj* bad, hurtful,
evil, maltreat, abuse,
injurious, deleterious,
detrimental, noxious,
pernicious, mischievous,
malignant, vile, mean,
wrong, depraved,
shocking, reprehensible,
disapprove, abominable,
detestable, execrable,

cursed, confounded,
damned, infernal, diabolic,
(admirable, estimable,
praiseworthy, pleasing,
tolerable, best, choice,
select, goodness,
beneficial valuable,
serviceable,
advantageous, edifying,
favorable)
have-*v* possess, own, hold,
tenure, occupy, depend,
monopoly, heritage,
inheritance, heir, engross,
recreate, acquire, get,
gain, win, earn, obtain,
procure, gather, collect,
assemble, pick, find, reap,
secure, draw, confute,
(lose, bereft, dispossess,
rid, minus, deprive, lapse,
forfeit, mislay, exempt)
hazard-*n* chance, accident,
hap-hazard, random, luck,
casualty, contingence,
adventure, probability,
possibility, odds,
undetermined, fortuitous,
causeless, incidental,
unintentional, danger, peril,
insecurity, jeopardy, risk,
venture, precariousness,
slipperiness, instability,
defenseless, exposure,
imperil, (safety, security,
surety, impregnability,
invulnerability, safeguard,
palladium, guardian)
heap-*n* big, huge, large,
ample, abundant, full,
intense, heavy, plenary,
high, zenith, vast,
immense, enormous,

extreme, inordinate,
excessive, extravagant,
exorbitant, outrageous,
preposterous, monstrous,
over-grown, towering,
stupendous, prodigious,
astonishing, incredible,
accumulate, lump, pile,
pyramid, (disperse, adrift,
here and there, smallness,
little, few, insignificant,
mediocrity, moderation,
atom, minute,
inconsiderable, paltry,
scant, limited, meager,
sparing, few)
heart-*n* love, fondness,
liking, inclination, regard,
admiration, affection,
sympathy, fellowship,
tenderness, benevolence,
attachment, passion,
devotion, fervor, adoration,
idolatry, Cupid, lover,
amour, betrothed, fiance,
beloved, adorable, sweet,
enchanting, (hate,
disaffection, repugnance,
dislike, antipathy, detest,
abominate, abhor, loathe,
recoil, shatter, shrink,
hateful, irritate)
hearty-*adj* healthy, well,
sound, hale, fresh, green,
whole, florid, flush,
staunch, brave, robust,
vigorous, weather-proof,
willing, voluntary, propend,
inclined, geniality,
cordiality, goodwill,
readiness, earnestness,
forward, eager,
(grudgingly, unwillingly,

adverse, reluctant,
backward, repugnant,
delicate, loss of health,
invalidate, atrophy, decay,
decline, consumption,
fatal)
heat-*n* hot, warm, mild,
genial, tepid, lukewarm,
unfrozen, thermal, fervent,
sunny, torrid, tropical,
estival, canicular, close,
sultry, stifling, stuffy,
suffocating, oppressive,
reeking, baking, burning,
sweltering, glow, flush,
bask, smoke, stew,
simmer, seethe, boil, burn,
broil, blaze, flame,
smolder, parch, fume,
pant, contend, strife,
contest, struggle,
opposition, rivalry, match,
race, steeplechase,
handicap, regatta,
(peaceful, pacific, calm,
tranquil, halcyon, quiet,
cold, frigid, ice, snow,
glacial frosty, freezing,
brutal, hibernal, bitter,
chilly, shiver, fresh,
inclement)
heave-*v* raise, heighten,
elevate, raise, lift, erect,
stick, perch, tilt, upheave,
exalt, hoist, cast, uplift,
remain, stay, stand, lie,
bring, draw-up, hold, halt,
stop, rest, pause, anchor,
(move, motion, shifting,
mobile, restless, nomadic,
lower, depress, dip,
reduce, fall, sink, trample,
duck)

heaven-*n* god like, kingdom,
throne, paradise, eden,
celestial, resurrection,
supernal, unearthly,
beatific, eternal home,
bliss, happiness, felicity,
beatitude, enchantment,
transport, rapture, ecstasy,
Elysium, (grieve, mourn,
yearn, repine, droop,
languish, sink, despair,
afflicted, demoniacal,
haunted, supernatural,
weird, uncanny, evil)

hedge-*n* compensate,
equate, indemnification,
compromise, counter,
retaliate, counter-balance,
hinder, impede, prevent,
forefend, retard, slacken,
preclude, inhibit, shackle,
obstruct, stop, block,
barricade, (aid, assist,
help, support, lift, advance,
further, promote, relief,
advocate, reinforcement)

heir-*n* benefactor, grantee,
trustee, holder, generative,
descendant, heredity,
descent, lineage

hell-*n* abyss, hollow, pit,
shaft, well, crater,
bottomless pit, unfortunate,
unblest, unhappy, unlucky,
poor, speculate, venture,
stake, random shot,
adversity, evil, failure,
disaster, gamble,
adventure, risk, hazard,
stake, (intention, purpose,
project, design, ambition,
undertake, aim)

helm-*n* handle, hilt, haft,
shaft, heft, shank, blade,
trigger, tiller, treadle, key,
turn screw, screwdriver,
direct, manage, govern,
conduct, order, prescribe,
head, lead, regulate,
guide, steer, pilot, drive,
throne, chair, dais,
(anarchy, relaxation,
misrule, subordinate,
dethronement, deposition,
abdication)

hence-*adv* thence,
therefore, since, on
account of, because,
owing to, wherefore,
attribute, impute, refer,
derive, theorize, reason,
argue, discuss, debate,
dispute, wrangle, canvass,
comment, (unreasonable,
illogical, false, unsound,
invalid, unwarranted,
inconclusive, casual,
fortuitous, accidental,
causeless, incidental,
contingent, undetermined)

herald-*n* precursor,
antecedent, precedent,
predecessor, forerunner,
leader, bell-weather,
harbinger, dawn, prelude,
preamble, preface,
prologue, prefix,
introduction, heading,
frontispiece, groundwork,
(sequel, suffix, successor,
tail, train, wake, trail, rear,
retinue, appendix,
postscript)

heritage-*n* heirs, posterity,
future, next, near,
eventual, ulterior,

prospective, tomorrow,
eventual, ultimately,
possess, own, occupy,
hold, tenure, depend,
retain, inheritance, revert,
engross, (exemption,
absence, devoid,
unobtained, past, gone by,
ancient, former, antiquity,
immemorial, bygone,
forgotten, irrecoverable
obsolete)

hermitage-n abode,
dwelling, lodging, domicile,
residence, address,
habitation, berth, seat, lap,
housing, quarters,
headquarters, tabernacle,
throne, ark, home,
fatherland, country,
homestead, stall, fireside,
hearth, stone, household

hesitate-v uncertain,
suspense, perplexity,
embarrassment, doubt,
dubiety, vague, haze, fog,
obscurity, contingency,
puzzle, bewilder, bother,
indecisive, ambiguous,
questionable, precarious,
disputable, (certain,
necessary, assured,
reliable, gospel, positive,
solid, authoritative,
authentic, official, evident,
infallible)

hinder-v impede, prevent,
preclude, obstruct, stop,
interrupt, retard,
embarrass, restrict,
restrain, inhibit, interfere,
discourage, drawback,
stumbling block, foreclose,

prohibit, forbid, disallow,
interdict, exclude,
unauthorized (grant,
empower, charter,
enfranchise, privilege,
warrant, sanction, entrust,
permit, allow, admit,
concede, recognize, favor,
license, authorize, aid,
helpful, subservient)

hiss-n sound, hoot, gibe,
flout, jeer, scoff, taunt,
sneer, quip, fling, wipe,
slap in the face,
disrespect, disregard,
slight, trifle, discourteous,
dishonor, desecrate, insult,
affront, outrage, (respect,
regard, consideration,
courtesy, attention,
reverence, honor, esteem,
admiration, homage)

hit-v blow, dint, stroke,
knock, tap, rap, slap,
smack, pat, dab, slam,
bang, whack, squash,
dowse, whop, swap,
probability, possibility,
contingency, odds, long
odds, run of luck, hammer,
mall, knock, strike, (duck,
recoil, rebound, revulsion,
repercussion)

hobble-v creep, craw, lag,
slug, draw, linger, loiter,
saunter, plod, trudge,
stump along, move-slowly,
slouch, stagger, mince,
slacken, moderate, easy,
leisurely, deliberate,
gradual, slow-paced, (trip,
speed, hasten, move
quickly, scuttle, scud,

scamper, race, run, shoot,
tear, whisk, sweep, brush,
accelerate)

hobby-*n* pursuit, purse,
prosecute, enterprise,
adventure, quest, game,
desire, wish, whim,
devotee, aspirant,
solicitant, avid, (indifferent,
neutral, of no interest,
have no desire, cold, frigid,
lukewarm, avoid, shun,
steer clear, deny)

hollow-*adj* vanish,
unsubstantial, incomplete,
deficiency, short measure,
shortcoming, insufficient,
imperfect, concave, dip,
indentation, cavity, pit,
follicle, depressed,
excavate, furrow, trough,
basin, valley, (convex,
project, sell, bilge, bulge,
protrude, tumor, hump,
hunch, bulb, node, nodule)

holocaust-*n* kill, put to
death, slay, shed blood,
murder, assassinate,
butcher, slaughter,
suffocate, sacrifice,
destroy, ravage, (creation,
produce, generate,
establish, give life to,
complete)

homely-*adj* plain,
disfigured, blemished,
pitted, freckled, discolored,
imperfect, injured, simple,
ordinary, chaste, severe,
(polished, festoon, garland,
adorned, decorated,
embellished, detailed,
fleur-de-lis)

honest-*adj* veracity, truthful,
frank, sincerely, candor,
fidelity, true, scrupulous,
trustworthy, probity,
integrity, rectitude, upright,
honor, purity, fair, just,
equity, impartiality,
principle, grace,
constancy, faithful,
warrant, apologize,
advocate, plead ignorance,
(accuse, charge, tax,
impute, taunt, reproach,
slur, false, deception,
untruth, guile, lying,
misrepresentation, perjury,
forgery, fabrication)

honor-*n* glory, distinction,
reputation, notability,
notoriety, dedication,
consecration,
enthronement,
canonization, celebration,
enshrinement, glorification,
immortalize, exalt, glitter,
distinguished, great,
eminence, height,
important, (disrepute,
discredit, repute, dishonor,
disgrace, shame,
humiliation, scandal, vile,
turpitude, tarnish, disgrace,
degrade, vile, stain,
shameful, degrading)

hoodwink-*v* deception,
false, untruth, fraud,
deceit, guile,
misrepresentation,
delusion, trickery,
circumvention, chicane,
juggle, hocus, feint, ignore,
bewilderment, shallow,
superficial, empty, half-

learned, uninformed,
unaware, (knowing, aware,
cognizant, conscious,
acquainted, instructed,
learned, familiar,
scholastic, profound,
accomplished,
ascertained)

hook-*n* attach, fix, affix,
saddle on, fasten, bind,
secure, clinch, twist, tie,
string, strap, sew, lace,
stitch, tack, pin, nail, join,
fast, close, tight, taut, inseparable, entangle,
parting, (sunder, divide,
disengage, subdivide,
sever, cut, snip, nib, nip,
cleave, rend, slit, split,
carve, hack, lacerate,
mangle, rupture, shatter,
shiver, crunch, chop)

hop-*v* leap, jump, spring,
bound, vault, station,
dance, caper, curvet,
caracole, skip, frisky,
bounce, flounce, agitation,
fun, frolic, merriment,
pleasure, amusement,
sport, laughter, reel,
festivity, play, game,
(wearisome, tediousness,
drag, tiresome,
uninterested, monotonous,
humdrum, slow, plunge,
dip, dive, duck, submerge,
douse, sink, engulf,
wallow)

hope-*v* desire, expectation,
trust, confidence, reliance,
faith, belief, assurance,
reassurance, promise,
optimism, enthusiasm,

encouraging, cheering,
bright, rose-colored,
prosperity, welfare, well-
being, affluence, blessings,
thrive, flourish, (adverse,
disastrous, calamitous,
ruinous, dire, deplorable,
unfortunate, unhappy,
unlucky, hapless, despair,
despondence,
abandonment)

horn-*n* receptacle,
recipient, receiver,
reservoir, compartment,
vessel, vase, utensil,
sharp, keen, pyramidal,
spindle, needle-shaped,
spiked, thorny, bristling,
barbed, copious,
abundant, abounding,
enough, rich, sufficient

horrify-*v* annoyance,
grievance, nuisance,
vexation, mortification,
sicken, bore, bother,
plague, pest, sea of
troubles, misfortune,
irritation, painful, disgust,
revolt, nauseate,
disenchant, repel, offend,
shock, fear, apprehensive,
solicitude, anxiety,
mistrust, suspicion, alarm,
tremble, shake, shiver,
shudder, (hopeful, trust,
encourage, aspire,
optimistic, pleasant,
agreeable, pleasure,
delectable, loveliness,
sunny, bright, sweet,
goodness, satisfy, gratify,
satiate, refresh, attract,
allure)

hostile-*adj* disagreeing, discordant, discrepant, incompatible, irreconcilable, inconsistent, uncomfortable, incongruous, unharmonious, inapt, unapt, unaccommodating, opposed, antagonistic, counteractive, clashing, conflicting, against, disfavor, (cooperation, complicity, participation, collusion, association, alliance, confederation, coalition, fusion, unanimity, combined)

humility-*n* meek, lowliness, submission, resignation, modest, blush, suffusion, confusion, sense of shame, disgrace, mortification, servile, condescending, courteous, pious, faith, holiness, religious, devout, devoted, reverent, godly heavenly, pure, spiritual, saintly, sacred, solemn, (wicked, evil, unjust, reprobate, irreverence, desecration, sacrilege, dignity, self-respect, pride, haughtiness, vain, arrogance, stately, proud)

I

idea-*n* notion, conception, thought, apprehension, impression, perception, image, sentiment, reflection, observation, consideration, abstract idea, point of view, theory, fancy, imagination, topic, thesis, text, business, affair, matter, argument, motion, inkling, (indifference, incurious, impassive, ignorance, remote)

identification-*n* identity, sameness, coincidence, exactness, similar, copy, recognize, equality, comparable, deduce, derived, gather, collect, draw an inference, make a deduction, whet, ween, estimate, appreciate, (discover, find, determine, evolve, contrary, oppose, differ, invert, reverse, turn the tables, contradict, antagonize, oppose)

idiosyncrasy-*n* essence, endowment, capacity, capability, moods, declension, features, aspects, peculiarities, diagnostic, principle, nature, specialty, particularity, characteristic, mannerism, specific, singularity, version, state, (general, universal, common, ecumenical, transcendental, prevalent, every all, unspecified, impersonal, implanted, extraneousness)

idle-*adj* shallow, imbecility, incapacity, vacancy of mind, poverty of intellect, weak, wanting, dull,

powerless, frivolous, petty,
inane, ridiculous,
worthless, (paramount,
essential, vial, all-
absorbing, serious,
earnest, grand, impressive,
commanding, imposing)
idol-n favorite, pet, spoiled,
desire, devotee, aspirant,
solicitant, heretic,
antichrist, pagan, heathen,
bigot, (orthodox, sound,
strict, faithful, evangelical)
ignore-v neglect,
carelessness, trifling,
omission, default,
inactivity, inattention,
nonchalance, insensibility,
imprudence, recklessness,
inconsiderate, heedless,
thoughtless, uninformed,
ignored, (knowledge,
cognizance, acquaintance,
insight, familiarity, intuition,
perception, enlightenment)
illegitimate-adj illegal,
unlawful, smuggling,
poaching, prohibited, illicit,
contraband, despotic,
deceitful, delusive,
insidious, untrue, feigned,
fraudulent, artificial,
unsound, (legal,
legitimacy, rule, regulation,
equity, enact, vested,
constitutional, permitted)
illuminate-v light, ray,
beam, stream, gleam,
streak, sun, aurora,
shining, luminous, lucid,
bright, vivid, reflection,
refraction, lighten,
irradiate, color, hue, tint,

intense, unfaded, gay,
(pale, faded, colorless,
decolorize, bleached,
tarnished, blanch, dull,
muddy, dingy)
illustrate-v exemplify, cite,
quote, exemplary,
example, uniformly, in
point, interpretation,
definition, explicit,
translate, define, construe,
decipher, expound,
unravel, disentangle,
resolve, (misrepresent,
pervert, garble, distort,
travesty, stretch,
aberration, irregularity,
exemption)
imbed-v locate, place,
situate, seat, station,
lodge, quarter, post, install,
establish, stow, house, fix,
pin, root, graft, deposit,
vest, pack, give, furnish,
afford, supply, lend,
support, bottom, found,
base, ground, maintain,
(depend, suspend, loose,
flowing, tail, caudate,
hang, displace, vacate)
imitation-n copy,
duplication, repetition,
mirror, reflect, mimic,
reproduce, repeat, echo,
match, parallel, counterfeit,
parody, travesty,
caricature, burlesque,
imitative, verbatim,
duplicate, transcript,
shadow, parody, similar,
impersonate, (original,
prototype, model, pattern,
precedent, standard)

immaculate-*adj* perfect, best, pure, good, paragon, unparalleled, supreme, superhuman, divine, approbation, faultless, spotless, impeccable, unblemished, ripen, mature, scathless, intact, harmless, purity, clean, purify, (decay, corrupt, mold, must, rot, putrefy, fester, rank, reek, stink, dirty, soil, smoke, tarnish, spot, dirty, filthy, grimy)

immature-*adj* new, novelty, recent, youth, innovation, modernism, recent, fresh, neoteric, new-born, young, vernal, renovated, brewing, hatching, forthcoming, (old, ancient, antique, venerable, elder, archaic, classic, seniority, mature, decline, senility)

immense-*adj* great, large, considerable fair, above par, big, huge, ample, abundant, enough, full, intense, strong, sound, passing, heavy, plenary, high, goodly, noble, precious, might, sad, grave, serious, vast, enormous, extreme, extravagant, preposterous, monstrous, (inappreciable, evanescent, minute, inconsiderable, paltry, small, diminutive, mere, simple, sheer, scanty, bare)

immortal-*adj* perpetual, eternal, everlasting, perpetuity, continual, endless, unending, ceaseless, incessant, unfading, evergreen, never-ending, enthrone, signalize, consecrate, dedicate, enshrine, (discredit, disrepute, dishonor, disgrace, humiliation, momentary, sudden, instant, abrupt, hasty, quick)

immovable-*adj* stable, unchangeable, constancy, immobile, soundness, stiffness, fixture, rock, pillar, tower, foundation, permanence, remain firm, settle, establish, determined, master over self, self-control, perseverance, tenacity, obstinacy, (vacillating, unsteady, volatile, frothy, weak, feeble minded, inconstancy, versatility, instability, fluctuation, vicissitude, alteration, restless)

impartial-*adj* impartiality, intelligent, keen acute, alive, discerning, wise, sage, sapient, reasonable, sensible, fair, upright, straightforward, frank, candid, conscientious, scrupulous, (undignified, partial, disloyal, untrustworthy, corrupt, debased, thoughtless, want of intelligence, week, feeble minded)

impeach-*v* condemnation,

reflection, disparage, ostracism, dispraise, censure, detract, depreciate, exception, rebuke, reprehension, reprobation, admonition, reproach, reprimand, castigate, lecture, disapprove, blame, frown upon, (approbation, approval, sanction, advocacy, esteem, good opinion, praise, applaud, commend, compliment, laudatory)

imperative-*adj* required, need, necessary, essential, indispensability, urgency, prerequisite, uncompromising, inflexible, relentless, peremptory, absolute, unsparing, ironhanded, oppressive, ruthless, (moderate, lenient, moderation, tolerant, mildness, forbearing, compassion, indulge)

imperceptible-*adj* mere, simple, sheer, stark, bare, inappreciable, infinitesimal, diminutive, inconsiderable, slight, scanty, limited, meager, sparing, impalpable, intangible, invisible, molecular, rudimentary, embryonic, (hugeness, enormous, corpulent, fat, plump, squab, full, lusty, strapping, consummate, excessive, stupendous, astonishing, inexpressible)

imperious-*adj* command, reign, dynasty, director, dictatorship, authority, influence, patronage, power, jurisdiction, divine right, administration, demagogy, socialism, feudalism, empire, monarchy, royalty, (anarchy, toleration, remission, lax, loose, dethrone, depose, abdicate, remiss, free rein)

impetuous-*adj* boisterous, violence, inclemency, vehemence, might, effervescence, turbulence, bluster, uproar, riot, row, rumpus, ferocity, rage, fury, hastily, precipitately, helter, skelter, urgency, acceleration, spurt, forced, march, rush, (leisure, slow, deliberate, quiet, calm, undisturbed, moderation, gentleness, sobriety, quiet, calmness, sedative, lenitive, demulcent, balmy, tranquilize)

imposition-*n* credulity, gull, infatuation, self-delusion, deception, superstition, simple, green, over-confident, infringe, encroach, exact, arrogate, violate, disfranchise, invalidate, misbehave, undue, unlawful, illicit, unconstitutional, unwarranted, unsanctioned, (due to, privilege, prerogative, right, prescription, title, claim,

pretension, demand,
incredulous, unbelieving,
inconvincible, distrustful)

impossible-adj
impracticable,
unachievable, infeasible,
insurmountable,
incompatible, inaccessible,
impassible, unobtainable,
refuse, rejection, declining,
repulse, rebuff, reject,
deny, decline, protest,
disclaimer, (offer, present,
tender, move, start, invite,
possibility, potentiality,
agree, compatibility,
feasibility, practicability,
perhaps, perchance,
surmountable, accessible,
achievable, within reach)

impoverish-v weaken,
debility, relaxation,
languor, impotence,
infirmity, femininity,
fragility, inactivity,
withered, haltered, shaken,
crazy, shaky, palsied,
decrepit, consumption,
expenditure, exhaustion,
dispersion, spend, expend,
use, consume, (provision,
supply, caterer, purveyor,
commissary, feeder,
reinforcement, strong,
might, vigorous, forcible,
hard, adamantine, robust,
sturdy, hardy)

Impression-n sensation,
excite, aesthetic,
perceptive, conscious,
aware, acute, sharp, keen,
vivid, lively, sharpen,
cultivate, tutor, idea,

notion, conception,
thought, apprehension,
image, sentiment,
reflection, observation,
consideration, theory,
conceit, fancy, fantasy,
imagination, (insensible,
unfeeling, senseless,
callous, hardened, case-
hardened)

impressive-adj sensational,
eloquent, vigorous,
nervous, powerful,
command of words, bold,
racy, slashing, pungent,
(feeble, tame, meager,
vapid, dull, dry, languid,
monotonous)

imprint-v propagate,
spread, advertise, affix,
type, figure, emblem,
cipher, device, represent,
motto, circumscribe,
enclose, imbedded

improper-adj inapt, unapt,
inappropriate, discordant,
hostile, incompatible,
irreconcilable, inconsistent,
unconformable,
exceptional, unjust, unfair,
wrong, encroach,
inequitable, unequal,
partial, unfit, (right, fit,
justice, equity, propriety,
impartiality, reasonable,
legitimate, justifiable)

impudent-adj insolence,
haughtiness, arrogance,
airs, overbearance,
domineering, impertinence,
sauciness, flippancy,
petulance, bluster,
swagger, presumption,

usurpation, assurance,
audacity, hardihood, front,
face, brass,
shamelessness, effrontery,
assumption of infallibility,
(servile, supple, oily, pliant,
cringing, fawning,
groveling, sniveling, mealy-
mouthed, precocious)

impulsive-adj impetus,
momentum, push, pulsing,
thrust, shove, jog, jolt,
brunt, booming, throw,
explosion, propulsion,
percussion, concussion,
collision, clash, encounter,
deceptive, illusive,
plausible, evasive, hollow,
irrelevant, (reason, argue,
discuss, debate, dispute,
logical, sequence,
examine, question,
rebound, reflex,
reverberation, rebuff,
return)

inane-adj nothing, naught,
nil, nullity, zero, cipher, no
one, nobody, never, no
such thing, insubstantiality,
nonsense, senseless,
inexpressible, undefinable,
(intelligent, clearness,
explicitness, lucidity,
perspicuity, legibility, plain
speaking, luminous,
transparent)

inaugural-adj precursor,
precedent, forerunner,
pioneer, prelude,
preamble, preface,
prologue, preliminary,
introductory, (sequel,
suffix, successor, trail,

rear, appendix, postscript,
codicil, epilogue)

inauspicious-adj untimely,
intrusive, unseasonable,
out of date, inopportune,
timeless, untoward,
unlucky, unpropitious,
unfortunate, unfavorable,
unsuited, inexpedient,
hopelessness, despair,
desperation, despondency,
pessimism, forlorn, (hope,
trust, confide, rely on,
harbor, indulge,
confidence, opportune,
timely, well timed,
seasonable, providential,
lucky, fortunate, happy)

incapable-adj impotence,
disability, impiousness,
imbecility, inapt, ineptitude,
invalidity, inefficiency,
incompetence,
disqualification,
helplessness, prostration,
paralysis, palsy, apoplexy,
exhaustion, collapse,
(capability, capacity,
faculty, quality, attribute,
endowment, virtue, gift,
property, qualification,
susceptibility, puissance,
might, force)

incase-v cover, superpose,
overlay, wrap, face,
veneer, pave, bind, cap,
coat, paint, incrust, limit,
bound, encystment,
imprisoned, enshrined,
(lining, inner coating,
covering, filling, stuffing,
padding)

incendiary-adj destructive,

subversive, ruinous, deleterious, suicidal, deadly, with a crushing effect, demolish, dispel, dissipate, consume, squelch, exterminate, devastate, extinguish, burn, inflame, roast, toast, fry, grill, singe, parch, scorch, cauterize, sear, char, incinerate, (cool, fan, refrigerate, refresh, ice, congeal, freeze, glaciate, solidification, produce, establish, constitute, generate)

Incessant-adj monotonous, harping, iterative, mocking, chiming, repeatedly, often again, over again, once more, ditto, encore, everlasting, continual, endless, ceaseless, (instantaneous, momentary, sudden, instant, abrupt)

Incidental-adj casual, fortuitous, accidental, adventitious, causeless, contingent, undetermined, indeterminate, possible, unintentional, hap-hazard, random probability, possibility, (attribution, theory, ascribe, impute, explanation, ascription, reference to, rationale, imputation)

Inclement-adj violence, vehemence, might, impetuosity, boisterousness, effervescence, ebullition, turbulence, bluster, uproar, riot, row, rumpus, severe, ferocity, rage, fury, exacerbation, exasperation, malignity, fit, paroxysm, force, convulsion, (moderating, temperateness, gentleness, sobriety, quiet, relaxation, remission, mitigation, tranquilization, assuagement, contemplation, pacification)

inclusive-adj addition, annexation, adjection, supplement, subjunctive, annex, affix, superpose, including, inclusive, component, integral, ingredient, element, constituent, contents, appurtenance, (extraneousness, foreign, alien, intruder, ulterior, excluded, exceptional, deduction, retrenchment)

income-n earnings, profit, winnings, proceeds, fruit, crop, harvest, benefit, gaining, acquire, obtain, procure, purchase, inheritance, recovery, retrieval, redemption, salvage, remuneration, wealthy, rich, affluent, opulent, moneyed, (poor, indigent, poverty stricken, impoverished, pauper, ruin, destitution, loss, forfeiture, bereaved, dispossessed, lapse, deprivation)

incomparable-*adj* superior, greater, major, higher, exceeding, great, distinguished, vaulting, ultra, supreme, utmost, paramount, preeminent, foremost, crowning, first-rate, important, excellent, paragon, unparalleled, unequaled, unapproached, unsurpassed, superlative, (inferior, minority, subordinate, shortcoming, deficiency, minimum, smallness, diminished, subordinate)

inconsistent-*adj* illogical unreasonable, false, unsound, invalid, unwarranted, inconsequential, unscientific, groundless, incorrect, fallacious, unproved, contrary, opposite, counter, opposed, contrasted, conflicting, negative, differing, (similar, identical, facsimile, exact. identical, equal)

increase-*v* enlargement, augmentation, extension, dilatation, expansion, increment, accretion, accession, development, growth, ascent, acerbate, sprout, raise, exalt, magnify, many, several, sundry, various, profusion, manifold, multiplied, multiple, multinominal, populous, (few, paucity, rarity, handful, minority,

scant, decrease, lessen, subtract, reduce, abate, decline, shrink, wane, reflux)

incredible-*adj* impossible, absurd, unreasonable, unfeasible, insurmountable, unobtainable, inaccessible, impervious, improbable, unlikely, contrary, rare, unimaginable, misbelief, doubtful, disputable, questionable, suspect, inconceivable, hard to believe, (worthy of, deserving, belief, credence, assurance, faith, trust, confidence, presumption, possible, conceivable, feasible)

increment-*n* augment, appendage, the addition of, affix, accrue, expand, extend, develop, measurement, (pare, reduce, contract, shrink, compress, diminish)

incumbent-*adj* inhabitant, resident, dweller, inmate, tenant, sojourner, settler, squatter, citizen, native, overhanging, overlying, prominent, superimposed, weighty, burdensome, cumbersome, heavy, ponderous, massive, unwieldy, (light, levity, imponderability, buoyancy, volatility, sublimated, floating, low, debasement, depressed)

incurable-*adj* hopeless, despair, despondency, forlorn, inconsolable, cureless, remediless, incorrigible, irreparable, irrecoverable, ruined, undone, immitigable, (hope, trust, confident, presumptuous, feed, foster, nourish, healthy, sound, hearty, fresh, unscathed)

indebted-*v* owing, debt, obligation, liability, arrears, deficit, default, insolvency, grateful, thankfulness, acknowledgement, allegiance, dueness, propriety, fitness, sense of duty, recognition, binding, imperative, behooving, (ungrateful, credit, trust, tick, score, tally, account, mortgagee)

indefinite-*adj* uncertain, incertitude, doubt, suspense, vague, haze, fog, obscure, ambiguity, casual, random, aimless, changeable, fallible, questionable, precarious, disputable, invisible, imperceptible, indistinct, concealment, confused, indistinct, (perceptibility, conspicuousness, appearance, exposure, manifestation, obvious, recognizable, certain, necessity, surety, assurance)

indemnity-*n* compensation, counteract, balance, hedge, square, give and take, compromise, excuse, exoneration, quitting, release, acquittal, conciliation, propitiation, reprieve, reward, recompense, remuneration, (penalty, retribution, confiscation, forfeit, revenge, vengeance, retaliation, rancor)

indenture-*n* compact, contract, agreement, bargain, affidavit, pact, bond, covenant, stipulation, settlement, convention, compromise, cartel, title, deed, authority, warrant, credential, diploma, (unattested, unauthenticated, check, destroy, weaken, contradict, vindicate, disproof)

indicate-*v* examine, scan, scrutinize, consider, inspect, review, rivet, direct, observe, mean, signify, express, convey, imply, bespeak, suggest, allusive, significant, symbolism, feature, diagnostic, recognize, (without meaning, senseless, nonsensical, void, vacant, insignificant, undefinable)

indigence-*n* insufficiency, inadequacy, incompetence, impotence, deficiency, emptiness,

scarcity, want, need, lack,
poverty, famine, poor,
depletion, vacancy,
(sufficient, enough,
adequate, commensurate,
competent, satisfactory,
valid, tangible, copious,
abundant, abounding,
flush)

Individual-n human being,
person, creature, mortal,
body, somebody, earthling,
party, head, personal,
individuality, special,
particular, realize,
designate, determine,
private, characteristic,
originality, (general,
universal, miscellaneous,
generic, broad, collective,
every, all, unspecified)

Indomitable-adj strong,
might, vigorous, forcible,
hard, adamantine, stout,
robust, sturdy, hardy,
powerful, potent, puissant,
valid, resistless,
irresistible, invincible,
impregnable,
unconquerable,
determined, resolute,
(vacillating, unsteady,
changeable, cowardly,
facile, pliant, reversible,
weak)

induce-v cause, origin,
source, principle, element,
genesis, procure, draw
down, evoke, entail,
provoke, reason, ground,
call, principle, keystone,
element, consideration,
attraction, magnet,

enticement, allurement,
witchery, cajolery,
seduction, (dissuade,
deport, against,
remonstrate, expostulate,
warn, consequence, result,
upshot, issue, outgrowth)

indulge-v lenient, mild,
gentle, soft, tolerant, easy
going, clement,
compassionate, forbearing,
permission, allow, leave,
sufferance, tolerance,
liberty, law, license,
concession grace, favor,
dispensation, exemption,
connivance, (prohibit,
disallow, veto, embargo,
taboo, restrictive, forbid)

ineffectual-adj useless,
inefficacy, futile, inaptitude,
inadequate, inefficiency,
unskillful, inoperative,
incompetent, superfluous,
dispensable, redundant,
unskillful, inadequate,
incapable, invalid,
helpless, exhaustion,
(capable, effective,
endowed, virtuous,
qualified, powerful, potent)

inert-adj dull, inactivity,
torpor, languor, latency,
sloth, irresolution,
obstinacy, passive,
sluggish, heavy, tame,
slow, blunt, lifeless, dead,
uninfluential, latent,
dormant, smoldering,
insensibility, apathy,
lethargic, neutrality,
vegetation, (sensitive,
impressionable,

enthusiastic, spirited,
excitable)
inexorable-*adj* unavoidable,
necessity, obligation,
compulsive, subjection,
imperious, iron, adverse,
fate, compel, inevitable,
irrevocable, impulsive,
(volition, voluntary, willful,
intended, spontaneity,
original, optional,
discretionary, willing)
inexperience-*n* ignorance,
incomprehensive,
simplicity, unexplored,
uncertainty, incapable,
unknown, bungling,
awkward, clumsy,
maladroit, incompetent,
rusty, without former
knowledge, unskillful,
disqualification, (skill,
dexterity, experience,
accomplish, competence,
talent, capacity)
infatuation-*n* impulsive,
impetuous, passionate,
uncontrolled,
ungovernable,
irrepressible,
inextinguishable, burning,
simmering, volcanic,
vehement, demonstrative,
furious, fierce, over-
zealous, enthusiastic,
impassioned, fanatical,
eager, (submission,
resignation, fortitude, even
tempered, tranquil,
tolerance, patience)
infernal-*adj* bad, hurtful,
virulence, wrong, arrant,
rank, foul, vile,

abominable, detestable,
cursed, confounded,
damned, diabolic,
malevolent, grudge, annoy,
malicious, rancorous,
spiteful, caustic, bitter,
envenomed, acrimonious,
grinding, galling,
(benevolent, benignity,
brotherly love, charity,
sympathy, tenderness,
goodness, excellence,
value, merit, virtue,
superiority)
infidelity-*n* dishonor,
dishonest, disgrace,
fraudulent, faithlessness,
betrayal, degrade,
derogate, stoop, grovel,
sneak, unscrupulous,
contemptible, abject,
untrustworthy, (upright,
honest, virtuous,
honorable, fair, right, just,
equitable, impartial, even
handed, square,
straightforward, honest)
infiltrate-*v* intervene,
interference, introduce,
import, throw, insinuate,
dovetailing, permeation,
passage, transmission,
transudation, ingress,
instill, mix, join, combine,
transfuse, tincture, season,
infect, (eliminate,
purification, simple,
uniform, disentangle,
encompass, beset)
infinitesimal-*adj* small,
little, tenuity, paucity,
fewness, mediocrity,
moderation, vanishing

point, atom, particle,
molecule, diminutive,
minute, inconsiderable,
paltry, unimportant,
slender, meager, few,
inappreciable, evanescent,
mere, (vast, immense,
enormous, extreme,
excessive, preposterous,
monstrous, stupendous,
astonishing, incredible,
marvelous)
influence-n change,
alteration, mutation,
permutation, variation,
modification, modulation,
mood, qualification,
innovation, deviation, turn,
diversion, break,
transformation,
transfiguration, pressure,
preponderance,
dominance, reign,
authority, capability,
interest, power, carry
weight, leverage,
(impotence, inertness,
powerless, irrelevant,
permanence, stability,
persistence, endurance,
persist)
information-n knowledge,
cognizance, acquaintance,
privity, insight, intuition,
familiarity, recognition,
appreciation, light,
enlightenment, learning,
lore, scholarly, conceive,
comprehend, understand,
enlightenment, publicity,
communication, intimation,
notice, representation,
(concealment, hiding,

masquerade, secret,
recondite, ignorance,
uninformed,
unconsciousness,
incomprehension)
infraction-n disobey,
violate, infringe, shirk,
defiance, uncomplying,
unsubmissive, unruly,
insubordinate, resisting,
insurgent, riotous,
unbidden, retraction,
repudiation, protest,
forfeiture, lawlessness,
discard, protest, (observe,
perform, compliance,
obedience, satisfaction,
discharge,
acknowledgement, satisfy,
fulfill, carry out)
infringe-v
transgression, trespass,
encroach, transcendence,
surpass, go beyond,
redundance, strain,
disobey, violate, shirk,
defiance, uncomplying,
(obedient, complying,
loyal, faithful, devoted,
restrainable, resigned,
passive, submissive,
henpecked)
infuse-v mix, alloy,
junction, combination,
impregnation, infiltration,
seasoning, springing,
interlard, instill, imbue,
infiltrate, dash, tinge,
tincture, season sprinkle,
attempter medicate, blend,
(pure, eliminate, sift,
uniform, homogeneous,
single, neat, clear, sheer)

ingrained-*adj* custom, usage, use, prescription, practice, prevalence, observance, conventional, conformity, rule, standing order, precedent, routine, rut, groove, habit, combine, unite, incorporate, amalgamate, embody, absorb, impregnate, (decomposition, analysis, dissection, resolution, unravel, catalytic, disuse, unusual)

inhibit-*v* restraint, hindrance, coercion, constraint, repression, discipline, control, confinement, durance, duress, imprisonment, emancipation, limbo, captivity, blockade, disallow, interdict, injunction, embargo, ban, taboo, proscription, (permit, allow, sufferance, tolerance, liberty, law, admit, authorize, warrant, sanction, entrust)

Injury-*n* impairment, damage, loss, detriment, laceration, outrage, havoc, contamination, canker, corruption, adulteration, alloy, decay, dilapidation, deteriorate, weaken, hurt, harm, scathe, injurious, deleterious, malignant, nocuous, evil, wrong, (beneficial, valuable, advantageous, profitable, edifying, improve,

betterment, mend, amendment, refine)

inkling-*n* supposition, assumption, postulation, condition, hypothesis, postulate, theory, proposal, suggestion, conceit, rough guess, conjecture, surmise, suspicion, hint, insinuate, allude, desire, wish, fantasy, leaning, (indifferent, neutral, unconcern, nonchalance, earnestness, anorexia, apathy)

innocuous-*adj* good, harmless, hurt, unobnoxious, beneficial, valuable, serviceable, advantageous, profitable, edifying, salutary, unerring, above suspicion, impeccable, (guilty, blame, culpable, reprehensible, enormity, atrocity, outrage, deadly, malpractice)

inoculate-*v* insert, forcible ingress, implantation, introduction, insinuation, intervention, injection, importation, infusion, immersion, submersion, dip, plunge, interment, imbed, dovetail, inculcate, indoctrinate, infuse, instill, infiltrate, ingraft, (misinform, misdirect, misrepresent, render unintelligible, perversion, extraction, removal, elimination, eradication, extirpation, educe, elicit)

inquisition-*n* inquiry,

request, search, quest,
pursuit, examination,
review, scrutiny,
investigation, indication,
exploration, exploitation,
ventilation, sifting,
calculation, analysis,
dissection, resolution,
study, tyrannical
extortionate, grinding,
withering, oppressive,
ruthless, (lenient, mild,
gentle, soft, tolerant,
indulgent, forbearing,
answer, respond, reply,
rebut, retort, rejoin,
acknowledge, explain)
insidious-*adj* deceitful,
deceived, cunning,
delusive, elusive, covens,
untrue, false, fraudulent,
trick, cheat, wile, blind,
feint, sly, stealthy,
underhanded, hidden,
crooked, shrewd,
(artlessness, simplicity,
innocence, candor,
sincerity, honesty, frank,
open minded, free, plain,
outspoken, downright)
insinuate-*v* cast reflection,
reproach, disapprove,
disparage, condemnatory,
damnify, denunciate,
abusive, objurgatory,
clamorous, vituperative,
defamatory, satirical,
severe, withering,
trenchant, sarcastic,
hypercritical, fastidious,
critical, hint, suggestion,
innuendo, (manifest,
apparent, salient, striking,

demonstrative, prominent,
flagrant, notorious,
approbation, approval,
sanctioned, advocate)
insipid-*adj* tasteless,
savorless, flat, stale, fade,
mild, gutless, ingestible,
mawkish, indifferent, cold,
frigid, lukewarm, cool,
unconcerned, phlegmatic,
easy-going, (avidity,
greediness, covetous,
grasping, craving, voracity,
taste, savor, smack, gusto)
insist-*v* argue, reason,
discuss, debate, dispute,
wrangle, bandy, controvert,
canvass, rational,
argumentative, claim,
warrant, controversial,
dialectic, command, order,
ordinance, act, instruct,
dispatch, demand,
imposition, require, charge,
prescribe, (unreasonable,
illogical, false, unsound,
invalid, unwarranted,
inconsequential)
insolvent-*adj* destitute,
indigence, penury,
pauperism, want, need,
distress, difficulties, needy,
poor, poverty-stricken,
debt, obligation, liability,
arrears, deficit,
impecuniosity, mendicant,
nonpayment, (credit, trust,
tally, account, accredited,
wealth, riches, fortune,
opulence, affluence,
independence)
inspire-*v* encourage, infuse,
give, reassure, embolden,

inspirit, cheer, nerve, put,
enliven, elate, exhilarate,
gladden, animate, raise
the spirits, perk up, give
pleasure, (depress,
discourage, dishearten,
dispirit, damp, dull, deject,
lower, sink, dash, knock-
down)

instance-*n* example,
specimen, sample,
quotation, exemplification,
illustration, accommodate,
conformity, illustrate,
accordance, cite, quote,
inducement, consideration,
attraction, enticement,
allurement, (disincline,
indispose, shake,
dissuade, remonstrate,
warn, without rhyme or
reason)

instant-*n* moment, second,
minute, twinkling, flash,
breath, crack, jiffy, burst,
hasty, quick, flash of
lightning, present, actual,
current, important,
consequence, prominence,
consideration, (whenever,
occasion, upon, sooner or
later, perpetual, eternal,
everlasting, immortal,
undying)

instinct-*n* intellect, mind,
understanding, thinking,
principle, rationality,
faculties, senses,
consciousness,
observation, percipience,
association of ideas,
conception, judgment, wit,
capacity, ability, instinctive,

impulsive, gratuitous,
hazarded, unconnected,
(absence of intellect,
imbecility, argumentative,
controversial, debatable)

institution-*n* school,
academy, university,
college, seminary, alma
mater, party, faction, side,
denomination, communion,
set, crew, band, society,
association, alliance,
league, legal, legitimate,
link, banded, bonded,
unite, join, associate,
corporation, syndicate,
establishment

instruct-*v* teach,
edification, education,
tuition, guidance,
qualification, preparation,
discipline, exercise, direct,
guide, impress upon,
convince, expound,
command, message,
direction, requirement,
order, (misinform, mislead,
misrepresent, lie, bewilder,
deceive, mystify)

insult-*v* rudeness,
discourtesy, ill-breeding,
ungainly manners,
disrespect, impudence,
barbarism, misbehavior,
stern, austerity,
modishness, acrimony,
acerbity, irreverence,
slight, neglect,
supercilious, affront,
(respect, consideration,
regard, courtesy, attention,
deference, reverence,
honor, esteem, veneration,

admiration, approbation)
integrate-v consolidate,
 whole, totality, integrity,
 totality, entirety,
 collectiveness, unity,
 completeness, integration,
 aggregate, gross amount,
 altogether, substantially,
 (incomplete, deficient,
 shortcoming, insufficiency,
 imperfect, defective,
 unfinished, fractional,
 fragmentary, sectional,
 divided)
intensify-v increase,
 augmentation,
 enlargement, extension,
 dilatation, expansion,
 increment, develop,
 magnify, enhance,
 aggravate, exaggerate,
 exasperate, stimulate,
 activity, agitation,
 effervescence, stir, bustle,
 perturbation, energize,
 kindle, excite, exert,
 (inertness, inactive,
 passive, torpid, sluggish,
 dull, heavy, uninfluential,
 decrease, diminish, lessen,
 shrink, wane)
intercede- v mediate,
 intercessor, peacemaker,
 negotiator, diplomat,
 arbitrate, deprecate,
 expostulate, protest,
 negative request, (request,
 motion, overture, demand,
 canvass, address, appeal)
interest-n influential,
 important, weight,
 prevailing, rampant,
 dominance, predominant,

curious, inquisitive, stare,
 gape, lionize, pry,
 paramount, essential, vital,
 all-absorbing, radical,
 cardinal, prime,
 (indifferent, passive,
 irrelevancy, uninfluential,
 powerless)
interlink-v join, junction,
 union, ligation, allegation,
 accouplement, marriage,
 inoculation, assemblage,
 pivot, hinge, dovetail,
 encase, graft, entwine,
 attach, intersect,
 transversely, cross, braid,
 knot, twine, twist, (disjoin,
 disconnect, separate, part,
 segregate, divorce,
 division, fracture)
intermediate-adj mean,
 medium, average, balance,
 mediocrity, generality,
 middle, compromise,
 neutrality, link, connect,
 hyphen, bracket, bridge,
 bond, tendon, tendril,
 intervention, insertion,
 partition, septum,
 diaphragm, midriff,
 (circumference,
 environment, outskirts,
 suburbs, precincts)
intermit-adj interrupt,
 interrupted sequence,
 discontinue, break,
 fracture, flaw, fault,
 suspend, interplay, cease,
 desist, break off, hold,
 stop,stick, pause, rest,
 halt, (continue,
 persistence, repetition,
 sustain, unvarying,

unreversed, unrevoked,
unvaried)
Interpose-v interject,
intercalated, intersperse,
interweave, intrusive,
(encompass, surround,
circumference, encircle,
embrace, circumvent)
Interrupt-v discontinue,
disjunction, break, fault,
pause, disconnect,
unsuccessful, spasmodic,
intermittent, few and far
between, alternation,
patchwork, episode,
cessation, resistance,
suspension, stop, rest, lull,
(continue, persist,
repetition, sustain, uphold,
hold up, perpetuate,
maintain, preserve)
Intervene-v mediate,
peacemaker, negotiator,
diplomat, moderate, time,
duration, period, term, last,
endure, remain, persist,
elapse, while, interim,
interval, intermission,
interlude, (circumvent,
around, about, without,
skirt, twine round, lap,
border)
Interview-n conference,
interlocution, converse,
conversation,
confabulation, talk,
discourse, verbal
intercourse, oral
communication,
commerce, chatty,
colloquial, parley, gossip,
tattle, visit, call,
assignation, appointment,

(seclusion, privacy,
retirement, reclusion,
estrangement,
sequestered, private, snug,
domestic)
Intolerance-n prejudice,
narrow-minded, intolerant,
impracticable, besotted,
infatuated, fanatical,
positive, opinioned,
bigoted, crotchety,
unreasonable,insolent,
impertinence, sauciness,
flippant, petulant, (servile,
obsequious, supple,
mealy-mouthed, settle,
pass, comment,
investigate)
Intricate-adj disorder,
derangement, irregularity,
unconformity, confusion,
confusedness, disarray
jumble, huddle, litter,
complexity, complexness,
implication, intricacy,
perplexity, network,
involved, raveled,
entangled, disarrange,
(order, regularity,
uniformity, symmetry,
progression, series,
subordination,
systematically, gradation,
uniform)
Intrinsic-adj inbeing,
inherence, inhesion,
subjectiveness, essence,
essentialness, incarnation,
principle, nature,
constitution, character,
type, quality, oral,
documentary, hearsay,
external, extrinsic, internal,

demonstration,
(countervail, rebut, refute,
subvert, destroy, check,
weaken, contravene,
objectiveness,
extraneousness, accident,
incidental, accidental)
introduce-v prefix, place
before, premise, prelude,
preface, preceding, prior,
before, former, foregoing,
aforementioned, prefatory,
introductory, preamble,
prologue, precession,
leading, heading,
precedence, (sequence,
coming after, follower,
attend, beset, succeeding,
sequent)
intrude-v disagree,
discordant, discrepant,
hostile, repugnant,
incompatible,
irreconcilable, inconsistent,
interfere, clash,
intervention, partition,
midriff, interpenetrate,
permeate, introduce,
import, interpose,
(surround, beset,
compass, encompass,
environ, enclose, encircle,
embrace)
inundate-v irrigate, deluge,
syringe, inject, gargle,
drench, douse, dilute, dip,
immerse, merge,
submerge, redundance,
many, super abundance,
saturation, transcendency,
exuberance, profuseness,
accumulation, (dry,
flatulent, effervescent,

atmospheric,
meteorological)
invalid-n powerless,
impotence, disability,
disablement, impiousness,
imbecility, incapacity,
indocility, inefficiency,
incompetence,
disqualification,
helplessness, prostration,
palsy, exhaustion,
inefficacy, failure, (power,
potency, might, force,
energy, ability, capability,
faculty, quality, attribute,
valid)
invariable-adj uniform,
homogeneity, accordance,
agreement, regularity,
constancy, always, without
exception, like clockwork,
symmetry, naturalization,
conventionality, example,
instance, specimen,
typical, normal, illustrative,
(exceptional, abnormal,
unusual, unaccustomed,
rare, varied, diversified,
irregular, uneven, rough,
multifarious, multiformity)
invasion-n attack, assault,
assail, charge, impugn,
aggression, offense,
incursion, inroad, irruption,
outbreak, investment,
obsession, bombardment,
fire, volley, platoon, beset,
besiege, beleaguer,
(defense, protection,
guard, ward, shielding,
preservation, guardianship,
resistance, safeguard)
inversion-n derangement,

disorder, eviction,
discomposure,
disturbance, dislocation,
perturbation, interruption,
corrugation, complicate,
involve, perplex, confound,
tangle, litter, scatter, mix,
(classify, divide, file, string,
together, thread, register,
catalog, tabulate, index,
graduate, digest,
methodize)

invest-v purchasing, buying,
procure, rent, expenditure,
expend, disburse,
circulate, remuneration,
fee, contingent, quota,
(premium, bonus, pension,
annuity, jointure, alimony,
pittance, proceeds)

invoke-v address,
allocution, speech,
apostrophe, interpolation,
appeal, invocation,
salutation, request,
entreat, beseech, plead,
supplicate, implore,
conjure, adjure, obtest,
evoke, impetrate,
imprecate, (deprecation,
expostulation, intercession,
mediation, protest)

involve-v include, contain,
hold, comprehend, take in,
admit, embrace, embody,
implicate, drag into,
compose, constitute, form,
containing, convoluted,
winding, twisted, tortile,
intricate, complicated,
perplexed, (simple
exclusion, omission,
exception, rejection,

repudiation, exile,
separation, segregation,
supposition, elimination,
inadmissible, relegate)

irregular-adj diverse,
unevenness, multiformity,
unconformity, varied,
rough, disorder, anomaly,
disunion, discord,
confusion, disarray,
jumble, complexity,
perplexity, turmoil, ferment,
disturbance, convulsion,
riot, unsymmetrical,
intricate, complicated,
(order, uniformity,
methodical, symmetrical,
uniform, arranged,
economy)

irreparable-adj hopeless,
despair, desperation,
despondency, pessimism,
forlorn, incurable, cureless,
remediless, beyond,
remedy, incorrigible,
unpromising, unpropitious,
threatening, hurtful,
painful, pestilence, hurt,
harm, (beneficial, valuable,
serviceable,
advantageous, profitable,
edifying, salutary, hope,
trust, confidence, reliance,
faith, assurance,
reassurance, security)

irrevocable-adj compulsory,
uncontrollable, inevitable,
unavoidable, inexorable,
involuntary, instinctive,
automatic, blind, stable,
unchangeable, constancy,
established, permanence,
fixed, steadfast, firm, valid,

irremovable, riveted,
rooted, settled,
(changeable, mutable,
variable, vagrant,
alternating)

J

jabber-v oquacity,
talkativeness, garrulity,
eloquent, jaw, gabble,
chatter, linguistic,
declamatory, open-
mouthed, fluency,
flippancy, flowing, tongue,
verbosity, stammer,
hesitation, impediment,
stutter, falter, mumble,
(oratory, elocution,
rhetoric, declamation)

jail-n bolt, bar, lock,
padlock, rail, prison, gaol,
cage, coop, den, cell,
stronghold, fortress, keep,
dungeon, Bastille,
bridewell, house of
correction, hulks, toll-
booth, penitentiary, guard-
room, (liberate,
disengagement, release,
emancipate, dismiss,
discharge)

jam-v squeeze, push,
reduce, extricate, express,
pulp, paste, dough, curd,
pudding, poultice, grume,
sugar, syrup, treacle,
molasses, honey, manna,
confection, nectar, pastry,
pie, (sour, vinegar, styptic)

jar-v clash, disagree,
interfere, intrude, discord,
capsule, vesicle, vessel,

pod, bottle, decanter,
ewer, cruise, carafe, crock,
kit, canteen, flagon,
demijohn, jug, pitcher,
mug, kettle, chalice,
tumbler, glass, rummer,
horn, saucepan

jargon-n paradox, riddle,
unintelligibility,
incomprehensible,
inconceivable, vagueness,
loose, beyond
comprehension, gibberish,
macaronic, confusion of
tongues, (verbal, literal,
titular, conjugate,
derivative, exact,
concordance, clear, plain
speaking, lucidity,
perspicuity, legibility)

jaundice-n yellow,
gamboge, cadmium,
aureate, golden, citron,
fallow, sallow, luteous,
tawny, bias, warped,
twisted, hobby, fad, quirk,
one sided, superficial,
partial, narrow, confined,
(deduce, derive, gather,
collect, judge, umpire,
assessor, discover)

jealousy-n envious, covet,
invidious, rival, suspicion,
scruple, qualm, unbeliever,
discredit, dissent, (believe,
credit, indifference,
serene)

jerk-v agitate, stir, tremor,
shake, ripple, jolt,
trepidation, quiver, quaver,
dance, disquiet, twitter,
flicker, flutter, traction,
draw, draught, pull, haul,

rake, drag, tug, tow, trail, train, wrench, twitch, tousle, propel, project, throw, fling, cast, pitch, chuck, toss, heave, hurl, flirt, flip, (repulse, repel, abduct, repellent, repulsive, diverge, divaricate, radiate, ramify, diverge)

jetty-n projection, prominent, protuberant, convex, nodular, mammillate, papule, arched, bold, bellied, tuberous, tumorous, cornute, odontoid, in relief, raised, salient, roadstead, anchorage, breakwater, mole, port, haven, harbor, pier, seaport, embankment, quay(precipice, breakers, shoals, shallows, bank, shelf, flat, iron-bound, coast, rock)

jilt-v disappoint, disconcerted, aghast, trick of fortune, deception, falseness, untruth, imposition, fraud, deceit, guile, knavery, misrepresentation, delusion, trick, cheat, deceiver, dissembler, hypocrite, shuffler, wolf in sheep's clothing, (dupe, gull, gudgeon, cull, victim, greenhorn, fool)

jobber-n tactician, genius, master mind, head, spirited, cunning, sharp, cracksman, strategist, proficient, expert, merchant, trader, dealer, monger, chandler, salesman, changer, shop-keeper, tradesman, retailer, Chapman, hawker, huckster, haggler, peddler, broker, (bungler, blunderer, fumbler, lubber, duffer, awkward,squad, notice, greenhorn)

jockey-n rider, horseman, equestrian, cavalier, rough rider, trainer, breaker, driver, coachman, whip, charioteer, postilion, post boy, carter, waggoner, drayman, cab-man, attendant, squire, usher, page, footboy, train-bearer, waiter, tapster, butler, livery servant, lackey, footman, valet, (master, padrone, lord, paramount, commander, captain, chief, sachems, sheik, runner, courier, pedestrian)

jog-v push, walk, march, step, tread, pace, plod, wend, promenade, trudge, tramp, stalk, stride, straddle, strut, foot it, stump, bundle, bowl along, toddle, paddle, roving, vagrancy, marching and countermarching, nomad, vagabondism, migration

join-v connect, union, attachment, attach, fix, affix, fasten, bind, secure, clinch, twist, pinion, string, strap, sew, lace, stitch, tack, knit, gird, tether,

moor, harness, chain,
fetter, firm, fast, close,
tight, taut, group, cluster,
accumulation, assemble,
compile, associate,
(disperse, dissipate,
distribute, apportionment,
spread, cut, scatter, sow,
disseminate, diffuse,
separate, parting, detach)

jolt-*v* impulse, impetus,
momentum, push, pulsing,
thrust, shove, jog, brunt,
booming, throw, strike,
knock, tap, rap, slap, flap,
dab, pat, thump, beat,
bang, slam, dash, punch,
thwack, whack, hit,
agitate, shake, convulse,
toss, tumble, (recoil,
revulsion, rebound,
reflection, reflex, reflux,
reverberation, rebuff,
repulse, return)

journal-*n* almanac,
calendar, register,
chronicle, annals, diary,
chronogram, record, note,
memorandum,
endorsement, inscription,
copy, duplicate, docket,
affidavit, certificate,
gazette, newspaper,
magazine, calendar,
ephemeris, diary, log,
archive, scroll, (efface,
obliterate, erase, scratch,
delete, unregistered,
undocumented, without)

judgment-*n* instinct,
conception, wits, capacity,
intellect, understanding,
reason, rationality,
cogitative, faculties,
senses, observation,
intuition, discrimination,
distinction, differentiation,
(indiscrimination,
uncertainty, indistinctness,
imbecility, without reason)

judicial-*adj* judge, tribunal,
municipality, bailiwick,
officer, bailiff, sit in
judgment, magistrate,
authority, prefiguration,
auspices, forecast, omen,
prognostication,
premonition, (weak, feeble
minded, fatuous, idiotic,
imbecile, blatant, babbling,
bewildered)

jump-*v* sudden change,
transilience, leap, plunge,
jerk, start, explosion,
spasm, convulsion, throe,
revulsion, cataclysm, hop,
spring, bound, vault,
saltation, frisky, skip,
dance, caper, curvet,
flounce, start, agitation,
(submerge, douse, sink,
engulf, send to the bottom,
plunge, dip, souse, duck)

jury-*n* judge, justice,
chancellor, recorder,
magistrate, jurat, assessor,
arbiter, arbitrator, umpire,
referee, archon, tribune,
scapegoat, stop-gap

K

keen-*adj* strong, energetic,
forcible, active, intense,
severe, vivid, sharp, acute,
incisive, trenchant, brisk,

rousing, irritating, poignant, virulent, caustic, mordant, harsh, stringent, double-edged, (inertness, dull, inert, inactivity, torpor, languor, inaction, lithe, passive, heavy, flat)

keep-v retain, retention, custody, tenacity, firm hold, grasp, grip,clutches, tongs, forceps, pincers, undisposed, tenacious, preserve, safe keeping, conserve, maintain, support, sustentation, salvation, hygienic, (relinquish, abandonment, renunciation, expropriation, dereliction, surrender, dispensation, resignation, riddance, jettison, discard)

key-n opener, perforate, wide open, ajar, gaping, patent, tubular, aperient, cause, origin, source, element, principle, occasioned, pivot, hinge, turning-point, lever, proximate cause, ground, reason, rationale, (derived, derivative, hereditary, dependent upon, owing to, resulting from, due to, closure, occlusion, blockade, shutting up. obstruction,hindrance, plug, block, cork, bar, shut)

kick-v assault, thrust, lunge, pass, push, cut, fire, volley, assail, strike, impulse, whip,attack, aggressive, strike out, fling, insolent, flippant, pert, forward,

impertinent, (defense, protect, guard, ward, shield, self-defense, preservation, resistance, safeguard, repel, stand one's ground)

kidnap-v take, reception, deglutition, appropriation, prehension, presentation, capture, apprehension, seizure, abduction, subtraction, abstraction, confiscation, eviction, rapacity, extortion, clutch, swoop, wrench, grip, haul, take, catch, scramble, (return, restitution, restoration, reinvestment, recuperation, release, give up, bring back, recoup, reimburse, recuperate, recover, revert)

kill-v destroy, violent death, homicide, manslaughter, murder, assassination, massacre, mortal, fatal, lethal, dead, deathly, suicidal, strangle, smother, kill with kindness, consume, burn, idle, trifle, (life, vivacity, spirit, dash, energy, animation)

kindle-v excite, affect, touch, move, impress, strike interest, animate, inspire, impassion, smite, infect, stir, provoke, raise up, summon up, arouse, fire, enkindle, apply the torch, sent on fire, inflame, stimulate, produce, work, handiwork, fabric, performance, creature, upshot, develop, (tranquil, passive, impassibility, coolness, unexcitable, imperturbable, dispassionate, sedate)

king-*n* potentate, sovereign, monarch, despot, tyrant, crowned head, emperor, majesty, protector, president, judge, empire, royalty, regal, dominant, paramount, supreme, influential, imperial, stringent, (absence of authority, anarchy, relaxation, loosening, remission, misrule, insubordination, depravation of power, remiss, unwarranted)

kiss-*v* endearment, caress, embrace, salute, smack, buss, osculation, courtship, wooing, suit, philander, flirt, obeisance, bow, courtesy, curtsy, scrape, loving, love token, (repulsive, noncomplacent, accommodating, gallant, ungentle, rough,rugged, bluff, blunt, gruff, tart, sour, surly)

kleptomania-*n* steal, theft, thievery, robbery, deception, abstraction, pillage, light-fingered, piratical, predaceous, plunder, rifle, sack, loot, ransack, spoil, spoilt, despoil, strip, monomania, eccentricity, fanaticism, infatuation, craze, oddity, (sane, rational, generous, restitution, return, restore, reimburse, reforge, recoup, redeem, recuperate, remit, rehabilitate)

knavery-*n* deception, falseness, untruth, imposition, fraud, guile, misrepresentation, delusion, gullible, conjuring, cunning, craftiness, subtlety, chicanery, juggler, concealment, sharp practice, (natural, pure, native, simple, plain, inartificial, untutored, unsophisticated, unaffected, sincere, frank, open)

knee-*n* angular, bent, crooked, aduncous, uncinate, aquiline, jagged, serrated, furcate, forked, dovetailed, knock-kneed, obeisance, homage, genuflection, courtesy, curtsy, prostration, kneel to, (deprecation, expostulation, intercession)

know-*v* knowledge, cognizance, acquaintance, privily, insight, familiarity, appreciation, intuition, consciousness, conceive, comprehend, take, realize, understand, aware, ascertained, (ignorance, shallow, superficial, green, rude, empty, half-learned, illiterate, unread, uninformed, empty-headed)

kowtow-*v* bow, depress, lower, take-down, subvert, prostrate, level, fell, cast, genuflection, obeisance, surrender, succumb, submit, yield, bend, resign, (elevate, raise, lift, sublimation, exaltation, prominence, heighten, erect)

L

labor-*n* work, action, performance, perpetration, movement, operation, evolution, procedure, execution, handicraft, business, deed, act, transaction, job, doings, dealings, proceeding, measure, achieve, inflict, (indolent, lazy, slothful, idle, lust, remiss, slack, inert, torpid, sluggish, languid, supine, heavy, dull leaden, lumpish, listless, dilatory, laggard)

lack-*n* insufficient, inadequate, impotence, deficiency, imperfection, shortcoming, paucity, stint, scantiness, scarcity, dearth, want, need, poverty, exigency, inanition, starvation, famine, drought, dole, pittance, short-allowance, (sufficient, adequate, enough, satisfaction, competence, fullness, abundance, copiousness, galore, lots, profusion, full

measure, rich, luxuriant, ample)

lackadaisical-*adj* indifferent, cold, frigid, lukewarm, cool, unconcerned, insouciant, phlegmatic, easy-going, devil-may care, careless, listless, half-hearted, unambitious, unaspiring, unsolicitous, inactive, dilatory, laggard, lagging, slow, tottering, irresolute, (active, briskness, liveliness, animation, life, vivacity, spirit, dash, eager, quick, prompt, instant, ready, alert, spry, sharp, spry)

ladle-*n* receptacle, shovel, trowel, spoon, spatula, watch-glass, thimble, receiver, cup, goblet, chalice, soup, decant, draft off, transfuse, spoon, hod, paddle, hoe, spade, spud

lag-*v* linger, slow, retard, relax, slacken, check, moderate, slack, tardy, dilatory, inactive, gentle, easy, leisurely, deliberate, gradual, insensible, imperceptible, languid, sluggish, slow-paced, tardigrade, snail-like, creeping, follow, attendant, shadow, dangler, get behind, (lead, in advance, before, ahead, precede, forerun, introduce)

lame-*adj* incomplete, imperfect, defective, deficient, wanting, failing,

meager, half and half,
perfunctory, sketch, crude,
mutilated, garbled, lopped,
truncated, helplessness,
prostration, paralysis,
palsy, apoplexy, syncope,
collapse, exhaustion,
emasculation, (ability,
ableness, togetherness,
faculty, quality, attribute,
endowment, virtue, gift,
property, qualification,
susceptibility, valid,
effective)

lampoon-*n* censure, scoff
at, point at, twit, taunt,
satirize, defame,
depreciate, find fault with,
criticize, disparaging,
condemnatory, damnify,
denunciatory, reproachful,
abusive, objurgatory,
clamorous, vituperative,
defamatory, satirical,
sarcastic, sardonic, cutting,
severe, hypercritical,
(applaud, praise, laud,
good work, homage,
blessing, benediction,
plaudit, shout, approval)

lance-*n* pierce, perforate,
tap, bore, drill, mine,
tunnel, enfilade, impale,
spike, spear, gore, spit,
stab, puncture, stick, prick,
riddle, punch, shooter,
shot, archer, propel,
project, throw, dart, tilt,
fling, cast, pitch, chuck,
toss, jerk, heave,
(repulsion, repulse,
abduction, dispel, abduct,
repellent, keep at arms's

length, send away)

land-*n* arrive, reach, attain,
get to, come to, overtake,
light, alight, dismount,
debark, disembark, here,
hither, detrain, welcome,
converge, meet,
completion, earth, ground,
continent, coast, shore,
mainland, peninsula, delta,
soil, globe, clay, loam,
acres, real estate, (ocean,
brine, water, waves,
departure, cessation,
decampment,
embarkation, outset, start,
exit, egress, exodus,
farewell)

landscape-*n* agriculture,
management of plants,
cultivation, husbandry,
farming, gardening,
horticulture, floriculture,
ornamental, flower garden,
vineyard, till, scenery,
dress the ground,
undeformed, undefaced,
unspotted, (deformed,
defaced, ugly, uninviting)

languid-*adj* weak, poor,
infirm, fantasia, sickly, dull,
slack, spent, short-winded,
effete, weatherbeaten,
decayed, rotten, worn,
seedy, wasted, washy, laid
low, pulled down, frail,
fragile, shatter,
decrepit,feeble, debilitate,
impotent, soft, effeminate,
femininity, womanly,
colorless, (strength, power,
stoutness, strong, might,
vigorous, forcible, hard,

adamantine, stout, robust,
sturdy, hardy)
lap-_n_ abode, dwelling,
lodging, domicile,
residence, address,
habitation, berth, seat,
sojourn, housing, quarters,
head-quarters, residence,
tabernacle, throne, ark,
supporter, aid, prop, stand,
anvil, stay, shore, skid, rib,
truss, bandage, sleeper,
stirrup, stilts, shoe, heel,
splint, bar, rod, (suspend,
loose, flowing, hang, slip,
hitch, fasten to, append)
lapidate-_v_ kill, homicide,
manslaughter, murder,
assassination, attack,
assault, onset, onslaught,
charge, aggression,
offense, incursion, inroad,
cut, thrust, fire, volley,
platoon, (defend, protect,
guard, ward, shield,
preservation, guardianship,
fortify, resistance)
lapse-_n_ elapse, course,
progress, process,
succession, flow, flux,
stream, tract, current, tide,
march, run, expire,
duration, past, gone, gone
by, over, passed away,
bygone, foregone, expired,
exploded, forgotten,
former, pristine, (future,
hereafter, approaching,
prospectively, hereafter,
tomorrow, eventually,
ultimately)
large-_adj_ quantity, vast,
immense, enormous,

extreme, inordinate,
excessive, extravagant,
exorbitant, outrageous,
preposterous,
unconscionable, swinging,
monstrous, big, great,
considerable, bulky,
voluminous, ample,
massive, mass, capacious,
comprehensive, spacious,
might, towering, fine,
magnificent, (dwarf,
pygmy, chit, minute,
diminutive, microscopic,
inconsiderable, exiguous,
puny)
lash-_v_ enforce, force, impel,
push, propel, whip, goad,
spur, prick, urge, hurry-on,
exhort, advise, advocate,
impulsive, seductive,
attractive, fascinating,
provocative, exciting,
violent, vehement, warm,
acute, sharp, rough, rude,
ungentle, bluff, boisterous,
impetuous, rampant,
turbulent, (moderation,
lenitive, gentleness, quiet,
mental calmness, sobriety,
relaxing, remission,
mitigation, tranquilization,
pacification)
last-_n_ final, end, close,
termination, dissonance,
conclusion, period, term,
extreme, verge,
consummation, finish,
conclude, expire, definitive,
ending, durable, lasting,
standing, permanent,
chronic, long-standing,
macrobiotic, perpetual,

lingering, (transient,
impermanence, temporary,
brief, quick, brisk,
extemporaneous,
summary, sudden,
momentary)
laud-v praise,
commendation, approval,
sanction, advocacy,
esteem, good opinion,
admiration, love, worship,
benediction, blessing, clap,
cheer, hosanna,
compliment,
complimentary, uncritical,
lavish of praise,
(disapprove, dislike,
lament, reprehension,
remonstrance,
expostulation, admonition,
reproach, rebuke,
reprimand, castigation,
lecture, curtain lecture,
blow up)
laugh-v ridicule, derision,
sardonic, smile, grin,
scoffing, mockery, quiz,
banter, irony, squib, satire,
skit, quip, quibble, grin,
parody, burlesque, satirize,
caricature, travesty, giggle,
titter, snigger, cheer,
chuckle, shout, (lament,
wail, complaint, plaint,
murmur, mutter, grumble,
groan, moan, whine,
whimper, sob, sigh,
suspiration, mourning,
condolence, deplore,
grieve)
launch-v beginning,
commencement, opening,
outset, incipience,

inception, introduction,
initial, inauguration,
embarkation, outbreak,
fresh start, origin, source,
rise, bud, germ, egg,
genesis, birth, nativity,
cradle, start, (end, close,
termination, dissonance,
conclusion, period, term,
extreme, consummation,
finish)
lavish-adj profuseness,
redundance, too much,
super abundance,
inordinate, excessive,
replete, prodigal,
overweening, extravagant,
overcharged,
supersaturated, drenched,
overflowing, superfluous,
(receive, take, catch,
miser, waste, scrubby,
touch, acquire, reception,
susceptibility, release)
law-n statute, rule, canon,
code, rubric, stage,
regulation, technicality,
precept, direction,
instruction, prescription,
receipt, golden rule,
maxim, permit, give
permission, grant,
empower, charter,
enfranchise, privilege,
license, authorize, warrant,
sanction, entrust,
(disallowance, interdiction,
injunction, embargo, ban,
taboo, proscription,
restriction, hindrance,
forbid, disallow, bar,
forefend)
lax-adj slackness, loose,

toleration, anarchy,
interregnums, loosening,
remission, dead, letter,
misrule, dethrone, depose,
abdicate, careless, weak,
free rein, unbridled,
unauthorized, (authority,
influence, patronage, hold,
rasp, grip, reach, clutch,
talons, power,
preponderance, credit,
jurisdiction)

lazy-*adj* inactive, inertness,
obstinacy, idle, remiss,
sloth, indolence,
indulgence, dawdling,
languor, sluggishness,
procrastination, torpidity,
somnolence, drowsiness,
drone, droll, nothingness,
slow, slack, moderate,
linger, loiter, tortoise,
(active, brisk, liveliness,
animation, life, vivacity,
spirit, dash, energy,
nimbleness)

lead-*v* direct, management,
government, gubernatorial,
conduct, legislate,
regulate, guide, steer, pilot,
administer, prescribe, cut
out work for, head, show
the way, authority,
influence, patronage,
power, jurisdiction,
despotism, command, (lax,
loose, slackness,
toleration, freedom,
loosening, remission,
misrule, relax, unbridled,
unauthorized, dethrone,
depose, abdicate)

leak-*n* crack, interval,

interspace, separation,
break, gap, opening, hole,
chasm, interruption, cleft,
mesh, crevice, chink,creek,
cranny, chap, slit, fissure,
scissure, rift, flaw, breach,
gorge, defile, transude, run
out, strain, distill, perspire,
sweat, filter, filtrate,
dribble, gush, spout, flow,
(excretion, discharge,
emanation, exhalation,
exudation, extrusion,
contiguity, contact,
proximity, apposition, join,
adjoin, graze, meet,
osculate, coincide, adhere,
touching)

lean-*adj* thin, narrowness,
closeness, exiled, exiguity,
tenuity, emaciation,
shaving, slip, skeleton,
shadow, anatomy, spindle,
meager, gaunt, tendency,
aptness, proneness,
proclivity, bent, turn, tone,
bias, set, (breadth, width,
latitude, amplitude,
diameter, bore, caliber,
radius, superficial,
thickness, corpulence,
dilation, wide, broad,
ample, extended, thick)

leap-*v* sudden change,
revolution, subversion,
break up, destruction,
radical, sweeping,
transilience, jump, plunge,
jerk, start, explosion,
spasm, convulsion, throe,
revulsion, storm, ascent,
ascension, rising, rise,
upgrowth, acclivity, hill,

rocket, lark, sky-rocket,
ascend, rise, mount, climb,
clamber, ramp, scramble,
(descent, dissension,
declination, fall, drop,
cadence, subsidence)

leave-*v* fissure, breach,
rent, split, rift, crack, slit,
incision, fission, dissection,
anatomy, disjoin,
disconnect, disengage,
sunder, divide, sever,
abscind, relinquish,
abandon, defection,
secession, withdrawal,
discontinuance,
renunciation, abrogation,
resignation, (arrive,
reunion, remain,
confinement, restrict,
forbid, hindrance, taboo,
embargo, ban)

leaven-*n* component,
integral, element,
constituent, ingredient, part
and parcel, contents,
appurtenance, feature,
member, to be implicated
in, cause, origin, source,
principle, element, agent,
groundwork, foundation,
(effect, consequence,
result, upshot, issue,
produce, work, handiwork,
fabric, performance,
creature)

ledge-*n* shelf, support,
ground, foundation, base,
basis, bearing, fulcrum,
footing, prop, stand, anvil,
shore, skid, rib, truss,
bandage, stirrup, stilts,
tower, pillar, column,

obelisk, monument,
steeple, spire, escarpment,
edge, brae, height,
(lowness, neap, debased,
nether, flat, level with the
ground)

left-*adj* residuary,
remaining, remainder,
residue, remnant, rest,
relic, leavings, heel-tap,
odds and ends, surplus,
overplus, excess,
complement, sinistrality,
left-handed, port, (dextral,
right-handed,
ambidextrous, adjunct,
affix, appendage,
reinforcement,
accompaniment, adjective)

leg-*n* support, travel,
wayfaring, journey,
excursion, expedition, tour,
trip, grand tour, circuit,
peregrination, discursion,
ramble, pilgrimage, course,
ambulation, march, step,
tread, pace, plod, wend,
promenade

legal-*adj* permit, leave,
allow, sufferance,
tolerance, liberty, law,
license, concession, grace,
indulgence, favor,
dispensation, exemption,
release, connivance,
vouchsafement,
authorization, warranty,
accordance, admission,
warrant, sanction, (forbid,
prohibit, disallowance,
injunction, embargo, ban,
taboo, hindrance, bar,
forefend)

legend-*n* record, trace, vestige, transactions, proceedings, debates, chronicles, annals, history, biography, tabulation, entry, booking, signature, identification, recorder, journalism, register, (efface, obliteration, erasure, cancellation, circumscribe, deletion, expunge, cancel, blot, deface)

legion-*n* multitude, numerousness, multiplicity, profusion, host, enormous number, array, sight, army, sea, galaxy, scores, peck, bushel, shoal, armed force, troops, soldiery, military, standing army, volunteers, (few, paucity, small number, small quantity, rarity, infrequency, handful, minority, thin)

leisure-*n* spare time, slow, deliberate, quiet, calm, undisturbed, slack, tardy, dilatory, gentle, easy, gradual, insensible, imperceptible, languid, sluggish, slow-paced, tardigrade, creeping, (speed, velocity, celerity, swiftness, rapidity, expedition, eagle speed, haste, spurt, dash, race, lively)

lend-*v* loan, advance, accommodation, federation, mortgage, investment, pawnbroker, money lender, usurer, advance, intrust, invest, let, lease, demise, aid, assistance, help, support, lift, patronage, countenance, favor, interest, advocacy, (prevention, preclusion, obstruction, stoppage, interruption, restriction, borrow, pledge, hire, rent, farm brace, touch, hold up)

lenient-*adj* moderate, temperateness, gentleness, sobriety, quiet, mental calmness, relaxation, remission, mitigation, tranquilization, assuagement, contemplation, pacification, measure, (violence, inclemency, vehemence, might, impetuosity, boisterousness, uproar, riot, severity)

lessen-*v* decrease, subtraction, reduction, abatement, declination, shrinking, abridgment, diminish, abridge, shrink, fall away, waste, wear, wane, ebb, decline, subside, compression, compactness, collapse, emaciation, atrophy, (expansion, enlargement, extension, augmentation, growth, development, increase, additional, undiminished, exaggerate, exasperate)

let-*v* permit, leave, allow, tolerance, liberty, law, license, concession, grace,

indulgence, favor,
dispensation, exemption,
release, connivance,
vouchsafement,
authorization, warranty,
lend, advance,
accomodate, (prohibition,
disallowance, borrow,
interdict, injunction,
embargo, ban, taboo,
restriction, release,
hindrance, exclusive)

lethargic-*adj* inactivity,
inaction, inertness,
obstinacy, drowsiness,
nodding, hypnotism,
heaviness, sleep, coma,
trance, nap, doze, snooze,
relaxation, idle, drone,
droll, dawdle, insensibility,
(active, briskness,
liveliness, animation, life,
vivacity, spirit, dash,
energy, nimbleness, agility,
quickness)

letter-*n* mark, character,
hieroglyphic, writing,
printing, abc's, consonant,
vowel, diphthong, mute,
liquid, labial, dental

levity-*n* lightness,
imponderability, buoyancy,
volatility, feather, dust,
mote, down, thistle down,
flue, cobweb, gossamer,
straw, cork, bubble, float,
ether, air, leaven ferment,
barm, yeast, (gravity,
weight, heaviness, specific
gravity, ponderous,
pressure, load, burden,
ballast, counterpoise, lead)

libation-*n* drunkenness,

intemperance, drinking,
inebriety, insobriety,
intoxication, tipsy, sot,
potable, draught, carousel,
nourishment, sustenance,
nurture, (excretion,
discharge, exhalation,
exudation, extrusion,
secretion, sobriety,
teetotaler)

liberty-*n* freedom,
independence, immunity,
exemption, emancipation,
franchise, liberalism,
permission, leave, allow,
sufferance, tolerance, law,
concession, grace,
indulgence, favor,
dispensation, release,
(prohibit, disallowance,
interdict, unlicensed,
contraband, subjection)

lick-*v* eat, feed, fare,
devour, swallow, take,
gulp, bolt, snap, dispatch,
pick, peck, crunch, chew,
masticate, nibble, gnaw,
mumble, strike, deal a
blow to, smite, slap, face,
smack, (discharge,
emanation, exhalation,
exudation, extrusion,
secretion, effusion, saliva,
outpour)

limbo-*n* purgatory, hell,
bottomless pit, place of
torment, everlasting fire,
torment, Gehenna, abyss,
inferno, mental suffering,
pain, ache, smart,
displeasure, vexation of
spirit, (pleasure,
gratification, enjoyment,

fruition, relish, zest,
satisfaction, heavenly,
paradise, eden, celestial)
limit-*n* restrain, hindrance,
restraint, coercion,
constraint, repression,
discipline, control,
confinement, durance,
duress, imprisonment, end,
close, termination,
conclusion, finish, (begin,
commence, originate,
conceive, initiate, open,
dawn, liberation,
disengagement, free,
deliverance)
linear-*adj* continuity,
consecutive, progressive,
gradual, serial, successive,
immediate, unbroken,
entire, uninterrupted,
unremitting, perennial,
paternity, parentage,
consanguinity, maternal,
family, ancestral,
patriarchal, (discontinue,
pause, interrupt, intervene,
break, disconnect, break)
liniment-*n* ointment,
linseed, unguent,
glycerine, stearin, grease,
suet, remedy, help,
redress, antidote,
antiseptic, corrective,
restorative, sedative,
physic, medicine, drug,
potion, (bane, curse, evil,
hurtfulness, painfulness,
scourge, sting, fang, thorn)
link-*n* pin, nail, bolt, hasp,
clasp, clamp, screw, rivet,
impact, solder, set, weld,
fuse-together, wedge,

rabbet, mortise, mire, jam,
dovetail, encase, graft,
ingraft, inosculate, close,
tight, taut, (sunder, divide,
subdivide, sever, dissever,
abscind, saw, snip, nib,
nip, cleave, rive, rend, slit)
lion-*n* courage, hero,
demigod, tiger, panther,
bull-dog, prowess,
heroism, chivalry,
manliness, nerve, pluck,
mettle, game, spunk, face,
virtue, prodigy,
phenomenon, potent,
(coward, timidity,
effeminacy, poltroonery,
baseness, dastardliness,
sneak, recreant, shy)
liquid-*n* fluid, inelastic,
liquor, humor, juice, sap,
serum, blood, serosal,
succulent, sappy, flowing,
soluble, lymph,
(atmospheric, airy, aerial,
meteorological weather-
wise, ventilate, climate)
list-*n* catalog, inventory,
schedule, register,
account, file, index, book,
ledger, synopsis, bill of
lading, prospectus,
statistics, directory, score
listless-*adj* inattentive,
inconsiderateness, absent,
abstracted, lost,
preoccupied, engrossed,
napping, dreamy,
disconcerted, (attention,
mindfulness, observance,
consideration, notice,
regard)
literary-*adj* lingual, dialectic,

vernacular, polyglot, book,
writing, work, volume,
publication, portfolio,
periodical, style, diction,
phraseology, wording,
manner, strain, literary
litigation-*n* citation,
arraignment, prosecution,
impeachment, accusation,
apprehension, arrest,
committal, writ, summons,
subpoena, strife, warfare,
outbreak, disagreement,
variance, difference,
(concord, accord,
harmony, symphony,
agreement, sympathy,
response, union, unison)
litter-*n* disorder, irregularity,
anomaly, unconformity,
anarchy, confusion,
disarray, jumble, huddle,
lumber, mess, mash,
hodgepodge, (order,
regularity, uniformity,
symmetry, gradation,
progression, series,
subordination, routine,
method, disposition)
little-*adj* small, quantity,
vanishing,diminutive,
minute, inconsiderable
paltry, faint, unimportant,
weak, slender, light, slight,
scanty, scant, limited,
mere, simple, sheer, stark,
bare, dwarf, pygmy, chit,
(corpulent, stout, fat,
plump, squab, full, lusty,
strapping, bouncing, portly,
burly, huge, immense)
live-*v* exist, being, entity,
subsistence, reality,

actuality, positiveness,
fact, matter of fact, real,
actual, absolute, true,
permanence, persistence,
endurance, standing,
maintenance, present,
occupying, inhabiting,
dwell, reside, stay, sojourn,
abide, lodge, (absence,
inexistent, empty, void,
vacant, inexistent,
extinction, annihilate,
nullify, abrogate, destroy,
negative, blank, missing)
livery-*n* outfit, equipment,
uniform, regimentals,
canonical, gear, harness,
turn out, accouterment,
caparison, suit, rigging,
trappings, traps, slops,
masquerade, color, hue,
tint, tinge, dye,
complexion, shade,
tincture, cast, coloration,
glow, flush, tone, key,
(hueless, pale, pallid,
muddy, leaden, nudity,
bareness, undress,
dishabille, molting,
exfoliation, divest, uncover,
denude)
load-*n* cargo, contents,
lading, freight, shipment,
bale, shipload, stuff,
oppress, care, anxiety,
solicitude, trouble, trial,
fiery ordeal, shock, blow,
dole, fret, burden,
(pleasure, gratification,
enjoyment, fruition, relish,
zest, gusto, satisfaction,
complacency, well-being)
loadstar-*n* motion toward,

attraction, pulling toward,
adduction, magnetism,
gravity, siderite, beacon,
cairn, seamark, lighthouse,
guide, address, direction,
heliograph
loathe-v dislike,
repugnance, disgust,
queasiness, turn, nausea,
averseness, antipathy,
abhorrence, horror, hatred,
detestation, animosity,
hydrophobia, insulting,
irritating, provoking,
abomination, aversion,
(love, fondness, liking,
inclination, affection,
sympathy, tenderness)
local-adj location,
lodgement, reposition,
stow, package, settlement,
installation, fixation,
insertion, anchorage,
mooring, encampment,
plantation, colony, place,
situate, locate, localize,
station, house,
(displacement,
transposition, eject, exile,
removal, dislocation,
unload, empty)
lock-v fasten, attach, fix,
affix, bind, secure, clinch,
twist, string, strap, firm,
close, knot, shackle, rein,
padlock, rivet, stake, hook,
latchet, resistance, stand,
front, oppugnant,
opposition, reluctant,
(separate, parting,
detachment, segregation,
divorce, divide, unlock,
detach, isolate)

locomotion-n moving,
stream, flow, flux, run,
course, evolution,
kinematics, step,
transitory, shifting,
movable, mobile,
mercurial, restless,
nomadic, erratic, cadence,
(quiet, tranquility, calm,
repose, peace, dead calm,
immobility, fixed, stay,
stagnate, rest, pause, lull)
lodge-n location, place,
situate, locate, localize,
put, lay, set, seat, station,
quarter, post, install,
house, stow, establish, fix,
pin, root, graft, plant,
people, inhabit, dwell,
reside, stay, sojourn, live,
abide, nestle, present,
(absent, missing, empty,
void, vacant, devoid,
truant, displacement)
lofty-adj height, altitude,
elevation, eminence, pitch,
sublimity, colossus, tall,
gigantic, Patagonian,
vehement, impassioned,
poetic, eloquent, petulant,
(feeble, tame, meager,
vapid, trashy, cold, frigid,
dull, dry, monotonous,
weak, careless, inexact)
log-n fuel, firing,
combustible, coal,
anthracite, culm, coke,
carbon, charcoal, turf,
peat, firewood, bobbing,
faggot, cinder, record,
note, minute, register, roll,
list, entry, memorandum,
document, deposition,

affidavit, certificate,
(efface, obliterate, erase,
expunge, cancel, blot,
scratch)

long-*adj* durable, lasting,
permanent, chronic, long-
standing, protracted,
prolonged, lengthy, drawn
out, profuse, verbose,
copious, exuberant,
rambling, broad, wide,
ample, extended, thick,
dumpy, streak,
outstretched, elongate,
extend, stretch, (short,
little, abbreviated, brief,
curt, compact, stubby,
temporary, cursory, short-
lived, deciduous, mortal,
summary, concise, terse)

longevity-*n* age, oldness,
senility, anility, climacteric,
declining years,
decrepitude, caducity,
seniority, eldership,
matronly, anile, ripe,
mellow, wrinkled, (youth,
juvenility, cradle, nursery,
green, budding)

longitude-*n* situation,
position, locality, status,
footing, standing,
standpoint, post, stage,
aspect, attitude, posture,
place, site station, seat,
length, span, linear,
measure of length,
(shortness, brevity,
littleness, shortening,
abbreviation, abridgment,
concision, retrenchment,
curtailment)

look-*v* see, vision, sight,
view, glance, glimpse,
peep, gaze, stare, leer,
contemplation, squint,
visual, ocular, optic,
appear, aspect, phase,
guise, complexion, color,
image, apparent, seeming,
ostensible, (invisible,
imperceptible, conceal,
blind, sightless)

loop-hole-*n* hole,
perforation, opening, vent,
orifice, path, thoroughfare,
escape, avocation,
elopement, flight, evasion,
retreat, narrow, hair-
breadth, impunity,
reprieve, livery, liberation,
refugee, elude, (closure,
occlusion, blockade,
shutting up, obstruction,
plug, block, shut, bolt,
stop, seal, unopened)

loose-*adj* detach, sunder,
divide, subdivide, sever,
dissever, abscind, saw,
snip, nib, nip, cleave,
rupture, shatter, shiver,
lacerate, scramble,
mangle, gash, hash, slice,
whittle, carve, dissect,
liberate, disengagement,
release, enlargement,
emancipation,
enfranchisement,
discharge, dismissal,
(restraint, hindrance,
coercion, compulsion,
constraint, repression,
discipline, control)

lose-*v* loss, depredation,
forfeiture, lapse, privation,
bereavement, deprivation,

dispossession, riddance,
lost, irretrievable,
hopeless, farewell, adieu,
failure, miscarriage,
repulse, rebuff, defeat, fall,
downfall, defeat, rout,
overthrow, (success,
fulfillment, advance,
progress, surmount,
overcome, triumph,
proficiency, gain, attain,
carry, acquire, obtainment,
purchase, descent, inherit)

love-*v* desire, wish, fancy,
fantasy, want, need,
exigency, longing,
hankering, inkling,
solicitude, anxiety,
yearning, coveting,
aspiration, liking, fondness,
relish, passion, rage,
mania, ambition,
eagerness, zeal, ardor,
breathless, impatience,
impetuosity, (indifferent,
cold, frigid, lukewarm, cool,
careless, listless,
lackadaisical, half-hearted,
apathy, insensibility)

lucid-*adj* luminous, lighten,
enlighten, shine, glow,
glitter, glisten, twinkle,
gleam, flare, glare, beam,
shimmer, glimmer, flicker,
sparkle, scintillate, dazzle,
transparent, pellucid,
diaphanous, limpid, clear,
serene, crystalline, glassy,
hyaline, (opacity,
opaqueness, film, cloud,
dim, turbid, thick, muddy,
opaques, obfuscated,
cloudy, hazy, misty, foggy,

vaporous, dark, black,
shade, shadow, extinction)

lush-*adj* vegetation, rank,
drunkenness,
intemperance, drinking,
inebriety, insobriety,
intoxication, tipsy, guzzle,
swill, soak, sot, lush, bib,
carouse, (sobriety,
teetotaler, abstainer)

luxury-*n* enjoyment,
pleasure, gratification,
relish, complacency,
comfort, ease, cushion,
joy, gladness, delight, glee,
cheer, sunshine,
happiness, felicity, bliss,
paradise, ecstasy,
Elysium, indulgence, high
living, excess, sensuality,
(temperance, moderation,
forbearance, self-denial,
frugality, total abstinence,
sufficient, care, anxiety,
solicitude, concern)

lymph-*n* fluid, liquid, liquor,
humor, juice, sap, serum,
blood, transparent,
pellucid, lucid, relucent,
limpid, clear, serene,
crystalline, vitreous,
watery, aqueous, aquatic,
lymphatic, drenching,
diluted, week, wet, moist,
(airy, ventilate, flatulent,
effervescent, windy,
opaque, smoky, murky,
dirty, opaque)

M

maceration-*n* saturation,
water, serum, serosal,

lymph, rheumy, delude,
dilution, dip, immerse,
submerge, plunge, souse,
duck, drown, soak, steep,
pickle, sprinkle,
atonement, reparation,
compromise, composition,
compensation, quitting,
expiation, redemption,
(atmospheric, airy)

mad-*adj* insane, disordered,
lunacy, madness, mania,
mental alienation,
aberration, demented,
frenzy, raving,
incoherence, wandering,
delirium calenture of the
brain, delusion,
hallucination, vertigo,
dizziness, fanaticism,
(sanity, soundness,
rationality, sobriety,
lucidity, senses, sound
mind)

madcap-*n* buffoon,
humorist, wag, with,
repartee, life of the party,
wit-snapper, joker, jester,
farceur, tumbler, acrobat,
harlequin, clown, motley,
motley fool, zany, dandy,
caricaturist, lunatic,
maniac, dreamer,
excitable, impetuosity,
boisterousness,
impatience, (passive,
coolness, calmness,
serene)

madrigal-*n* solo, duet, duo,
trio, quartet, descant, glee,
catch, round, chorus,
antiphon, accompaniment,
composer, musician,
perform, attune,
instrumental, vocal, choral,
lyric, operatic, harmonious,
poetry, versification,
rhyming, (unpoetical,
unrhymed)

magistrate-*n* authority,
influence, patronage,
power, preponderance,
credit, prestige,
jurisdiction, divine right,
despotism, command,
empire, auspicious,
propitious, master,
padrone, paramount,
(servant, subject, retainer,
follower, henchman,
menial, attendant, squire,
usher, page, footboy)

magnetism-*n* power,
potency, puissance, might,
force, energy,
almightiness,
omnipotence, authority,
strength, ability, ableness,
competency, efficiency,
validity, cogency,
enablement, pressure,
elasticity, gravity,
electricity, galvanism,
(impotence, disability,
disablement, impiousness,
imbecility, incapacity)

magnificent-*n* grand,
ostentation, display, show,
flourish, parade, pomp,
array, state, solemnity,
dash, splash, glitter, strut,
pomposity, magnificence,
splendor, demonstration,
celebration, pageant,
spectacle, form, elegance,
brace, beauty, unadorned,

symmetry, refined,
delicate, (ugly, graceless,
inelegant, ungraceful,
ungainly, uncouth, stiff,
rugged, rough, gross, rude,
awkward, clumsy)

magnify-v increase,
augment, enlargement,
extension, expansion,
increment, accretion,
accession, development,
intensify, enhance,
redouble, exaggerate,
exasperate, heighten,
overestimate,
oversensitive, vanity, over-
rate, (underestimate,
depreciate, detraction,
undervalue, modesty)

magnitude-n size, quantity,
dimension, amplitude,
mass, amount, quantum,
measure, substance,
strength, more or less,
greatness, multitude,
immense, enormity,
infinity, might, volume,
heap, (minimum, particle,
molecule, corpuscle, small,
diminutive, minute,
inconsiderable)

main-adj important,
consequence, moment,
prominence, consideration,
mark, materialistic, import,
significance, concern,
emphasis, interest, gravity,
seriousness, solemnity,
conduit, channel, duct,
(unimportant, insignificant,
nothingness, immaterial,
triviality, levity, frivolity,
minor detail, nonsense)

maintain-v sustain, act
upon, perform, play,
support, strain, take effect,
quicken, strike,
preservation, safe keeping,
conservation, keep,
prophylactic, unimpaired,
unbroken, continue,
persist, perpetuate,
undying, unvaried,
(discontinue, cease, desist,
stop, slacken, decay,
deteriorate, suspend,
interrupt)

major-adj greater, supreme,
higher, exceeding,
distinguished, vaulting,
utmost, paramount,
foremost, crowning, first-
rate, excellent,
transcendent, sovereign,
superlative, inimitable,
incomparable, potentate,
lord, sovereign, monarch,
autocrat, despot, tyrant,
(servant, subject, flunky,
inferior)

make-v constitute,
composition, combination,
inclusion, admission,
comprehension, reception,
form, compose, contain,
embrace, embody, involve,
implicate, produce, create,
fabricate, manufacture,
establish, perform,
achievement, (destruction,
waste, dissolution, ruin,
annihilation)

makeshift-n substitute,
supplanting, supersession,
stop-gap, jury-mast,
dummy, scapegoat,

double, alternative,
representative, supersede,
replace, ostensible motive,
ground, plea, pretext,
pretense, lame, excuse,
(interchanged, reciprocal,
mutual, communicative,
intercurrent)

malaise-n pain, suffering,
bodily, physical pain, dolor,
ache, smart, twinge, twitch,
ripe, headache, hurt, cut,
sore, discomfort, spasm,
mental suffering,
annoyance, irritation,
infliction, plague, (happy,
blest, blessed, blissful,
beatified, comfortable,
overjoyed, entranced,
enchanted)

malaria-n contagious,
infectious, catching, taking,
epidemic, insalubrious,
noxious, deleterious,
pestilent, poisonous, bane,
curse, evil scourge,
leaven, virus, mephitis,
(remedy, help, restorative,
corrective, tonic,
therapeutic, sedative)

malformation-n distortion,
twist, crookedness,
grimace, deformity,
monstrosity, misproportion,
contort, twist, warp, writhe,
irregular, unsymmetrical,
awry, askew, ugliness,
misshape, (symmetry,
shapeliness, finish, beauty,
proportion, uniformity,
regular, uniform, balanced,
parallel, coextensive)

malign-v bad, hurtful,

virulence, bane,
malevolence, ill-treatment,
annoyance, molestation,
abuse, oppression,
persecution, outrage,
misusage, injury, damage,
wrong, aggrieve,
(goodness, excellence,
merit, virtue, value, worth,
price, beneficial, profitable,
edifying, healthful,
salutary)

man-n adult male, he,
manhood, gentlemen, sir,
master, yeoman, swain,
fellow, blade, beau, chap,
gaffer, good man,
husband, masculine,
manly, hero, demigod,
bully, courageous, lion-
hearted

manager-n director,
manager, governor, rector,
comptroller,
superintendent, over-seer,
inspector, surveyor,
moderator, monitor,
taskmaster, leader,
conductor, property man,
machinist, prompter, call-
boy, (unmanaged,
abandoned, without
direction)

mangle-v separate, part,
detachment, segregation,
divorce, fissure, breach,
split, rift, crack, slit,
incision, sunder, divide,
haggle, lacerate, gash,
hash, slice, scramble,
whittle, impairment, injury,
damage, infect, (improve,
mend, revise, refine,

rectify, enrich, mellow, elaborate, fatten)

mania-*n* disordered, abnormal, unsound, derangement, insanity, lunacy, madness, mental alienation, aberration, demented, frenzy, raving, incoherence, wandering, hallucination, dizziness, kleptomania, dipsomania, hypochondriasis, hysteria, (sane, rational, reasonable)

manifold-*adj* multiform, variety, diversity, multifariousness, many-sided, omnifarious, irregular, diversified, different, all sorts and kinds, many, several, sundry, divers, various, profusion, populous, numerous, (fewness, paucity, small number, rarity, infrequency, handful, maniple, minority, scattered)

manner-*n* description, denomination, designation, character, stamp, predicament, sort, genus, species, variety, family, race, tribe, clan, type, kit, sect, assortment, feather, kidney, suit, range, style, mode of expression, method, way, manner, wise, gait, form, mode, fashion, tone, guise

mannerism-*n* special, particular, individual, specific, proper, personal,

original, private, respective, definite, determinate, especial, characteristic, ideocracy, distinctive feature, (general, universal, miscellany, collective, common, prevalent, transcendental)

many-*adj* frequent, repetition, many times, incessant, perpetual, continual, constant, numerous, multiplicity, profusion, plenty, majority, huge numbers, several, sundry, various, manifold, multiplied, thick, studded, (fewness, reduction, weeding, elimination, decimation, scanty, thin)

marble-*n* hard, rigid, stubborn, stiff, firm, starched, stark, unbending, unlimber, unyielding, inflexible, tense, indurate, adamantine, concrete, stony, granitic, vitreous, (soft, tender, supple, pliant, lithe)

march-*v* advance, precession, leading, heading, precedence, priority, forerun, proceed, progress, roving, vagrancy, countermarching, nomad, vagabondism, (regression, withdrawal, retirement, recession, follow, pursue, shadow, trail, lag)

margin-*n* edge, verge, brink, brow, brim, border, skirt, rim, flange, side,

space extension, extent,
expanse, room, field, way,
expansion, compass,
sweep, play, swing,
spread, capacity, stretch,
range, latitude, scope,
(center, interior, surface,
climate, zone, meridian)

mark-*n* indication, sign,
symbol, type, figure,
emblem, cipher,
representation, epigraph,
motto, characteristic,
pointer, note, token, line,
stroke, dash, score,
witness, voucher, position,
place, period, pitch, stand,
(insignificant, disregard,
non-representative, without
affirmation)

market-*n* purchase, buying,
shopping, bribery, patron,
client, customer, invest in,
procure, rent, spend, mart,
place, bazaar, staple,
exchange, hall, stall,
booth, wharf, office,
chambers, warehouse,
establishment, (sale,
seller, vendor, dispose of,
dispense, merchant, vent)

marry-*v* combine, unite,
incorporate, amalgamate,
embody, absorb, re-
embody, blend, merge,
fuse, melt into one,
consolidate, cement in a
union, impregnate,
matrimony, wedlock,
union, nuptial, tie, match,
betrothment, bridal,
spouse, join, couple,
betroth, (divorce, separate,

widowhood,
decomposition, dissection,
resolution, dissolution,
corruption, dispersion)

martial-*adj* warfare, fighting,
hostilities, war, arms, battle
array, campaign, crusade,
expedition, mobilization,
battle, campaigning,
service, havoc, tribunal,
court, board, bench, law,
arbitration, inquisition,
(pacification, conciliation,
reconciliation,
accommodation, terms,
compromise, amnesty)

martyrdom-*n*
unselfishness, self-
denying, sacrificing,
devoted, generous, liberal,
benevolence, elevation,
loftiness of purpose,
exaltation, magnanimity,
chivalry, heroism,
sublimity, (selfishness,
indulgence, worldliness,
self-seeking, mean,
narrow-minded,
mercenary, earthly,
mundane)

marvelous-*adj* great,
wonderful, admire,
surprise, astonish, amaze,
astound, dumbfound,
dazzle, wondrous,
overwhelming,
stupendous, indescribable,
inexpressible, awesome,
aghast, agape, spellbound,
(common, ordinary,
expected, foreseen,
astonished at nothing)

mash-*v* mix, blend, tincture,

sprinkle, cross, alloy,
amalgamate, compound,
adulterate, infect, instill,
infiltrate, confusion,
disorder, disarray, jumble,
huddle, litter, lumber,
mess, muddle, hash,
hodgepodge, (uniformity,
symmetry, orderly, neat,
tidy, well regulated,
correct, methodical)

mask-v conceal, hide,
mystification, seal of
secrecy, screen, disguise,
masquerade, stealthiness,
reticence, reserve,
evasion, suppression,
white lie, cover, blind,
gauze, veil, mantle, cloud,
mist, shade, shadow,
(inform, acquaint,
announce, tell, impart,
mention, make known,
enlighten, specify)

master-v understand,
comprehend, take in,
catch, grasp, follow,
collect, make out, easily
understood, clearness,
simplify, explain, plain,
distinct, explicit, positive,
precise, graphic,
expressive, conceive,
accomplished, profound,
book-learned, (shallow,
superficial, rude, empty,
illiterate, uninformed)

mate-n similar,
resemblance, likeness,
affinity, approximation,
parallelism, sameness,
fellow, analog, pair, twin,
double, counterpart,

likeness, wife, espouse,
marry, join, spousal, bridal,
helper, auxiliary, recruit,
assistant, associate,
midwife, colleague,
(opposition, enemy,
adversary, dissimilar,
unlike, unmatched,
unlikeness, diversity,
dissemblance, difference)

matter-n substance, body,
flesh and blood, thing,
object, article, tangible,
material, essential,
physical, sensible,
ponderable, palpable,
objective, impersonal,
neuter, unspiritual, subject,
idea, argument, text, sum
and substance, gist,
suggestive, (immaterial,
unextended, disembodied,
personal, subjective,
groundless, nothingness,
nonentity, unsubstantial)

mature-adj old, age,
antiquity, decline, decay,
seniority, eldership,
tradition, custom,
venerable, time-honored,
prime, adolescent,
pubescent, of age, grown
up, virile, adult, (new,
novel, recent, fresh, young,
green, immature, virgin,
modern, late, neoteric)

maze-n convolution,
winding, circumvolution,
wave, undulation,
tortuosity, coil, roll, curl,
buckle, spiral, helix,
corkscrew, worm, volute,
tendril, dilemma,

embarrassment, perplexity, intricacy, entanglement, awkwardness, mesh, (ease, feasibility, flexibility, smoothness, round, rounded, oval)

meager-*adj* small, little, tenuity, paucity, few, mediocrity, moderation, minute, slight, limited, sparing, incomplete, insufficient, immature, deficit, omission, lack, hollow, (complete, large, entirety, full, sufficiency, replenish, whole, quantity, volume, unlimited, vast, immense, enormous, extreme)

mean-*adj* contemptible, wretched, vile, scrubby, pitiful, sorry, trashy, worthless, medium, intermediate, average, balance, mediocrity, generality, compromise, neutrality, commonplace, (gravity, seriousness, solemnity, pressure, urgency, stress, matter of life and death)

meander-*v* winding, convolution, sinuosity, undulation, tortuosity, twirl, snake-like, involved, intricate, complicated, perplexed, stray, straggle, sidle, diverge, trailing, digress, wander, twist, rove, drift, go astray, adrift, (bearing a straight course, set, directly, straight, point blank, straightforward)

measure-*n* compute, survey, valuation, appraisement, assessment, estimate, reckoning, gauging, standard, rule, compass, calipers, gage, meter, scale, coordinates, degree, extent, amount, ratio, intensity, strength, quantity, mass, comparative, gradual, limits

mediocrity-*n* mean, medium, average, generality, intermediate, neutral, compromise, imperfect, deficiency, inadequacy, fault, defect, weak point, flaw, blemish, indifferent, middling, ordinary, passable, secondary, limited, (perfect, faultless, model, standard, complete, intact, inimitable, harmless, immaculate, impeccable)

medley-*n* alloy, mixture, jumble, sauce, mash, instill, infiltrate, blend, cross, amalgamate, compound, infect, complex, intricacy, perplexity, disarrange, entangled, deranged, haphazard, random, luck, (orderly, regularity, subordination, methodical, unconfused, arranged)

meet-*v* assemble, crowd, throng, flood, rush, deluge, rabble, mob, horde, body, tribe, crew, gang, group, cluster, muster, convene, gather, converge, concur, come together, unite, concentrate, expedite, convenient, due, proper, eligible, seemly, (exit, emergence, burst, evacuation, diverge, repel, push, dispel, leave, depart, disperse, dismember)

mellow-*adj* advance, ascend, increase, fructify, ripen, pick up, come about, rally, better, improved, enrich, cultivate, enhance, render, elaborate, season, bring to maturity, mature, nurture, (crude, raw, virgin, unprepared, improvise, coarse, deteriorate, degenerate, impair, weaken)

melt-*v* convert, pervert, render, mold, form, merge, liquefy, dissolve, solvent, boil, heat, calcination, ignite, inflammation, adust, incendiary, caustic, smelt, digest, stew, cook, seethe, simmer, (cool, fan, refrigerate, refresh, congeal, freeze, glaciate, benumb, starve, quench, extinguish)

memory-*n* remembrance, retention, tenaciy, readiness, reminiscence, recognition, recurrence, recollection, retrospect, reminder, memento, souvenir, keepsake, relic, memorandum, memorabilia, tenacious, (oblivion, forgetfulness, short, efface, mindless, insensible, escape, failing memory)

menagerie-*n* collection, clan, brotherhood, association, gang, swarm, shoal, school, covey, flock, herd, drove, array, bevy, vivarium, zoological garden, aviary, aquarium, domestication, breeding, (disperse, scatter, disseminate, diffuse, shed, spread)

mendicant-*adj* beggar, sturdy, cadger, canvasser, touter, loss of fortune, pauper, poor, indigent, penniless, insolvency, (wealth, richness, fortune, affluence, sufficiency, livelihood)

mental-*adj* intellect, understanding reason, rationality, cogitative, faculties, senses, consciousness, observation, percipience, under consideration, thought, reflect, consider, deliberate, (unendowed with reason, imbecility, vacant, thoughtless, diverted, irrational)

mercy-*n* leniency, moderation, tolerance, mildness, gentleness, favor, clemency, forbearance, compassion, tolerance, pity, commiseration, sympathy, ruthful, humane, exorable,

melt, thaw, relent,
unhardened, (severity,
strictness, harshness,
rigor, stringency, austerity,
inclemency, relentless)
merge-v combine, mixture
union, unification,
synthesis, incorporation,
amalgamation,
embodiment, coalescence,
fusion, blending,
absorption, centralization,
impregnate, ingrained,
(decompose, analysis,
dissect, catalysis,
dissolution, corruption,
unravel, disperse)
merit-n goodness,
excellence, virtue, value,
worth, price, perfection,
prime, flower, cream,
champion, beneficial,
profitable, advantageous,
salutary, favorable, good,
superior, fine, genuine,
admirable, praiseworthy,
(vile, oppressive,
burdensome, malign,
corrupting, corrosive,
destructive, destroy)
merriment-n cheerful,
geniality, gaiety, cheer,
good humor, high spirits,
liveliness, vivacity,
animation, joviality, jollity,
jocularity, mirth, hilarity,
exhilaration, laughter,
rejoicing, elate, exhilarate,
gladden, inspire, perk up,
delight, (dejection,
depression, lowness,
heaviness, melancholy,
sadness, dismal)

mesh-v interval, interspace,
separation, break, gap,
opening, hole, chasm,
interruption, interstice,
cleft, crevice, chink, rime,
creek, cranny, crack, chap,
slit, flaw, breach, rent,
gash, cut, crossing,
intersection, transversely,
network, web, twill, skein,
chain, braid, entanglement,
(coexist, adhere, graze,
touch, meet, osculate,
contact, proximity,
meeting)
mess-n mixture, combine,
intermix, mingle, shuffle,
knead, brew, impregnate
with, instill, imbue,
infiltrate, compound, infect,
among, amongst, amid,
amidst, miscellaneous,
dilemma, embarrassment,
perplexity, intricacy,
entanglement,
awkwardness, delicacy,
maze, vexed, quandary,
(ease, facilitate, smooth,
emancipate, free,
manageable, light, simple,
eliminate, single, pure,
clear)
messenger-n envoy,
emissary, legate,
ambassador, diplomat,
marshal, flag-bearer,
herald, crier, trumpeter,
courier, runner, errand-
boy, reporter, mail,
telephone, wireless,
heliograph, subject,
retainer, follower,
henchman, menial, help,

attache, handmaid,
secretary, assistant,
(master, lord, padrone,
paramount, commander,
captain, chief, authority,
corporal)

meteor-*n* heavenly body,
cosmically, mundane,
terrestrial, solar, heliacal,
lunar, celestial, sphere,
starry, stellar, luminary,
light, flame, spark,
phosphorescence, star,
blazing, (shade, sunshade,
gauze, veil, mantle, mask,
cloud, mist, umbrageous)

mettle-*n* sensible,
impressionable,
susceptive, impassion,
gushing, warm-tender,
soft-hearted, romantic,
enthusiastic, highflying,
spirited, vivacious, lively,
expressive, mobile,
trembling, excitable,
fastidious, (insensible,
inertness, apathy, dull,
frigid, cold-hearted,
indifferent, lukewarm,
careless)

middle-*n* midst, half-way,
navel, equidistance,
bisection, half-distance,
equator, diaphragm,
midriff, intermediate,
equatorial, midship,
compromise,
compensation, middle
term, meet one half way,
give and take, arrange,
adjust, agree, moderate,
average, mediocrity

midst-*n* centrality, center,

core, kernel, nucleus,
heart, pole, axis, navel,
backbone, marrow,
symmetry, center of
gravity, bring to focus,
intermediate, intervention,
introduce, (surround,
beset, encompass)

mild-*adj* moderate,
temperate, relaxation,
remission, mitigation,
tranquilization, pacification,
gentleness, sobriety, quiet,
contemplation, appease,
soothe, lull, swag, calm,
cool, hush, quell, tame,
(violent, fury, storm, rough,
vehement, warm, acute,
sharp, rude, impetuous,
rampant)

mill-*v* reduce, grind,
pulverize, comminute,
granulate, triturate,
levigate, scrape, file,
abrade, rub down, grate,
rasp, pound, bray, bruise,
contuse, beat, crush,
crunch, crumble,
disintegrate, (lubricate, oil,
glycerine, lather, grease,
lather, smooth)

millennium-*n* period,
second, minute, hour, day,
week, month, quarter,
year, decade, lifetime,
generation, century, age,
prospectively, hereafter,
eventually, ultimately,
whereupon, (lapse, elapse,
advance, progress,
succession, proceed, slip,
slide, past, gone, foregone,
extinct, forgotten, over)

mince-_v_ cut up, separate, sunder, divide, subdivide, rescind, segregate, keep apart, sever, abscind, chop, chip, crack, snap, break, tear, burst, rend, wrench, rupture, shatter, shiver, hack, slash, mangle, slice, tear, whittle, (join, unite, annex, attach, hinge, seam, suture, stitch, link, miter, close, combine)

mind-_n_ intellect, understanding, reason, thinking, rationality, cogitative, faculties, senses, consciousness, observation, percipience, intuition, association of ideas, instinct, conception, judgment, wits, capacity, genius, ability, thoughtful, reflect, speculate, contemplate, consider

mine-_n_ sap, destroy, waste, dissolution, breaking up, disruption, consumption, disorganization, fall, downfall, ruin, perdition, annihilation, demolition, overthrow, subversion, suppress, abolish, ruinous, incendiary, deleterious, (produce, perform, operate, form, construct, fabricate, frame, contrive, forge)

minister-_n_ subserve, mediate, intervene, instrumental, useful, give, bestow, donation, presentation, accordance, delivery, consignment, dispensation, communication, endowment, award, generosity, liberality, offering, bequest, legacy, devise, deliver, present, (receive, acquire, accept, assign, admit)

minor-_adj_ inferior, shortcoming, deficiency, minimum, smallness, less, lesser, minus, lower, subordinate, second-rate, least, lowest, diminished, decrease, infant, babe, youth, youngster, master, (veteran, old, seer, patriarch, superior, supreme, major, great, noble, higher, exceeding)

minute-_adj_ small, little, diminutive, inconsiderable, paltry, faint, slender, light, slight, scanty, limited, sparing, inappreciable, infinitesimal, mere, simple, sheer, stark, bare, period of time, duration of, moment, instant, second, twinkling, flash, breath, burst, sudden, instantaneous, hasty, quick, lightning, (perpetuity, eternity, ever, everlasting, great, magnitude, considerable, ample)

mirror-_n_ imitate, copy, repetition, duplication, quotation, reproduction, mimicry, simulation, reflector, speculum, looking glass, pier, model,

standard, pattern, best,
inimitable, paragon,
unparalleled, supreme,
perfect, (imperfect, faulty,
unsound, deficient,
unimitated, original,
unmatched)

misbehave-*v* coarse,
indecorous, ribald, gross,
unseemly, unpresentable,
ungraceful, ill-mannered,
underbred, ungentlemanly,
unladylike, unpolished,
uncouth, heavy, rude,
awkward, (good taste,
cultivated, delicacy,
refinement, gust, finesse,
nicety, polish, elegance,
grace, connoisseur)

miscalculate-*v* misjudge,
prejudgment, foregone
conclusion, narrow-
minded, intolerant,
besotted, dogmatic,
opinioned, unreasonable,
false judgment, weak,
feeble, poor, flimsy, loose,
vague, irrational, foolish,
frivolous, (logical
sequence, good sense,
deduce, conclusive)

mischief-*n* evil, harm hurt,
nuisance, disaster,
accident, casualty, mishap,
calamity, bale, mental
suffering, outrage, wrong,
injury, foul play, grievance,
disastrous, bad, aggrieve,
oppress, persecute, inflict,
maltreat, abuse,
(goodness, admirable,
estimable, praise-worthy,
satisfactory, favorable)

misconduct-*n* mismanage,
misapplication, absence of
rule, bungling, blunder,
unskillful, quackery,
mistake, misguided,
foolish, inconsistent,
ignorant, (accomplished,
expert, skillful, competent)

miserable-*adj* suffering,
pain, dolor, ache, smart,
displeasure,
dissatisfaction, discomfort,
discomposure, malaise,
uneasiness, dejection,
annoyance, irritation,
worry, infliction visitation,
care, anxiety, solicitude,
trouble, trial, ordeal, shock,
burden, unhappiness,
misery, tribulation,
(pleasure, gratification,
enjoyment, well-being,
comfort, ease, joy,
gladness, delight, mind at
ease)

misfortune-*n* adversity, evil,
failure, bad fortune,
trouble, hardship, curse,
blight, blast, load,
pressure, mishap, disaster,
calamity, catastrophe,
accident, casualty, ruin,
failure, affliction,
(prosperity, welfare, well-
being, affluence, wealth,
success, thrift, roaring,
prosper, thrive)

mishap-*n* source of
irritation, annoyance,
grievance, nuisance,
vexation, mortification,
bore, bother, plague, pest,
infestation, molestation,

(pleasant, inviting,
attractive, lovely,
enchantment, seduction)
misjudgment-*n* bias, warp,
twist, hasty conclusion,
preconceived,
partisanship, partial,
narrow, blind side,
confined, error, fallacy,
laxity, mistake, fault,
blunder, (accuracy,
exactness, honest,
precise)
mismatch-*v* different,
diverse, varied, modified,
various, dissimilarity,
disagreement, disparity,
discord, unconformity,
conflict, unfitness,
inaptitude, impropriety,
inconsistency, disjoining,
(conformity, uniformity,
concert, relevancy,
admissibility, compatibility,
relation)
misrepresent-*v* lie,
falsehood, deception,
untruth, guile, mendacity,
perjury, forgery, invention,
fabrication, suppression of
truth, perversion,
distortion, exaggeration,
misinterpretation,
misconstrue, mistake,
parody, equivocation,
evasion, fraud, (veracity,
truthfulness, frankness,
sincerity, honesty)
miss-*v* girl, lass, wench,
damsel, maiden, virgin,
fail, unsuccessful, labor,
toil in vane, miscarry,
omission, oversight, slip,

trip, stumble, mess,
mishap, misfortune,
collapse, (success,
advance, lucky, fortunate,
prosperity, triumph, gain,
advantage, conquest,
victory)
mist-*n* cloud, bubble, foam,
froth, head, spume, lather,
spray, surf, yeast, barm,
vapor, fog, haze, stream,
effervescence,
fermentation, nebulous,
(semi-fluid, stickiness,
viscidity, adhesiveness)
mistake-*n* error, fallacy,
misconception, miss, fault,
blunder, oversight,
misprint, slip, blot, flaw,
trip, stumble, heresy,
hallucination, laxity,
miscount, untrue, false,
unreal, ungrounded,
failure, unsuccessful,
mishap, split, collapse,
(true, infallible, successful,
fortunate, prosperous)
mitigate-*v* abate, moderate,
soften, temper, mollify,
leniency, dull, take off the
edge, blunt, obtund,
sheathe, subdue, chasten
sober, tone, smooth down,
lessen, palliate, tranquilize,
assuage, appease,
(violent, sharpen, quicken,
excite, explode, convulse,
infuriate, madden, lash)
mix-*v* combine, instill,
imbue, transfuse, join,
intermix, mingle, shuffle,
knead, brew, impregnate,
infiltrate, dash, stir-up,

together, compound,
adulterate, (simple, purity,
homogeneity, eliminate)

mob-*n* crowd, assemblage,
throng, flood, rush, press,
crush, horde, body, tribe,
crew, gang, knot, squad,
band, party, swarm,
school, covey, flock, herd,
drove, array, bevy, galaxy,
company, troop, group,
cluster, clump, (disperse,
scatter, sow, disseminate,
diffuse, shed, spread,
disembody)

mobile-*adj* motion,
movement, going, unrest,
stream, flow, run, coarse,
stir, evolution, kinematics,
step, transitional, motor,
motive, shifting, mercurial,
unquiet, restless, nomadic,
inconstancy, versatility,
mobility, unstable,
restlessness, fidget,
disquiet, agitation, (stable,
constant, immobility, stand,
established, fixture,
foundation, permanence,
durable)

mock-*v* imitate, copy,
mirror, reflect, reproduce,
repeat, echo, catch,
transcribe, match, mimic,
ape, simulate,
impersonate, counterfeit,
parody, modeled after,
verbatim, word for word,
repetition, sameness, pair,
mate, double, parallel,
(dissimilar, unlike,
unmatched, originality,
different kind)

mode-*n* state, condition,
category, estate, lot, case
trim, mood, plight, aspect,
schuss, tone, tenor, trim,
guise, light, complexion,
style, character, structural,
organic, method, way,
manner, fashion, form,
habit, (infraction of usage,
unaccustomed, leave off,
unusual, unaccustomed)

model-*n* represent,
imitation, illustration,
delineation, depiction,
imagery, portraiture,
design, art, personation,
impersonation, image,
likeness, (misrepresent,
distort, exaggerate, daub)

moderate-*adj* small, allay,
slow, sufficient, cheap,
temperate, low,
reasonable, inexpensive,
depreciated, nominal,
bargain, sufficient,
adequate, enough,
satisfactory, competent,
mediocrity, fill, (scarcity,
want, need, lack, poverty,
insufficient, inadequate)

modesty-*n* humility, timidity,
diffidence, bashfulness,
blushing, self-knowledge,
shy, nervous, skittish, coy,
sheepish, shamefaced,
unpretending, reserved,
constrained, demure,
private, without ceremony,
(vanity, conceit, self-
confidence, airs,
pretension, egotism,
gaudery, elation,
ostentation)

mold-*n* frame, fabric,
constitute, habitude,
stamp, set, fit, mode, form,
shape, tone, tenor,
prototype, original, model,
pattern, precedent,
standard, type, rush, weed,
fungus, mushroom,
toadstool, lichen, moss,
conferva, growth, (result
copy, facsimile, duplicate)
molestation-*n* wrong,
aggrieve, oppress,
persecute, trample, tread,
run down, victimize,
overburden, maltreat,
abuse, ill-use, ill-treat,
buffet, bruise, scratch,
smite, scourge, violate,
destroy, hurt, harm,
(admire, excellent, best,
choice, select,
praiseworthy, beneficial,
serviceable, edifying,
salutary)
monotonous-*adj* uniform,
consistent, even,
invariable, always, without
exception, regularity,
routine, conformity, equal,
even, match, symmetrical,
(uneven, countervail,
varied, diversified,
irregular)
monstrous-*adj* huge, giant,
gargantuan, mammoth,
corpulent, stout, fat, plump,
immense, enormous,
might, vast, stupendous,
monstrous, gigantic,
(small, dwarf, pygmy,
inconsiderable, puny,
atom)

monument-*n* memorial,
cenotaph, shrine, grave,
tombstone, hatchment,
slab, tablet, trophy,
achievement, obelisk,
pillar, column, monolith,
commemoration,
celebration, (obliterate,
erasure, cancellation,
deletion)
mood-*n* affection, character,
disposition, nature, spirit,
tone, temper, idiosyncrasy,
propensity, humor, grain,
mettle, sympathy, passion,
temperament, vein,
tendency, aptness, prone
more-*adj* added, addition,
annex, affix, extra, plus,
likewise, furthermore,
further, including, inclusive,
besides, to boot, et cetera,
supplement, accessory,
appendage, reinforce,
(subtract, deduct, retrench,
minus, without, except,
diminish)
mortal-*adj* fatal, kill,
assassination, massacre,
butcher, slayer, lethal,
dead, deathly, suicidal,
internecine, transient,
impermanence, fugacity,
caducity, mortality,
temporary, (durable,
lasting, permanent, long-
standing, chronic,
perennial)
mortar-*n* cement, glue,
gum, paste, size, wafer,
solder, lute, putty, bird-
lime, stucco, plaster, grout,
arms, weapon, missile,

bolt, projectile, shot, ball,
canister, cannon, grenade,
shell, bomb, rocket

mortification-n humility,
meek, lowness, modesty,
blush, suffusion, confusion,
disgrace, condescend,
demean, stoop,
submissive, service,
affable, resigned, abashed,
ashamed, brow-beaten,
(dignified, stately, proud,
haughty, lofty, high,
mighty, vainglorious,
arrogant)

motion-n movement, going,
stream, flow, flux, run,
course, stir, evolution,
kinematics, progress, offer,
proffer, presentation,
tender, bid, overture,
proposal, invitation,
advances, (refusal,
rejection, projection,
disclaimer, dissent,
revocation, remain, stay,
stop, stagnate, halt)

motley-adj variegated,
mottled, marbled, dappled,
clouded, mosaic, pied,
diverse, variety,
multifariousness, manifold,
heterogeneous, epicene,
indiscriminate, (uniform,
constant, routine, custom,
standard, conformity,
punctual)

mount-v ascend, rising,
ascension, upgrowth, leap,
acclivity, ladder, arise,
apprise, climb, escalade,
soar, display, show,
flourish, parade,

magnificence, splendor,
mountain, hill, elevate,
high, (low, neap, debased,
flat, under, descent,
declination, fall, drop,
lapse, downfall, slip, tilt,
trip)

mournful-adj melancholy,
sadness, depression,
dejection, prostration,
despondency, dismal,
spiritless, unhappy,
somber, dark, gloomy,
lamenting, dreadful,
(cheerfulness, geniality,
gaiety, good humor, glee,
light, liveliness, vivacity,
merriment, hilarity,
exhilaration, animation,
jovial)

mouth-n entrance,
beginning, opening, outset,
incipience, inception,
inchoation, introduction,
initial, origin, source,
receptacle, recipient,
receiver, reservoir, gizzard,
ventricle, bread-basket,
(end, close, termination,
dissonance, conclusion,
consummation, finish,
terminate, conclude)

muddy-adj moist, damp,
watery, undried, humid,
wet, dank, muggy, dewy,
swampy, soft, sodden,
swashy, soggy, dabbled,
reeking, dripping, soaking,
(dry, anhydrous, arid,
dried, undamped)

multifarious-adj
disconnection,
independence, strange,

alien, foreign, outlandish,
exotic, diverse, variety,
diversity, manifold, motley,
mosaic, indiscriminate,
irregular, (regularity,
uniformity, constant,
punctual, routine, normal,
natural, ordinary, steady)

multitude-*n* numerous,
multiplicity, profusion,
legion, host, great,
enormous, quantity,
number, array, army, sea,
galaxy, scores, peck,
bushel, shoal, swarm,
many, several, sundry,
various, (few, small
quantity, rarity,
infrequency, handful,
maniple, minority,
reduction)

musical-*adj* melody,
rhythm, measure, rhyme,
pitch, tone, modulation,
temperament, syncopation,
song, glee, madrigal,
compose, perform strains,
(discord, harshness,
tuneless, unmusical,
dissonance)

mute-*adj* silent, stillness,
peace, hush, lull, solemn,
dead, render, hold one's
tongue, stifle, muffle,
muzzle, inaudible, faint,
suppress, smother, dumb,
(vocal, cry, utter, exclaim,
pronounce)

mysterious-*adj* obscure,
dark, muddy, dim,
nebulous, undiscernible,
invisible, indefinite,
perplexed, confused,
undetermined, vague,
loose, ambiguous, mystic,
transcendental, occult,
recondite, undefinable,
(intelligent, clear, explicit,
lucid, perspicuity, legibility,
plain speaking,
understandable)

N

name-*n* imprint, label,
indicate, symbolize, mark,
note, stamp, earmark,
ticket, docket, score, dash,
trace, print, appoint,
nominate, return, charter,
ordinate, install,
inaugurate, investiture,
accession, coronation,
enthronement,
(countermand, disclaim,
abolish, dissolve, dismiss,
nullify, annul, cancel)

napping-*v* dull,
unentertaining, depress,
humdrum, monotonous,
inactive, heaviness,
absent, bemused,
dreaming, unreflective,
(attentive, observant,
absorption of mind)

native-*adj* inhabitant,
resident, dweller, occupier,
householder, lodger,
inmate, tenant, incumbent,
sojourner, settler, squatter,
indigent, aborigines, free,
plain, outspoken, blunt,
downright, (cunning, craft,
artful, skillful, subtle, alien,
foreign)

naught-*n* nothing, zero,

cipher, none, nobody, complete absence, insubstantiality, vacant, vacuous, empty, blank, hollow, nominal, null, inane, (numerous, many, several, some, profuse, multiple)

near-adv loom, impending, destined, about to happen, coming, eventually, prospective, approaching, future, precipitation, anticipation, premature, soon, shortly, (now, occurring, happening, immediate)

necessity-n requirement, need, want, have occasion for, needful, essential, indispensable, prerequisite, demanding, urgent, obligatory, involuntary, compulsive, inevitable, (willing, volition, free-will, voluntary, optional, discretionary, intentional, spontaneous)

neglect-v abandon, negligent, careless, omit, default, thoughtless, remiss, perfunctory, inconsiderate, reckless, (care, watchful, vigilant, survey, alert, regardful, cautious, considerate, prepared)

negotiate-v mediate, intervene, peacemaker, diplomat, moderate, arbitrate, intercede, bargain, agree, promise, stipulate, barter,

compromise, settle, conclude, come to an understanding

net-n remainder, residue, remains, remnant, rest, relic, leavings, result, left, unconsumed, sedimentary, surviving, exceeding, over and above, outlying, superfluous, (adjunct, addition, addendum, affix, appendage, augment, increment)

neutralize-v opposition, contrariety, antagonism, polarity, clashing, compensation, cross, interfere, conflict with, jostle, antagonize, withstand, counterpoise, retroactive, reactionary, contrary, (concur, conspire, cooperate, agree, consent)

nice-adj pleasing, savory, good, fastidious, agreeable, delectable, lovely, beatify, satisfy, refreshing, comfortable, genial, glad, sweet, luxurious, voluptuous, sensual, attractive, enticing, appetizing, charming, (annoying, painful, grievance, vexation, mortification, bother, displeasing, disturbing)

nightmare-n fright, affright, alarm, dread, awe, terror, horror, dismay, consternation, panic, scare, stampede,

intimidation, terrorism,
reign of terror, demonic,
scarecrow

nil-*n* inexistent, negative,
annihilation, extinction,
destruction, abrogate,
destroy, take away, perish,
blank, missing, omitted,
absent, exhausted, gone,
lost, departed, defunct,
dead, (subsist, presence,
positive, realty, actuality,
live, breathe, real, actual,
positive, substantial)

nip-*v* cut, destroy, shorten,
sunder, divide, subdivide,
sever, dissever, abscind,
saw, snip, nib, cleave, rive,
rend, slit, split, splinter,
crack, snap, carve, dissect,
hinder, impede, obstruct,
stop, (attach, join, hinge,
seam, suture, stitch, link,
miter, close, combine, fix,
affix, fasten)

noble-*adj* great,
virtuousness, morality,
ethical, rectitude, integrity,
cardinal virtues, merit,
worth, desert, excellence,
credit, self-control,
resolution, self-denial,
exemplary, saintly,
seraphic, godlike,
commendable,
praiseworthy, (wicked,
immoral, impropriety,
weak, fault, deficient,
vicious, sinful)

nod-*v* signal, wag, gesture,
wink, glance, leer, shrug,
beck, touch, nudge,
oscillate, undulate, wave,

beat, waggle, bob, curtsy,
play, dangle, assent,
acquiescence, admission,
accordance, agreement,
recognition,
acknowledgment, avowal,
(dissent, discordance,
contradiction, protest, noncompliance)

nomination-*n* commission,
delegation, assignment,
procuration, deputation,
legation, mission,
embassy, agency,
appointment, return,
charter, ordination,
installation, inauguration,
investiture, accession,
coronation, enthronement,
(dismiss, abolish, dissolve,
cancel, repeal, revocation,
annul)

nonsense-*n* absurdity,
vagary, tomfoolery,
mummery, imbecility,
blunder, muddle, farce,
absence of meaning,
meaningless, empty,
jargon, gibberish,
balderdash, insanity,
(significant, expression,
substantial, literal, plain,
simple, suggestive,
convey, imply, indicate)

nook-*n* limited space, lieu,
spot, pint, dot, niche, hole,
compartment, premises,
station, abode, angle,
cusp, bend, fold, notch, for,
corner, recess, oriel

noose-*n* snare, trap, pitfall,
decoy, bait, cobweb, net,
meshes, mouse-trap,

mine, scaffold, block, axe,
guillotine, stake, cross,
gallows, gibbet, drop, rope,
halter, bowstring

normal-*adj* regular, intrinsic,
fundamental, implanted,
inherent, essential, natural,
innate, inborn, inbred,
radical, incarnate,
thoroughbred, immanent,
instinctive,
(extraneousness,
incidental, accidental)

note-*n* remark, examine,
scan, scrutinize, consider,
revise, pour over, inspect,
review, indication, observe,
look, see, view, notice,
regard, give, heed,
contemplate, attentive,
mindful, watchful,
(inattentive, blind, deaf,
inconsiderate, absent,
abstracted, lost, overlook,
disregard, dismiss)

noteworthy-*adj* exceptional,
non-conformity,
unconventional, unusual,
uncommon, extraordinary,
unparalleled, fantastic,
exceptional, (conventional,
usual, common, ordinary,
natural)

notorious-*adj* famous,
notability, notoriety, vogue,
celebrity, renown, popular,
glory, honor,
illustriousness, regard,
respect, reputable,
respectable, dignity,
stateliness, solemnity,
grandeur, splendor, noble,
majesty, sublime,

(shameful, disgrace,
tarnish, blot, taint,
discredit, degrade, vilify)

null-*adj* powerless,
impotent, disable,
impiousness, invalidity,
inefficiency, incompetence,
disqualification,
helplessness, prostration,
paralysis, palsy, apoplexy,
exhaustion, emasculation,
(power, potency, ability,
ableness, energy, force,
control, authority, strength,
influence, magnetism)

nurture-*n* feed, food,
nourishment, nutriment,
sustenance, fodder,
provision, ration, keep,
commons, board,
commissariats, pasture,
dietary, eatable, edible,
culinary, succulent,
potable, (starve, excrete,
deject, perspire, sweat,
diarrhea, salivation,
discharge)

O

oak-*n* strong, mighty,
vigorous, forcible, hard,
adamantine, stout, robust,
sturdy, hardy, powerful,
potent, puissant, valid,
courage, brave, valor,
resolute, bold, gallant,
intrepid, defiant, (coward,
timid, poltroonery,
baseness, dastard, sneak,
weak, relaxed, frail, fragile,
shatter, flimsy)

oar-*n* paddle, navigate, fin,

flipper, natation, handle,
hilt, haft, shaft, heft, shank,
blade, trigger, tiller, helm,
treadle, key, turn screw,
screwdriver
oasis-*n* separation, parting,
detachment, segregation,
divorce, supposition,
deduction, discerptible,
unconformable,
exceptional, abnormal,
continent, mainland,
peninsula, delta, isthmus,
(attach, fix, affix, fasten,
bind, secure, clinch, twist,
pinion)
obdurate-*adj* obstinate,
tenacious, stubborn, case-
hardened, inflexible,
immovable, inert,
unchangeable, severe,
strictness, harshness,
rigor, stringency, austerity,
inclemency, (lenitive,
moderation, tolerance,
mildness, gentleness,
favor, indulgence,
clemency, mercy)
obey-*v* rules, observance,
compliance, submission,
subjection, resignation,
allegiance, loyalty, fealty,
homage, deference,
devotion, complying,
(violate, infringe, shirk,
insubordination,
disobedient)
object-*n* thing, matter, body,
substance, stuff, element,
principle, material, article,
something, still life,
decision, determination,
resolve, purpose,

ultimatum, resolution,
motive, intention, advise,
(speculation, venture,
stake, game of chance,
risk, hazard, fortuitous,
indiscriminate)
oblige-*v* accommodate,
consult the wishes of,
humor, cheer, encourage,
nurture, cultivate, foster,
cherish, support, sustain,
uphold, bolster,
compulsive, coercion,
coaction, constraint,
duress, enforcement,
press, conscription,
(prevention, preclusion,
obstruction, interruption,
hindrance)
obnoxious-*adj* source of
irritation, annoyance,
grievance, nuisance,
vexation, mortification,
bore, bother, burdensome,
oppressive, sinister,
maltreat, abuse,
persecute, abomination,
(excellence, merit, virtue,
value, worth, beneficial,
advantageous, edifying,
pleasant, agreeable,
enchanting)
obscure-*adj* dark, murky,
gloomy, extinguish, cloudy,
confused, indistinct,
shadowy, indefinite, ill-
defined, opaque, (visible,
conspicuousness, distinct,
exposure, discernible,
apparent, perceptible)
observation-*n*
understanding, reason,
rationality, cogitative,

intelligence, intuition,
association of ideas,
instinct, conception,
judgment, wits, capacity,
ability, attention,
mindfulness, intentness,
thought, consideration,
(abstraction, absorption,
preoccupation, distraction,
disregard)

obstruct-v hinder, prevent,
preclude, stoppage,
interruption, retard,
embarrassment,
restriction, impede,
obstacle, drag, stay, stop,
shut, blockage, bar, bolt,
seal, choke, occlusion,
(open, vent, vomiter,
perforate, pierce, puncture,
support, lift, advance,
assist, promote, favor,
relief, rescue)

obtain-v get, acquisition,
gaining, procuration,
purchase, descent,
inheritance, gift, recover,
retrieval, redemption,
salvage, gain,
remuneration, proceeds,
harvest, benefit, (deprived,
loss, lapse, bereft)

obtrude-v interfere,
intervention, introduce,
import, insinuate, smuggle,
infiltrate, ingrain, partition,
interpenetrate, permeate,
insert, implantation,
inoculation, immersion,
imbed, (removal,
elimination, extrication,
eradication, evolution,
wrench, evulsion)

occasion-n opportunity,
opening, room, suitable,
proper, tempestuous,
crisis, turn, juncture,
conjuncture, turning point,
given time, timely,
providential, lucky,
fortunate, happy,
favorable, propitious,
auspicious, critical,
(unsuitable, ill timed,
intrude, premature,
intrusion)

occult-adj concealed,
hidden, secret, recondite,
mystic, cabalistic, dark,
cryptic, private, privy,
auricular, clandestine,
close,inviolate, stealthy,
skulking, surreptitious,
(informant, enlightenment,
case, specification,
communicative, advice,
monition, statement,
affirmation)

occupation-n business,
employet, pursuit, affair,
concern, matter, case,
task, work, job, errand,
commission, mission,
charge, care, duty,
vocation, calling,
profession, industry, trade,
officiate, serve, capacity,
handicraft

occupy-v presence,
attendance, where,
permeation,
pervasion,diffusion,
dispersion, omnipresence,
inhabit, dwell, reside, stay,
sojourn, live, abide, lodge,
nestle, roost, perch, locate,

fill, domiciled, (truant,
absent, absence,
inexistent, emptiness, void,
vacant, deserted, devoid)

occur-v eventuality, event,
occurrence, incident, affair,
transaction, proceeding,
phenomenon, advent,
concern, circumstance,
casualty, accident,
adventure, passage, crisis,
pass, emergency,
contingency,
consequence, (impending,
threaten, loom, await,
approach, destined,
approaching)

odd-adj individuality,
idiosyncrasy, originality,
mannerism, exception,
peculiarity, infraction,
violation, infringement,
eccentricity, bizarre,
monstrosity, rarity, freak,
remainder, residue,
remains, relic,
(supplement, continuation,
rider, off-shoot, conformity,
symmetry, conventionality,
pattern, specimen)

ode-n poetry, poetics,
versification, rhyming,
making verses, prosody,
song, ballad, lullaby,
anthology, assonance,
accentuation, laureate,
lyrist, (prose, unpoetical,
unrhymed)

offensive-adj unsavory,
repulsive, nasty, acrid,
acrimonious, rough,
sickening, nauseous,
loathsome, unpleasant,

displease, annoy,
discompose, trouble,
disquiet, disturb, cross,
perplex, molest,
(refreshing, comfortable,
cordial, genial, glad, sweet,
delectable, good,
palatable, nice, dainty)

offer-v proposal,
presentation, tender, bid,
overture, motion, invitation,
candidature, move, start,
gift, donation, present,
fairing, favor, benefaction,
grant, oblation, sacrifice,
(receive, acquire,
reception, acceptance,
release, admission,
refusal, rejection, denial,
decline, repulse, rebuff,
discountenance)

official-adj authoritative,
influence, patronage,
power, preponderance,
absolute, command,
empire, rule, dominion,
sovereign, hold, grasp,
certain, necessity, surety,
unerring, infallible,
reliability, (uncertainty,
doubt, dubiety, hesitation,
precariousness,
unfortunate, fallible,
adverse, disastrous)

offset-n compensate,
equate, commutation,
indemnification,
compromise,
neutralization, nullification,
counteraction,
counterpoise, equivalent,
consideration, offshoot,
ramification, descendant,

often-adv repetition,
iteration, reiteration,
harping, recurrence,
succession, monotony,
rhythm, repeat, echo,
frequent, many times,
repeatedly, perpetually,
continually, constantly,
incessantly, (sometimes,
occasionally, at times,
rarity, fewness, seldom,
scarcely)

ogle-v look, view, espial,
glance, ken, glimpse,
peep, gaze, stare, leer,
contemplation, survey,
speculation, watch, sight-
seeing, longing, hankering,
inkling, solicitude, anxiety,
yearning, coveting,
(indifferent, cold, frigid,
lukewarm, cool,
unconcerned, blind,
hoodwink, dim sighted)

oil-n lubricate, anointment,
glycerine, grease, lather,
grease, soap, wax,
ointment, unctuous,
slippery, oleaginous,
adipose, sebaceous, fatty,
(pulpy, paste, dough, curd,
jam, poultice, watery)

old-adj age, ancient,
antique, long standing,
time-honored, venerable,
elder, prime, primitive,
igneous, primordial,
seniority, maturity, decline,
decay, senility, ripe,
mellow, longevity,
decrepitude, (young,
youthful, juvenile, green,
callow, budding, new,

novel, recent, fresh,
modern, recent, immature)

omission-n exclusion,
exception, rejection,
repudiation, exile,
seclusion, separation,
segregation, supposition,
elimination, bar, leave,
shut, reject, repudiate,
blackball, banish, (include,
admit, consist of, embrace,
embody, involve, implicate,
contain, constitute,
complete, entire,
supplement)

one-adj whole, total,
integrity, collectiveness,
unity, complete,
indivisibility, integration,
aggregate, main, essential,
identity, sameness,
monotony, identical,
(inversion, contrariety,
contrast, part, portion,
division, segment, fraction,
parcel, piece, morsel)

oneself-n identity,
sameness, coincidence,
facsimile, similar, alter ego,
identification, self,
monotony, exactness,
identical (opposite,
reverse, inverse, converse)

only-adj small, unity,
individual, sole, single,
solitary, apart, alone,
unaccompanied, isolation,
seclusion, lone, lonely,
desolate, dreary, simple,
purity, homogeneity,
uniform, neat, (mixture,
tinge, tincture, compound,
infusion, combination,

matrimony, accompany,
coexist, attend, part)
ooze-*v* emerge, exit, issue,
emersion, burst,
emanation, evacuation,
perspiration, sweating,
leakage, percolation,
distillation, gush,
outpouring, effluence,
effusion, disclose, divulge,
split, acknowledge, allow,
(screen, cover, mask,
masquerade, ingress,
enter, influx, invasion,
import)
opalescent-*adj*
semitransparent,
opalescence, milkiness,
pearliness, gauze, muslin,
film, mist, cloud,
variegation, iridescence,
play of colors, polychrome,
maculation, spottiness,
spectrum, rainbow,
(transparent, pellucid,
lucid, diaphanous,
relucent, limpid, clear,
serene, crystalline,
vitreous)
open-*adj* divulge, reveal,
break, split, disclose,
resection, unveiling,
deterred, revelation,
exposition,
acknowledgement, avowal,
confession, disclose, allow,
concede, grant, admit,
(ambush, screen, cover,
shade, blinker, veil,
curtain, blind, cloak, cloud,
mask, visor, disguise,
masquerade, dress)
operate-*v* cause,

groundwork, foundation,
support, spring, genesis,
descent, produce, perform,
fabricate, frame, construct,
manufacture, contrive,
forge, coin, carve, build,
raise, edify, rear, erect,
constitute, (extinction,
annihilation, destroy, ruin,
demolish, over-turn,
sacrifice, subvert)
operator-*n* agent, doer,
actor, agent, performer,
perpetrator, executor,
practitioner, worker,
stager, bee, ant, artisan,
handicrafts, workman,
artisan, craftsman,
mechanic, operative,
maker, journeyman,
pursuit, pursuing,
prosecution, (abstain,
refrain, spare, eschew,
maintain, spare)
opinion-*n* persuasion,
conviction, convince, self-
conviction, certainty, mind,
view, conception,
impression, surmise,
conclusion, judgment,
tenet, dogma, principle,
popular belief, (misbelief,
discredit, miscreant,
infidelity, dissent,
retraction, doubt,
skepticism, misgiving,
demur, mistrust)
opponent-*n* antagonist,
adversary, adverse party,
opposition, enemy,
assailant, obstructive,
brawler, wrangler,
disputant, malcontent,

demagogue, reactionary,
rival, competitor, (helper,
recruit, assistant, midwife,
colleague, partner, mate,
collaborator, ally, friend,
confidant)

opportunity-*n* occasion,
opening, room, suitable
time, proper time, crisis,
turn, juncture, turning
point, timely, lucky,
fortunate, happy,
providential, favorable,
propitious, auspicious,
suitable, (untimely,
intrusive, inopportune,
unlucky, inauspicious)

oppose-*v* contrary, contrast,
antithesis, contradiction,
antagonism, inversion,
opposite, invert, diverse,
conflicting, hostile,
diametrically opposite,
crossfire, clashing,
collision, conflict,
resistance, restraint,
hindrance, (cooperation,
association, alliance,
conference, coalition,
fusion)

oppressor-*n* tyrant, severe,
strictness, harshness,
rigor, stringency, austerity,
inclemency, arrogance,
arbitrary power, despotism,
dictatorship, autocracy,
tyranny, domineering,
assumption, usurpation,
inquisition, reign of terror,
disciplinarian, despot,
inquisitor, extortioner,
(lenient, mild, gentle,
clement, tolerant,

indulgent, easy-going,
forbearing)

oral-*adj* voice, vocal, organ,
lungs, bellows, cry,
utterance, breathe,
ejaculate, rap out,
articulate, distinct,
stertorous, melodious,
enunciate, pronounce,
accentuate, aspirate,
deliver, (stammer,
hesitation, impediment,
titubation, whisper, lisp,
drawl, twang, accent,
stutter, mumble, mutter,
whisper)

oratory-*n* speaking, speech,
locution, talk, parlance,
verbal intercourse, oral
communication, oration,
recitation, delivery, lecture,
harangue, sermon, formal
speech, rhetoric,
declamation

orb-*n* region, sphere,
ground, soil, area, realm,
hemisphere, quarter,
district, beat, circuit, circle,
department, domain, tract,
territory, country, canton,
county, shire, province,
parish, township, arena,
precincts, walk, clime,
climate, zone, meridian,
(spacious, roomy,
extension, extent,
superficial extent)

orbit-*n* world, creation,
nature, universe, earth,
globe, wide world, cosmos,
sphere, heavens, sky,
firmament, celestial
spaces, stars, asteroids,

nebulae, galaxy, milky
way, path, way, manner,
method, gait, form, mode,
fashion, tone, guise,
procedure

orchestra-*n* music, concert,
strain, tune, air, melody,
instrumental music, full
score, minstrels, band,
concerted, piece, stringed
instruments, wind
instruments, vibrating
surfaces

ordain-*v* appointment,
nomination, return, charter,
installation, inauguration,
investiture, accession,
coronation, enthronement,
vicegerency, regency,
regentship, viceroy,
consignee, commission,
accredit, (abrogate, annul,
cancel, destroy, abolish,
revoke, repeal, rescind,
reverse, retract, recall)

ordeal-*n* concern, grief,
sorrow, distress, affliction,
woe, bitterness, heartache,
broken hearted, anxiety,
solicitude, trouble, fiery
ordeal, shock, blow, dole,
fret, burden, load,
(happiness, felicity, bliss,
beatitude, enchantment,
transport, rapture,
ravishment, ecstasy,
paradise, pleasing)

order-*n* regular, uniformity,
symmetry, gradation,
progression, routine,
method, disposition,
arrangement, array,
system, economy,

discipline, orderliness,
rank, place, methodically,
systematically, periodically,
(disorder, derangement,
irregularity, confusion,
complexity, perplexity)

ordinary-*adj* indifferent,
middling, mediocre,
average, tolerable, fair,
passable, decent,
admissible, bearable,
secondary, inferior,
second-rate, second-best,
typical, normal, orthodox,
regular, steady, (irregular,
abnormal, unconventional,
unusual, perfect,
impeccability, model,
paragon)

organize-*v* arrange, plan,
preparation, distribution,
allocation, sorting,
assortment, allotment,
apportionment, taxis,
graduation, organization,
analysis, classification,
division, digestion, atlas,
(disorder, disturbance,
dislocation, perturbation,
interruption, shuffling,
inversion, misplace,
mislay)

original-*n* prototype, model,
pattern, precedent,
standard, scanting, type,
protoplasm, module,
exemplar, example,
ensample, text, (imitation,
copy, transcription,
repetition, duplication,
mimicry)

orthodox-*adj* conformity,
observance, symmetry,

naturalization,
conventionality, custom,
agreeable, example,
quotation, exemplification,
illustration, typical normal,
formal, canonical, sound,
strict, rigid, positive,
uncompromising, (unusual,
unaccustomed,
uncommon, remarkable,
extraordinary, curious)

oscillation-*n* motion,
vibration, liberation, motion
of a pendulum, nutation,
undulation, pulsation,
pulse, alternate, wave,
rock, swing, pulsate, beat,
waggle, fluctuate, dance,
curvet, reel, change,
inconstancy, vicissitude,
(stable, constant,
established, fixture,
permanence, solidity, firm,
steadfast)

osculation-*n* contact,
contiguity, proximity,
apposition, juxtaposition,
touching, abutment,
meeting, coincidence,
adhesion, (gorge, defile,
ravine, crevice, separation,
interval, opening, leak)

ostensible-*adj* probable,
likely, hopeful, to be
expected, in a fair way,
plausible, specious,
colorable, well-founded,
reasonable, credible,
presumable, presumptive,
apparent, apparently,
seemingly, (improbability,
unlikelihood, unfavorable,
possibility, incredibility,

rare, infrequent,
inconceivable)

oust-*v* eject, emit, exit,
dispatch, exhale, excerpt,
excrete, secrete, secern,
extravagate, shed, void,
evacuate, effuse, spend,
expend, pour forth, squirt,
spurt, spill, slop, perspire,
exude, (admit, receive,
import, introduce, ingest,
absorb, suction, sucking,
insertion)

outburst-*n* violence,
inclemency, vehemence,
might, impetuosity,
effervescence, turbulence,
ferocity, rage, fury,
exacerbation,
exasperation, (moderation,
lenitive, gentleness,
sobriety)

outcome-*n* profit, earnings,
winnings, innings, pickings,
net profit, proceeds, return,
harvest, benefit, get back,
recover, regain, retrieve,
redeem

outlandish-*adj* ridiculous,
ludicrous, comic, droll,
funny, laughable,
grotesque, farcical, odd,
whimsical, fanciful,
fantastic, queer, eccentric,
strange, awkward,
(tasteful, unaffected,
cultivated, refined)

outline-*n* origin, source,
rise, but, germ, egg,
rudiment, genesis, birth,
title page, heading,
rudiments, elements,
grammar, alphabet, begin,

commence, inchoate,
arise, originate, conceive,
initiate, open, (end, close,
finish, terminate, conclude,
expire, consummation,
definitive)

outlying-*adj* remaining,
unconsumed, sedimentary,
surviving, net, exceeding,
over and above,
outstanding, cast off,
superfluous, redundant,
surplus, overplus, excess,
(augment, appendage,
adjunct, addition, affix,
reinforcement,
supernumerary,
accessory)

outmaneuver-*v* deception,
falseness, fraud, deceit,
guile, fraudulence,
knavery, cunning,
misrepresentation,
delusion, gullible, juggling,
trick, cheat, feint, juggle,
defeat, conquer, vanquish,
over come, silence, quell,
checkmate, (fruitless,
ineffectual, inefficient,
impotent, efficacious)

outrage-*n* bad turn, affront,
disrespect, atrocity, ill
usage, intolerance,
persecution, malevolent,
grudge, abolish, malign,
molest, worry, harass,
haunt, wreck, impair,
wane, (benevolent, kind,
well meaning, amiable)

outrageous-*adj* violent,
vehement, warm, acute,
sharp, rough, rude,
ungentle, bluff, boisterous,

wild, brusque, abrupt,
impetuous, excite, incite,
urge, lash, stimulate,
irritate, inflame, kindle,
(tranquilize, assuage,
appease, swag, lull,
soothe, compose, still,
calm, cool, quiet, hush,
quell)

outrival-*adj* superior,
exceed, excel, transcend,
out-do, out-weigh,
dominate, prevail, come
first, culminate,
distinguished, vaulting,
greatest, paramount,
foremost, crowning,
excellent, important,
(inferior, minority,
subordinate, short-coming,
deficiency, minimum,
smallness, diminish)

outset-*n* beginning,
commencement, opening,
incipience, inception,
inchoation, introduction,
alpha, initial, inauguration,
embarkation, outbreak,
onset, brunt, initiative,
fresh start, (end, close,
finish, terminate, conclude,
be all over with, expire,
final, crowning, complete,
hinder)

outside-*n* exterior, surface,
eccentricity, face,
superficial, skin-deep,
frontal, external, outward,
covering, extramural,
(interior, inside, interspace,
innermost, indoor, inward,
enclosed)

outstanding-*adj* remainder,

residue, remains, remnant, rest, relic, leavings, heel-tap, odds and ends, left, unconsumed, sedimentary, surviving, exceeding, outlying, (adjunct, addition, affix, appendage, augment, increment, reinforcement, supernumerary, accessory, item, garnish, sauce)

outweigh-v exceed, excel, transcend, out-balance, out-do, pass, surpass, get ahead of, cap, beat, eclipse, preponderate, predominate, prevail, proceed, take precedence, come first, render larger, (inferior, smaller, decrease, contract, hide, lower, minor, less, lesser, deficient, minus)

ovation-n celebration, solemnization, jubilee, commemoration, triumph, jubilation, keep, signalize, rejoice, (nonobservance, evasion, failure, omission, neglect, laxity, informality)

overburden-adj redundant, luxury, excess, surplus, margin, remainder, duplicate, surplusage, extravagance, lavishness, superfluous, unnecessary, needless

P

pack-v arrange, dispose, place, form, collocate, marshal, size, rank, group,

parcel out, allot, distribute, dispose of, assign, assort, classify, divide, file, string, assembled, closely packed, dense, swarming, (dispersion, divergence, scattering, dissemination, misplace, mislay, disorder)

paddle-v walk, march, step, tread, pace, plod, wend, promenade, trudge, tramp, stalk, stride, straddle, strut, stump, bundle, handle, hilt, haft, shaft, heft, shank, blade, trigger, tiller, helm, treadle, key

padlock-n fasten, bolt, latch, latchet, tag, tooth, hook, holdfast, rivet, anchor, grappling, stake, post, tie, strap, tackle, rigging, brace, girder

page-n numeration, numbering, pagination, tale, recension, enumeration, summation, reckoning, computation, check, prove, demonstrate, balance, audit, part, issue, number, album, portfolio, periodical, serial, magazine, circular, paper, bill, sheet, broadsheet

pair-n couple, duality, duplicity, two, deuce, brace, cheeks, twins, duplex, analog, the like, match, similarity, resemblance, likeness, affinity, pendant, fellow, mate, double, counterpart, (dissimilar, unlike, disparate, of a different

kind, unmatched, nothing
of the kind)

palatable-*adj* savoriness,
zest, dainty, delicacy,
ambrosia, nectar, appetite,
relish, like, smack the lips,
well-tasted, good, nice,
dainty, delectable, gusty,
appetizing, lickerish,
delicate, delicious,
exquisite, rich, luscious,
(offensive, repulsive,
nasty, sickening,
nauseous, loathful,
unpleasant)

pale-*adj* dimness, darkness,
half-light, glimmer,
nebulosity, aurora, dusk,
twilight, shades, moonlight,
lackluster, dingy, dark,
pallid, tallow-faced, faint,
dull, cold, muddy, leaden,
discoloration, neutral tint,
monochrome, (pigment,
color, dye, tinge,
illuminate, emblazon,
bright, vivid, intense, deep)

pall-*n* cloak, mantle,
mantlet, mantua, shawl,
wrapper, veil, cape, tippet,
kirtle, plaid, muffler,
comforter, coffin, shell,
sarcophagus, urn, bier,
hearse, catafalque,
offensive, repulsive, nasty,
sickening, nauseous,
loathful, unpleasant,
(dainty, delicacy,
ambrosia, nectar, game,
relish, like)

palpable-*adj* material,
bodily, corporeal, physical,
somatic, sensible, tangible,

ponderable, substantial,
objective, impersonal,
neuter, unspiritual, plain,
distinct, definite, well
defined, marked, in focus,
recognizable, (invisible,
non-appearance,
concealment, dim,
confused, indistinct)

palpitate-*v* tremble,
agitation, stir, tremor,
ripple, jog, jolt, jar, jerk,
shock, succussion,
trepidation, tingle, thrill,
heave, pant, throb, quiver,
flutter, twitter, shake

pamper-*v* indulge, high,
living, self-indulgence,
voluptuousness,
dissipation, sensuality,
animalism, carnality,
pleasure, effeminacy,
silkiness, luxury, piggish,
gluttony, greed, epicurism,
gorge, overfed,
omnivorous, (fast, starve,
clam, famish, perish,
Lenten, unfed, frugality,
moderation)

panel-*n* partition, septum,
diaphragm, midriff, party-
wall, vail, between, betwixt,
sandwich, parenthesis, list,
catalog, inventory,
schedule, register,
account, bill, calendar,
index, table, contents,
(surround, beset,
compass, encompass,
environ, inclose, enclose,
encircle, embrace)

paper-*n* write, pen, copy,
engross, write out, fair,

transcribe, scribble, scrawl, scrabble, scratch, interline, stain paper, write down, record, sign, compose, indite, draw up, dictate, inscribe

paradox-*n* absurdity, imbecility, nonsense, inconsistency, blunder, muddle, bull, farce, rhapsody, farrago, extravagance, romance, obscure, dark, muddy, dim, nebulous, shrouded in mystery, invisible, (plain, distinct, explicit, positive, definite, graphic, expressive, illustrative, lucid)

parallel-*adj* similarity, resemblance, likeness, similitude, semblance, affinity, approximation, agreement, analogy, brotherhood, repetition, uniformity, imitation, copying, transcription, duplication, quotation, (unimitated, unmatched, unparalleled, original, dissimilar, unlike, disparate)

paramount-*adj* supreme, essential, vital, all-absorbing, radical, cardinal, chief, main, prime, primary, principal, leading, capital, foremost, over-ruling, of vital importance, significant, telling, trenchant, emphatic, pregnant, urgent, pressing, critical,

(poor, paltry, pitiful, contemptible, sorry, mean, meager)

paraphrase-*n* explanatory, expository, explicative, exegetical, polyglot, literal, significative, synonymous, equivalent, interpret, explain, define, construe, translate, phrase, expression, set phrase, sentence, paragraph, figure of speech, periphrase, (misrepresent, pervert, garble, falsify)

parody-*n* ridicule, derision, sardonic, smile, grin, scoffing, mockery, quiz, banter, irony, raillery, chaff, joke, twit, quiz, satirize, caricature, burlesque, travesty, servile, copy, imitation, counterfeit, deception, faithful, (prototype, original, model, pattern, precedent, standard, scanting, type, paradigm)

paroxysm-*n* passion, excitement, flush, heat, fever, fire, flame, fume, blood boiling, tumult, effervescence, ebullition, boiling, whiff, gust, storm, tempest, scene breaking out, agony, explosion, burst, (submission, resignation, suffer, forbearance, fortitude, compose, appease)

part-*n* divide, portion, dose, item, particular, aught, any, division, ward, subdivision,

section, chapter, verse,
article, clause, count,
paragraph, passage,
sector, segment, fraction,
fragment, parcel, (whole,
totality, integrity, entirety,
aggregate, gross amount,
sum total, bulk, mass,
lump, altogether)

particular-*adj* exact,
accurate, definite, precise,
well defined, just right,
correct, strict, close, rigid,
rigorous, punctual,
genuine, authentic,
legitimate, orthodox, pure,
natural, sound, sterling,
(error, fallacy,
misconception, mistake,
miss, fault, blunder,
oversight, misprint, slip,
blot, flaw, loose thread)

partner-*n* companion,
accompany, coexist,
attend, fellow associate,
escort, consort, spouse,
colleague, satellite,
concomitant, accessory,
spouse, mate, yokefellow,
husband, man, consort,
goodman, squaw, lady,
matron, wedded pair,
husband, wife, (separation,
divorce, unity, oneness)

pass-*v* move through,
transmission, permeation,
transudation, infiltration,
endosmose, ingress,
egress, opening, journey,
perforate, penetrate,
thread, conduit, gone, last,
latter, bygone, foregone,
elapsed, lapsed, expired,

(future, prospectively,
impending, next, stay,
eventual)

passion-*n* emotion,
character, qualities,
disposition, nature, spirit,
tone, temper, idiosyncrasy,
soul, pervading, spirit,
humor, mood, grain,
mettle, sympathy, desire,
wish, fancy, fantasy, want,
need, exigency, inclination,
leaning, (indifferent, cold,
frigid, lukewarm,
unconcerned, careless,
listless)

passive-*adj* inert, dullness,
inactivity, torpor, languor,
quiescence, latency,
inaction, sloth, sluggish,
heavy, flat, slack, tame,
slow, blunt, lifeless, dead,
uninfluential, dormant,
(strong, energetic, forcible,
active, intense, severe,
keen, vivid, sharp, acute,
incisive, trenchant, brisk,
poignant, caustic)

paste-*n* bond, tendon,
tendril, fiber, ribbon, rope,
cable,line, hawser, painter,
mooring, wire, chain,
fasten, tie, strap, tackle,
rigging, adhere, fuse

pat-*v* blow, stroke, knock,
tap, rap, slap, smack dab,
fillip, slam, bang, hit,
whack, thwack, cuff,
squash, dowse, whop,
swap, punch, thump, pelt,
kick, cut, thrust, lunge,
hammer, batter, (recoil,
retroaction, revulsion,

rebound, rebuff, reflux,
reverberation, return)
patch-*n* plot, enclosure,
close, arena, precincts,
tract, territory, country,
canton, county, shire,
domain, blemish,
disfigurement, deformity,
defect, flaw, injury, stain,
blot, spot, speck, freckle,
mole, blotch, disfigure,
pitted, (spacious, roomy,
extensive, expansive,
capacious, ample,
boundless)
patience-*n* perseverance,
resolution, determination,
desperation, devotion,
tenacity, obstinacy, self-
control, submission,
resignation, forbearance,
longanimity, fortitude,
(ruffle, hurry, fuss, stew,
ferment, fit, violence, rage,
fury, desperation,
madness, distraction,
raving, delirium, frenzy,
hysterics)
patter-*v* rap, snap, tap,
knock, click, clash, crack,
crash, pop, slam, bang,
clap, rustle, loquacity,
talkativeness, garrulity,
eloquent, jaw, gabble,
jabber, chatter, orate,
fluent, (silence, mute,
mum, still, reserved,
reticent, conceal, hush)
pause-*v* rest, lull, respite,
truce, drop, interregnums,
abeyance, cessation,
resistance, intermission,
interruption, stop, halt,

arrival, closure,
discontinue, quiet, tranquil,
calm, repose, stand still,
stagnate, quell, stationary,
anchor, (move, motion,
transitorily, restless,
changeable, nomadic)
pay-*v* remunerate, reward,
recompense, meed,
quitting, compensation,
reparation, redress,
retribution, reckoning,
acknowledgment, requital,
amends, salvage,
perquisite, allowance,
salary, (penalty, fine,
forfeit, escheat, amerce,
sconce, confiscate,
punishment, penalty,
atonement)
peace-*n* concord, accord,
harmony, symphony,
agreement, love,
response, union, unison,
unity, assent, unanimity,
friendship, alliance,
understanding,
conciliation, fraternize,
(dissension, odds, discord,
disagreement, division,
split, quarrel, squabble,
altercation, wrangling,
strife, embroilment)
peak-*n* summit, top, vertex,
apex, zenith, pinnacle,
acme, culmination,
meridian, utmost height,
pitch, maximum, climax,
tip, crown, garret, ceiling,
pediment, (bottom, base,
basement, foundation,
substructure, ground,
earth, pavement, floor)

peck-*n* multitude, numerous, multiplicity, profusion, plenty, legion, host, large, enormous, array, army, sea, scores, bushel, sundry, dilemma, stumbling block, pickle, stew, hot water, (smooth, unload, emancipate, easiness, capability, fewness, paucity, small number, handful, minority, scanty)

peculiar-*adj* unusual, unexpected, monstrous, wonderful, remarkable, noteworthy, nondescript, curiosity, abnormal, exception, infraction, distinctive, specific, original, respective, (general, generic, universal, every, unspecified, impersonal, conformity, conventional)

pedigree-*adj* continuity, sequence, succession, round, suite, progression, series, train, chain, entire, linear, uninterrupted, unbroken, paternal, maternal, family, ancestral, patriarchal, line, genealogy, descent, extraction, forefathers, (broken, discontinue, unsuccessful)

peep-*v* short sight, sharp, quick, piercing, penetrating, look, glance, glimpse, gaze, stare, leer, regard, watch, peer, pry, visible, perceptible, exposed to view, (invisible, obscure, misty, veiled)

peer-*n* equal, even, level, monotonous, coequal, symmetrical, co-ordinate, on a par, balanced, match, reach, keep pace with, peerage, house of lords, temporal, spiritual, grandee, aristocrat, (common, plebeian, bourgeois, peasantry, masses, inferior, unequal, uneven, disparate)

pelt-*n* skin, covering, pellicle, fleece, fell, fur, leather, hide, cuticle, scarf, mask, concealment, shield, stone, lapidate, hurl, beset, besiege, beleaguer, cut and thrust, kick, strike, impulse, (protect, guard, safeguard, shield, preserve)

pen-*n* enclosure, envelope, case, wrapper, receptacle, paddock, pound, net, wall, rail, railing, barrier, barricade, gate, door, hatch, restraint, hindrance, coercion, confinement, imprisonment, captivity, (liberation, release, emancipation, dismissal, discharge, free, unfetter, disengage, acquit)

penalty-*n* retribution, punishment, pain, amercement, forfeit, sequestration, confiscation, damage

penchant-*n* disposition, willing, inclination, leaning,

humor, mood, vein, bent,
aptitude, desire, geniality,
cordiality, goodwill,
readiness, earnestness,
forwardness, (unwilling,
grudgingly, indifferent)

pensive-adj thoughtful,
thinking, meditative,
reflective, museful, wistful,
contemplative, speculative,
deliberative, studious,
sedate, introspective,
(vacancy, unintellectual,
unoccupied, thoughtless)

people-n mankind, human
race, species, nature,
humanity, mortality, flesh,
generation, human being,
person, individual,
creature, mortal, body,
somebody, soul, living
soul, earthling, party,
persons, folk, general
public, national, realm,
population

pepper-n pungent, strong
taste, twang, sharp, rough,
unsavory, seasoning,
palatable, spice, full-
flavored, condiment, high-
tasted, biting, spicy, herb,
(insipid, weak, flat, vapid,
tasteless, mawkish)

perch-n place, locate,
situate, localize, put, lay,
set, seat, station, lodge,
quarter, post, install,
house, stow, camp, root,
shelve, deposit, reposit,
cradle, moor, tether,
picket, pack, vest,
(displace, eject, set aside,
remove, unload, empty,

dispel, banishment, exile,
vacate, cart-away)

perchance-adv possibility,
potentiality, compatibility,
agreement, practicability,
feasibility, practicable,
contingency, compatible,
chance, feasible,
(impossible, no chance
whatever, hopeless)

perdition-n destruction, fall,
downfall, ruin, crash,
smash, havoc, waste,
dissolution, breaking up,
disruption, consumption,
(production, creation,
construction, formation,
fabrication, manufacture)

peremptory-adj asserting,
declaratory, predictor,
pronunciation, affirmative,
positive, certain, express,
explicit, absolute,
emphatic, flat, broad,
confident, (negation,
denial, disavowal,
contradict, prohibit)

perennial-adj continual,
consecutive, progressive,
gradual, successive,
immediate, unbroken,
entire, evergreen,
constant, (discontinue,
pause, interrupt, intervene,
spasmodic, intermission,
alternate)

perfect-adj great, faultless,
immaculate, spotless,
impeccable, flawless,
inimitable, paragon,
unparalleled, supreme,
superhuman, divine, (fault,
weak, imperfect, deficient,

defective, cracked)
perform-*v* achieve,
accomplish, completion,
fulfillment, execution,
dispatch, consummation,
culmination, finish,
conclusion, close, issue,
(incomplete, shortcoming,
unfulfilled, neglect)
perhaps-*adv* possibly,
potentiality, feasibility,
conceivable, credible,
compatible, achievable,
chance, contingency,
practicable, within reach,
accessible, surmountable,
(impossible, absurd,
contrary)
perish-*v* die, death,
decease, demise,
dissolution, departure,
release, rest, loss,
bereavement, end,
cessation, extinction, death
rattle, (life, vitality,
animation, vivification,
alive, respire, subsist,
revive)
permeate-*v* pervade, fill,
present, occupy,
inhabiting, moored,
domiciled, omnipresent,
dwell, reside, diffusion,
haunt, revisit, sojourn,
abide, lodge, nestle, roost,
(empty, vacuum, truant,
absent, vacate)
perplex-*v* distressing,
bothersome, afflicting,
unlucky, uncomfortable,
disheartening, depressing,
distasteful, unpleasant,
unpopular, thankless,

(refreshing, comfortable,
cordial, genial, glad,
pleasant delightful, lovely,
felicitous)
persecute-*v* oppress,
wrong, aggrieve, trample,
tread, overburden, weigh-
down, victimize, molest,
maltreat, abuse, ill-use, ill-
treat, harm, injure,
(goodness, merit,
beneficial, valuable,
profitable)
persist-*v* continue, last,
endure, go on, remain,
intervene, elapse,
continue, seize an
opportunity, permanent,
duration, pending, interval,
(never, nevermore, at no
time, hesitant, doubtful)
persuade-*v* induce, prevail,
overcome, carry, bring
round, procure, enlist,
engage, invite, court,
tempt, seduce, entice,
allure, captivate, fascinate,
(discourage, dampen,
restrain, reluctance)
pertinent-*adj* relative,
bearing, reference,
connection, concern,
correlative, cognate,
association, nearness,
interest, relevancy,
comparison, correlation,
(incidental, parenthetical,
remote, far fetched)
pervert-*n* misrepresent,
garble, distort, travesty,
retort, stretch, strain,
misinterpreted, hardening,
backsliding, declination,

reprobation, (elected, adopted, regenerated, inspired, consecrated, converted)

pessimism-*n* underestimate, depreciate, detract, undervalue, modest, under rate, disparage, minimize, (over-estimation, oversensitive, vanity)

petrify-*v* density, solidity, solidness, constipation, solidified, compact, thickset, substantial, massive, impenetrable, impermeable, (rare, subtile, thin, fine, tenuous, compressible, flimsy, slight, spongy)

phantom-*n* imaginary, fancy, conceive, deal, realize, create, originate, devise, invent, fabricate, improvise, fertile, unreal, ideal, legendary, whimsical, fairy-like, mythological, illusory, fallacious

photography-*n* representation, illustration, delineation, depiction, portraiture, engraving, daguerreotype, image, likeness, facsimile, (misrepresent, distort, exaggerate, daub)

physical-*adj* materialistic, substantiality, condition, matter, body, substance, stuff, element, principle, object, article, (immaterial, disembody, spiritualize,

extramundane, earthy, pneumatolysis)

pick-*v* select, choice, option, discretion, volition, alternative, dilemma, adoption, decision, judgment, election, poll, ballot, exception, preference, (indifferent, neutral, abstain, refrain)

picket-*n* place, situate, locate, moor, tether, pack, tuck in, imbed, vest, make a place for, put, lay, set, seat, station, lodge, quarter, post, sentinel, watch, patrol, vedette, bivouac, scout, spy, spiel

pickle-*n* preserve, maintain, keep, embalm, dry, cure, salt, season, bottle, pot, tin, can, macerate, dilution, humectant, dilemma, embarrassment, perplexity, (easy, facile, feasible, easily managed)

picture-*n* description, set forth, portray, represent, characterize, particularize, narrate, relate, recite, recount, graphic, appearance, aspect, color, image, (vanish, disappear, missing, lost, departure)

piercing-*v* shrill, harsh sounds, acute, high note, scream, discordant, cry, roar, shout, hoop, whoop, yell, bellow, howl, scream, screech, shriek (muffled, dead silence, melodious)

pile-*v* heap, exaggerate, magnify, aggravate,

amplify, overestimate,
hyperbolize, overestimate,
accumulation, congeries,
lump, mass, pyramid, drift,
acervate, conglomeration,
quantity, greatness,
(disperse, scatter,
disseminate, diffuse, shed,
spread, overspread,
distribute, dispel)

pilot-*n* guide, direct,
manage, govern, conduct,
order, prescribe, regulate,
steer, take the helm,
superintend, sailor,
mariner, navigator,
skipper, gondolier,
steersman, seaman

pin-*v* fasten, restraint,
hindrance, coercion,
compulsion, constraint,
repression, discipline,
control, confinement,
durance, duress,
imprisonment, (liberate,
disengagement, release,
dismissal)

pinch-*v* requirement, need,
want, necessities, stress,
exigency, essential,
indispensability, urgency,
pain, suffer, ache, smart,
bleed, tingle, hurt, chafe,
(pleasure, bodily
enjoyment, gratification,
luxury)

pioneer-*n* precursor,
antecedent, precedent,
predecessor, forerunner,
van-courier, prodrome,
outrider, leader, herald,
prelude, prior, groundwork,
(sequel, suffix, successor,

tail, train, wake, rear)

pitch-*v* degree, grade,
extent, measure, amount,
ratio, stint, standard,
reach, amplitude, range,
scope, gradation, shade,
tenor, station, comparative,
gradual, limit, height

pith-*n* gist, intrinsically,
inherence, inhesion,
subjectiveness, ego,
essence, essential part,
quintessence, incarnation,
quiddity, marrow, sap,
lifeblood, backbone, heart,
soul, (outward, incidental,
extrinsic, extraneous,
accidental, objective,
derived from without)

place-*v* arrange, prepare,
plan, disposal, distribute,
sort, assort, allotment,
apportionment, analysis,
classification, division,
digest, (disorder,
misarrange, disturb,
confuse, perturb, jumble,
muddle)

placid-*adj* passive, tranquil,
collness, calmness,
composure, serenity, quiet,
peace of mind

plagiarism-*n* steal, theft,
thievery, borrowed,
forgery, imitator, echo,
transcribe, match, parallel,
simulate, impersonate,
represent, counterfeit,
parody, travesty,
caricature, burlesque

plain-*adj* simple, plain,
homeliness, undress,
chastity, unaffected,

chaste, severe, bald, flat,
dull, unvaried,
monotonous,
unornamented, blank,
(ornate, florid, rich, flowery,
elegant)

platform-*n* pulpit, desk,
reading, theater,
amphitheater, forum,
stage, rostrum, hustings,
tribune, plan, scheme,
design, project, proposal,
suggestion, sketch,
skeleton, outline, draught,
draft

plausible-*adj* probable,
likelihood, hopeful,
specious, ostensible,
founded, reasonable,
credible, presumable,
presumptive, apparent,
most-likely, (improbable,
unlikely, long odds,
unfavorable)

plea-*v* vindication,
justification, warrant,
exoneration, exculpation,
acquittal, whitewashing,
extenuation, softening,
mitigation, reply,
(accusation, charge,
imputation, slur, libel)

pleasant-*adj* flatter,
adulator, eulogist,
euphemism, optimist,
encomiast, laudatory,
whitewasher, toady,
sycophant, courtier, puffer,
touter, amuse, entertain,
diversion, relaxation,
solace, fun, frolic,
merriment, laughter, labor
of love, (weariness,

lassitude, disgust, nausea,
loathing)

pledge-*v* promise,
undertaking, word, troth,
plight, parole, word of
honor, vow, oath,
affirmation, assurance,
warranty, guarantee,
insurance, contract,
borrow, (demise, lease,
advance, loan,)

plenty-*n* sufficient,
adequate, enough, withal,
satisfaction, ample,
copious, abundant,
abounding, replete, rich,
luxuriant, affluent,
inexhaustible, liberal,
(scarcity, want, need, lack,
poverty, dole)

plod-*v* slow, languor, slow-
goer, linger, loiter,
sluggard, snail, dawdle,
creep, crawl, lag, drawl,
saunter, trudge, stump
along, retard, slacken,
(move quickly, trip, speed,
hasten, scuttle, scud)

pluck-*v* take, catch, hook,
nab, bag, sack, pocket,
receive, accept, assume,
possess, take possession
of, ravish, seize, pounce,
assault, intercept,
scramble for, snatch,
(return, restore,
recuperate, reinvest,
reparation, remit,
rehabilitate)

plump-*adj* huge, immense,
enormous, might, vast,
stupendous, monstrous,
colossal, gigantic, infinite,

large as life, hulky,
unwieldy, lumpish,
whopping, (dwarf, pygmy,
atom, microscopic, gaunt,
molecular, thin,
inconsiderable)

pocket-*n* receptacle,
compartment, hole, corner,
niche, recess, nook, crypt,
stall, chest, box, coffer,
caddy, case, basket,
pouch, sack, wallet, scrip,
poke, knit, knapsack,
haversack, satchel

point-*v* mark, topic, food for
thought, subject matter,
theme, thesis, text,
business, affair, argument,
motion, resolution, inquiry,
problem, question, (notion,
conception, reflection,
observation, idea)

polemic-*n* combatant,
disputant, controversial,
litigant, belligerent,
competitor, rival,
contention, strife,
opposition, rivalry,
handicap, contest, match,
race, (peace, amity,
friendship, harmony)

polished-*adj* polite,
courtesy, respect, good
manners, good behavior,
good breeding, urbanity,
presence, obeisance,
politeness, amiability,
complacency, (impudence,
disrespect, sternness)

pommel-*v* rotund, round,
circular, cylindrical,
columnar, spherical, ball,
boulder, oblong, oblate,

drop, vesicle, bulb, bullet,
barrel, drum, rolling pin,
rundle, cone

ponderous-*adj* judgment,
result, conclusion, upshot,
deduction, inference,
egotism, illation, corollary,
porism, estimation,
valuation, appreciation,
assessment, (detection,
discovery, find, determine,
trace)

poor-*adj* poverty, indigence,
penury, pauperism,
destitution, want, need,
lack, necessity, distress,
difficulties, bad,
embarrassed, reduced,
circumstances, slender,
stricken, (wealth, rich,
fortunate, opulence,
affluence, provision,
livelihood, maintenance,
dowry, means, resources)

pop-*v* abruptly,
unexpectedly, plump,
unaware, without notice,
startle, take aback,
electrify, stun, stagger,
astonish, surprise,
(expected, anticipating,
reckoning, suspense,
waiting, abeyance)

popular-*adj* celebrated,
distinction, mark, name,
figure, repute, reputation,
fame, renown,
approbation, notoriety,
illustriousness, hero,
nobility, glory, honor,
(disgrace, shame,
humiliation, tarnish,
scandal)

portable-*adj* transit,
transition, passage,
removal, conveyance,
relegation, portage,
carting, shoveling, freight,
convoy, bring, fetch, reach,
send, consign, deliver,
transpose, movable,
contagious

portfolio-*n* book, part,
issue, number, album,
magazine, periodical,
serial, annual, journal,
paper, bill, broadsheet

positive-*adj* certain,
necessity, certitude,
surety, assurance,
infallibleness, reliability,
gospel, scripture, absolute,
unqualified, inevitable,
infallible, unchangeable,
impeachable, conclusive,
authoritative, (uncertain,
doubtful, dubious,
indecisive, value,
ambiguous, undefined,
confused)

possess-*v* ownership,
tenure, occupancy,
holding, tenancy, heritage,
inheritance,enjoy, labor
under, come to pass,
conditional, (circumstance,
situation, phase, position)

posthumous-*adj* late, tardy,
slow, behind, belated,
unpunctual, backward,
slowly, leisurely,
deliberately, delay,
postponement,
adjournment, prorogation,
retardation, (punctual,
promptitude, prematurity)

posture-*n* form, figure,
conformation, make,
formation, feature,
lineament, turn, phase,
aspect, situation, locality,
latitude, footing, standing,
standpoint, stage, aspect,
attitude

potentiality-*n* possibility,
compatibility, agreement,
practicability, feasibility,
feasible, performable,
achievable, accessible,
superable, surmountable,
obtainable, contingent,
(impossibility, absurd,
unreasonable, incredible,
inconceivable, improbable,
prodigious, impervious)

potpourri-*n* fragrant,
aromatic, redolent, spicy,
balmy, scented, sweet-
smelling, perfumed,
muscadine, ambrosial,
scent, mixture, join,
combine, intermix, mingle,
instill, compound, medicate

pout-*v* moody,
discourteous, displacency,
grim, sullen, peevish,
acrimonious, surly, rough,
blunt, gruff

poverty-*n* indigence -
penury, pauper,
destitution, want, need,
necessity, privation,
distress, needy, difficulties,
beggar, (wealth, riches,
fortune, opulence,
affluence, livelihood)

practical-*adj* operative,
efficient, efficacious,
effectual, maintaining,

practice, procedure,
practical joking, ridicule,
sarcasm, mockery,
discourtesy
praiseworthy-*adj*
commendable, praise,
laud, good work, tribute,
eulogy, homage,
benediction, blessing,
applause,complimentary,
uncritical, (frown upon,
reprehend, admonish,
reprimand, chastise,
castigate, lash out,
trounce)
precedent-*n* coming before,
lead, superiority,
antecedent, anterior, prior,
former, foregoing,
prefatory, introductory,
precursor, (sequence,
coming after, succeed,
follow, ensure, alternate)
precious-*adj* valuable, dear,
extravagance, exorbitance,
superiority, goodness,
excellence, worth, rare
expensive, costly,
beneficial, serviceable,
advantageous, edifying,
(cheap, depreciated,
bargain)
precipice-*n* slope, obliquity,
inclination, slant, crooked,
leaning, bevel, tilt, bias,
twist, swag, cant, lurch,
rise, ascent, gradient,
rising ground, dip, fall
downhill, steepness, cliff,
escarpment
precocious-*adj* flippant,
pert, cavalier, saucy,
forward, impertinent,

malapert, assuming, bluff,
brazen, shameless,
aweless, unblushing,
unabashed, bold, bare,
impudent, audacious,
presumptuous, (servile,
obsequious, supple,
soapy, oily, groveling,
sniveling, mealy-mouthed,
beggarly, prostrate)
pregnant-*adj* productive,
fertility, luxuriance,
puberty, pullulating,
fructify, multiplication,
propagation, procreation,
superfetation, generate,
(sterile, waste, barren,
addle, unfertile, arid)
prejudice-*adj* misjudgment,
miscalculation, hasty
conclusion, foregone
conclusion, narrow-
minded, confined, illiberal,
intolerant, besotted,
infatuated, fanatical,
positive, dogmatic, bias,
underestimate,
overestimate, (solve,
resolve, render right, be
near the truth, recognize,
realize, verify, make
certain)
prepense-*v*
predetermination,
premeditation, deliberation,
foregone conclusion,
resolve, propend, intention,
project, redesigned,
advised, calculated, well-
laid, (impulse, sudden)
prerogative-*n* right,
privilege, prescription, title,
claim, pretension, demand,

birthright, immunity,
license, liberty, franchise,
vested interest, sanction,
authority, (impropriety,
emptiness, illegality)
prescribe-v advice,
counsel, suggestion,
recommendation,
advocacy, instruction,
charge, direct, manage,
govern, conduct, order,
lead
present-v bestowal,
donation, delivery,
consignment,
dispensation, endowment,
investment, almsgiving,
generosity, liberality,
charity, dispensation,
(receive, acquire,
admission, benefactor)
pretend-v feign, assume,
make believe, false,
simulate, counterfeit,
sham, malign, deceitful,
dishonest, evasive, hollow,
insincere, forsworn,
fabricate, prevaricate,
(veracity, truth, frankness)
primary-adj important,
significant, concern,
emphasis, greatness,
superiority, notability,
gravity, seriousness,
solemnity, no laughing
matter, urgent,
prominence, (trivial,
frivolous, paltry, small)
privacy-n seclusion,
exclusion, retirement,
reclusion, recess,
snugness, solitude,
solitary, isolation,

loneliness, voluntary exile,
aloofness, convent, exile,
ostracism, (social,
companionship,
association, acquaintance,
conversable, convivial,
jovial, hospitable)
probation-n verification,
test, assay, proof,
diagnostic, crucial test,
check, ordeal, experiment,
answerable, prove,
establish, make good,
show, conclusiveness,
(refutation, answer,
disproof, conviction,
invalidation, retort,
negative, parry, argument)
procreate-v productive,
prolific, teeming, fertile,
fruitful, frugivorous,
luxuriant, pregnant,
generative, life-giving,
spermatic, multiparous,
(sterility, infertility, waste,
desert, unprofitable)
profession-n part, cue,
province, function, look-
out, department, capacity,
sphere, orb, field, line,
routine, career, race,
vocation, calling, craft,
trade, actively employed,
employment
promise-v undertaking,
work, troth, plight, pledge,
parole, affirmation, vow,
oath, profession,
assurance, warranty,
guarantee, insurance,
obligation, contract,
(release, liberation,
absolute, free)

pronounce-*v* utter, breathe, give, ejaculate, vocalize, prolate, articulate, enunciate, accentuate, aspirate, deliver, mouth, phonetic, oral, (silence, render mute, muzzle, muffle, suppress, smother)

propagate-*v* productive, prolific, teeming, fertile, fruitful, circulate, promulgate, spread, publish, known, information, put forward, proclaim, announce, advertise, (sterile, unproductive, unfertile)

propitiate-*v* forgiveness, pardon, condonation, grace, remission, absolution, amnesty, oblivion, indulgence, reprieve, conciliation, reconciliation, pacification, (revenge, vengeance, avenged)

prosecute-*v* accuse, charge, imputation, slur, inculpation, elation, criminative, argument, condemnation, defendant, prisoner, charge, (vindication, justification, warrant, exoneration)

provide-*v* supply, purvey, commissariats, grist, resource, caterer, furnish, find, cater, victual, prepare, anticipate, foresight, arrange, ripening, maturation, evolution, (waste, expenditure, dispersion, consumption, exhaustion)

province-*n* region, sphere, ground soil, area, realm, hemisphere, quarter, district, beat, orb, circuit, circle, domain, tract, territory, country, canton, county, shire, parish, (abyss, free space)

prune-*v* retrench, cut short, scrimp, cut, chop up, hack, hew, clip, dock, lop, shear, shave, mow, reap, crop, snub, truncate, pollard stunt, nip, curtail, (long, lengthy, outstretched, elongate)

pulsate-*v* agitation, stir, tremor, shake, ripple, jog, jolt, jar, jerk, shock, succussion, trepidation, quiver, quaver, dance, twitter, flicker, flutter, disquiet, perturbation, commotion, turmoil, stagger

punctual-*adj* accuracy, exact, precise, delicacy, rigor, mathematical, clockwork precision, genuine, authentic, legitimate, substantial, tangible, valid, undistorted, (laxity, indefinite, erroneous, untrue)

pure-*adj* innocent, spotless, clear, immaculate, clean, not guilty, irreproachable, virtuous, above suspicion, exceptional, without flaw, blameless, (guilt, atrocity, fault, sin, error, transgression)

purpose-*n* intent, project, predetermination, design, ambition, contemplation, mind, view, proposal, study, decision, resolve, settled, resolution, wish, motive, deliberate, (speculation, venture, chance)

pursue-*v* continue, persist, keep, stick to, maintain, carry on, uninterrupted, sustain, uphold, hold up, perpetuate, preserve, harp upon, repeat, (cease, discontinue, desist, pause, rest, respite)

push-*v* propulsion, ejaculation, ejection, throw, fling, toss, shot, discharge, missile, projectile, motion, dart, lance, flirt, flip, shoot, launch, send forth, (draw, pull, haul, lug, rake, drag, tug, tow, trail)

Q

quackery-*n* unskillful, incompetency, inability, disqualification, folly, stupidity, indiscretion,neglect, thoughtless, absence of rule, blunder, (skill, dexterity, clever, talent, ability)

quadrant-*n* angular measurement, elevation, distance, velocity, sextant, miter, obtuse, salient, fusiform, wedge-shaped, cuneiform, triangular, rectangular, multilateral, cubical, pyramidal

quagmire-*n* marsh, swamp, morass, moss, fen, bog, slough, sump, wash, mud, squash, slush, embarrassing, awkward, unwieldy, unmanageable, intractable, (ease, feasibility, smooth)

quake-*v* flutter, trepidation, fear and trembling, perturbation, tremor, quivering, shaking, trembling, throbbing, palpitation, fright, affright, quiver, quaver, twitter, twirl, writhe, toss

qualify-*v* change, mutate, permutation, variation, modification, modulation, innovation, metastasis, deviation, turn, diversion, beat, transform, transfigure, metamorphosis, convert, alter, vary, diversity, (stable, permanent, persist, endure, standing, maintain, preserve, conserve)

qualm-*n* misbelief, discredit, infidelity, dissent, change of opinion, doubt, uncertainty, skepticism, misgiving, demure, suspicion, jealousy, scruple, unbeliever, (credence, assurance, faith trust)

quantity-*n* magnitude, amplitude, mass, amount, quantum, measure,

substance, strength,
quantitative, some, any,
more or less,
(comparative, gradual,
shading, range, scope,
caliber)

quantum-*n* dividend,
portion, contingent, share,
allotment, lot, measure,
dose, dole, meed, pittance,
ration, ratio, proportion,
quota, mess, allowance,
(insufficient, inadequate,
scarce, lack, famine)

quarrel-*n* dispute, tiff,
squabble, altercation,
words, big words,
wrangling, jangle, babble,
cross questions, strife,
broil, brawl, row, racket,
embroilment, (accord,
peace of mind, comfort,
harmony, unison,
agreement)

quarter-*n* quadratic,
quartile, tetracid, four,
tetrad, quartet, abode,
dwelling, lodging, domicile,
residence, address,
habitation, berth, seat, lap,
sojourn housing,
headquarters, throne

quasi-*adj* imitate, copy,
mirror, reflect, reproduce,
repeat, do like, echo,
catch, transcribe, match,
parallel, mock, mimic,
simulate, impersonate,
counterfeit, (original,
unique, unimitated)

quell-*v* becalm, hush, lull to
sleep, lay an embargo on,
remain, stay, stand, resting

place, bivouac, anchor,
rest, cast, quiet, tranquility,
repose, (motion, stream,
flow, restlessness,
nomadic)

quench-*v* dissuade, deport,
cry out against,
remonstrate, expostulate,
warn, contraindicate,
disincline, repel, damp,
cool, calm, quiet,
deprecate, (persuade,
prevail, overcome, carry,
procure)

question-*n* inquiry,
examination, review,
scrutiny, investigation,
exploration, sifting,
calculation, analysis,
dissection, resolution,
induction, (answer,
respond, reply, rebut,
retort, rejoin)

questionable-*adj* doubtful,
mistrust, suspect, raise a
question, unbeliever,
refuse to admit, harbor,
demure, suspicious, have
one's doubts,
inconceivable, (belief,
credence, credit, reliability,
assurance)

quibble-*v* sophism,
solecism, paralogism,
quirk, fallacy, subterfuge,
subtlety, quilled,
inconsistency, mockery,
pervert, equivocate,
mystify, evade, elude, the
absence of reason,
evasion, (logical
sequence, good cause,
sound, valid)

quick-_adj_ hurry, hasten, accelerate, quicken, swift, rapid, eagle speed, acceleration, spurt, rush, dash, fast, speedy, nimble, agile, expeditious, express, (slow, dawdle, retard, slacken, falter)

quid-_n_ barter, exchange, truck system, tit for tat, give and take, blow for blow, measure for measure, recrimination, accusation, revenge, (resist, rebuff, opposition, reluctant, withstand)

quiet-_adj_ moderation, lenitive, temperate, gentle, tranquilize, assuage, appease, hush, quell, sober, soothe, compose, lull, calm, pacify, (loud, violent, ear-breaking, blast, fury)

quip-_n_ cranks, jest, joke, conceit, quirk, merry, bright, happy, flash of wit, scintillation, witticism, work-play, riddle, smartness, retort, repartee, ridicule, (dull, uninteresting, unlively, stupid, slow, flat)

quirk-_n_ amusement, entertainment, reaction, relaxation, solace, pastime, sport, labor of love, fun, frolic, merriment, jollity, heyday, laughter, (weariness, lassitude, fatigue, disgust, loathing)

quit-_v_ relinquish, abandon, desertion, defection

secession, withdrawal, break off, desist, stop, vacate, renounce, forego, discard, abandon, discontinue, resignation, retirement

quiz-_v_ question, interrogate, interpolation, challenge, examination, cross-examination, inquire, investigate, seek, search, rummage, explore, (answer, respond, reply, rebut, unriddle)

quota-_n_ apportionment, dividend, contingent, allotment, measure, dose, dole, meed, pittance, ration, proportion, allowance, share, portion, assign, appropriate

quote-_v_ example, instance, specimen, sample, exemplification, illustration, case in point, pattern, agreement, illustrative, invariable, instance, cite

R

rabid-_adj_ longing, hankering, inkling, solicitude, anxiety, yearning, coveting, aspiration, ambition, eagerness, zeal, ardor, breathless, impatience, over-anxiety, (indifferent, cold, frigid, lukewarm)

race-_v_ run, spurt, rush, dash, steeplechase, lively, gallop, cantor, trot, round trot, scamper, lightening, rocket, arrow, dart, torrent, hustler, gazelle, (creep, crawl, shuffle, saunter, delay, sluggish)

rack-*n* care, anxiety, solicitude, trouble, trial, ordeal, shock, blow, dole, fret, burden, load, vessel, vase, bushel, barrel, canister, utensil, hamper, crate, cradle (well-being, good, snugness)

racket-*n* loudness, power, loud noise, din, clang, clatter, bombination, roar, uproar, peal, swell, blast, boom, resonance, vociferation, hullabaloo, thunder, resound, (whisper, inaudible, low, dull, muffled)

radical-*adj* cause, original, primary, aboriginal, embryonic, germinal, having a common,review, improve, refine upon, rectify, enrich, mellow, elaborate, fatten, promote, cultivate, advance

rage-*n* resentment, displeasure, animosity, anger, wrath, indignation, exasperation, violence, vehemence, impetuosity, boisterousness, effervescence, row, (calm, moderate, gentle, sobriety)

raise-*v* increase, augment, enlarge, extend, expand, increment, accretion, accession, develop, aggravate, ascent, acerbate, spread, exalt,

deepen, (decrease, diminution, lessen, subtraction)

rake-*v* drag, draw, pull, haul, lug, tug, tow, trail, train, take in tow, wrench, jerk, twitch, tousle, traction, rascal, scoundrel, villain, miscreant, wretch, reptile, viper, scamp, (model, paragon, good example)

rampant-*adj* influential, important, weighty, prevailing, prevalent, rife, dominant, regnant, predominant, run through, pervade, (impotence, inertness, irrelevant, uninfluential, powerless)

random-*adj* indiscriminate, aimless, promiscuous, undirected, drift, causeless, without purpose, casually, by the way, accidental, speculate, unintentional, (intentional, purpose, decision, motive)

ransack-*v* plunder, pillage, rifle, sack, loot, spoil, spoilt, despoil, strip, steal, abstract, appropriate, plagiarize, seize, poach, swindle, peculate, embezzle

rapid-*adj* advance, proceed, progress, move quickly, trip, speed, hasten, spank, scuttle, hurry, accelerate, quicken, fast, swift, quick, nimble, agile, expeditious, express, (relax, slow, regress, retreat, retrograde, withdraw, short, halt)

rapture-*n* love, fondness, liking, inclination, regard, admiration, affection, sympathy, yearning, tender passion, flame, devotion, (hate, detest, abominate, abhor, loathe, revolt against)

rare-*adj* unusual, extraordinary, singular, unique, curious, odd, strange, monstrous, unexpected, remarkable, noteworthy, queer, quaint, nondescript, original, (typical, normal, ordinary, conventional)

rate-*v* estimation, valuation, appreciation, judicature, result, conclusion, upshot, deduction, ponderous, assessment, deduce, derive, gather, collect, (result, discover, find, determine, evolve)

ratio-*n* degree, grade, extent, measure, amount, stint, standard, height, pitch, reach, amplitude, range, scope, caliber, gradation, shade, rate, sort, comparative, (absolute, quantity, mass)

rational-*n* intellect, mind, understanding, reason, thinking, principle, rationality, cogitative, faculties, senses, consciousness, observation, intuition, soul, spirit, (imbecility, brutality, brute-instinct)

rattle-*v* repeated noise, roll, drum, rumble, clatter, patter, clack, hum, trill, shake, chime, peal, toll, tick, beat, ding-dong, tantara, whir, rat-a-tat, rub-a-dub, racket, clutter, cuckoo, repetition, devil's tattoo

ravenous-*adj* appetite, sharp appetite, keenness, hunger, stomach, twist, thirst, avidity, greed, covetous, grasping, craving, voracity, gluttony, (earnestness, anorexia, inappetence, apathy)

raw-*adj* immaturity, crudity, abortion, disqualification, improvisation, dismantle, extemporize, non-preparation, neglect, improvidence, (preparation, ripen, maturation, evolution, elaboration, gestation)

reaction-*n* counteraction, opposition, contrariety, antagonism, polarity, clashing, collision, interference, resistance, renitency, friction, neutralization, recoil, compensation, hindrance, (concurrence, cooperation, cogency, union, agreement, consent)

ready-*adj* prepare, providing, provision, anticipation, foresight, precaution, rehearsal, note of preparation, arrangement, clearance,

tuning, array, ripening,
(extemporize, improvise,
undress)

reap-*v* acquire, get, gain,
win, earn, obtain, procure,
gather, collect, assemble,
find, receive, replevy,
redeem, advantageous,
gainful, remunerative,
paying, lucrative, (loss,
privation, bereavement,
deprivation, dispossession,
riddance, deprived, bereft,
irretrievable)

reason-*n* wisdom, sapience,
sense, common sense,
rationality, judgment,
solidity, depth, profundity,
caliber, enlarged views,
genius, inspiration,
aptitude, (shallow, wanting,
weak, idiotic, vacant,
blatant)

reassure-*v* hope, confident,
trust, rely on, presume,
optimism, enthusiasm,
aspiration, secure,
encouraging, cheering,
inspiriting, looking up,
bright, roseate, (hesitate,
falter, funk, cower, crouch)

rebuff-*v* repulse, defeat,
rout, overthrow,
discomfiture, beating,
drubbing, nonsuit,
subjugation, fall, downfall,
ruin, perdition, wreck, fail,
unsuccessful, (success,
speed, advance, progress,
good fortune)

recede-*v* recession, move
from, retirement,
withdrawal, retreat,

retrocession, departure,
recoil, flight, avoidance,
remove, shunt, shun,
shrink, depart, (approach,
approximate, near, access)

receive-*v* acquisition,
exception, introduction,
susceptibility, acceptance,
admission, assignee,
devisee, donor, grantee,
take in, (give, gift,
donation, delivery,
dispensation, generosity)

recess-*v* regress, retreat,
withdrawal, retirement,
recession, refluence, ebb,
return, reflection, recoil,
deterioration, recede,
retrograde, (progression,
advance, improvement,
proceed, forward, onward)

reciprocate-*v* interchange,
exchange, transposition,
shuffling, castling, barter,
retaliation, bandy, shuffle,
permute, in exchange, vice
versa, (consideration,
substitute, supersede,
replace, redeem)

reckon-*v* discharge, settle,
quit, acquit, account,
balance, square up,
disgorge, make
repayment, repay, refund,
reimburse, retribute, make
compensation, (default,
defalcation, protest,
repudiation)

· **recognize**-*v* see, behold,
discern, perceive, have in
sight, descry, sight, make
out, discover, distinguish,
spy, witness, contemplate,

speculate, cast, (blind,
hoodwink, dazzle, screen
from sight)

recommend-v approval,
approbation, sanction,
advocacy, esteem,
estimation, good opinion,
admiration, appreciation,
regard, account,
popularity, credit, repute,
(reprehension, admonition)

reconcile-v forgiveness,
pardon, condonation,
grace, remission,
absolution, amnesty,
oblivion, indulgence,
reprieve, conciliation,
excuse, exonerate,
(revenge, ruthless,
avenging, retaliation, feud)

recovery-n restitution,
restoration, return,
reinvestment,
recuperation, rehabilitation,
reconstruction, reparation,
atonement, release,
regurgitate,
(dispossession, relapse,
deterioration, return,
retrogression, confiscate,
eviction)

rectify-v restoration,
renovation, revival, refresh,
renaissance, redress,
recovery, restitution, return
to original state, curable,
heal, repair, (deterioration,
relapse, retrograde,
recidivism)

redeem-v recover, retrieval,
replevin, salvage, trove,
find, foundling,
compensate, equate,

indemnity, compromise,
neutralization, nullification,
retaliation, equalize

reduce-v decrease,
diminish, lessen, abridge,
shorten, shrink, contract,
discount, depreciate,
extenuate, lower, weaken,
fritter away, subtract,
(increase, enlarge, extend,
augment, magnify, gain)

reek-v unclean, impurity,
defilement, contamination,
abomination, taint, decay,
corruption, mold, must,
mildew, dirty, filthy, grimy,
soiled, stink, rank, (clean,
immaculate, spotless,
neat, tidy, trim)

refinement-n improvement,
betterment, melioration,
amendment, mend,
advancement, cultivate,
reformation, correction,
elaboration, purification,
repair, (deterioration,
impairment, injury,
damage)

reflux-v recoil, refluent,
react, spring, rebound,
revulsion, ricochet,
elasticity, reflection,
reverberation, resonance,
boomerang, (impulse,
impetus, momentum, push,
thrust, hammer, punch)

refrain-v avoidance,
forbearance, inaction,
abstention, neutrality,
evasion, elusion,
seclusion, avocation, flight,
escape, retreat, recoil,
departure, (pursuit,

prosecution, enterprising, undertaking)

refresh-*v* restoration, rehabilitation, reproduce, renovation, revival, resuscitation, renaissance, second youth, rejuvenescence, new birth, regeneration, (relapse, fall back, retrograde, return)

regard-*v* view, look, espial, glance, point of view, see, behold, discern, perceive, descry, make out, discover, distinguish, recognize, contemplate, speculate, (blindness, undiscerning)

register-*v* digest, synopsis, compendium, table, analysis, classification, division, atlas, classify, methodize, regulate, systematize, coordinate, settle, fix, (litter, scatter, mix, entangle, ravel, dishevel)

regret-*v* self-reproach, penitence, contrition, compunction, repentance, remorse, self-accusation, be sorry for, confess, reclaimed, disclose, (induration, obduracy, impenitence, uncontrite, shiftless)

rehabilitate-*v* restore, reinstatement, renovation, revival, refreshment, renaissance, redress, retrieval, reclamation, recovery, convalescence, resumption, recuperate,

curative, remedial, recover

rehearse-*v* repetition, iteration, reiteration, harping, recurrence, succession, monotony, rhythm, chimes, imitation, reverberation, recur, reappear, renew, repeated, often, again, over again, ditto

reinforce-*v* aid, assist, help, appellation, support, lift, advance, furtherance, promotion, relief, sustenance, nutrition, ministry, accommodation, supply, (prevent, preclude, obstruct, stop, block)

rejoice-*v* bless, beatify, satisfy, gratify, desire, slake, satiate, quench, indulge, humor, flatter, regale, refreshing, comfortable, cordial, glad, cheering, exciting, (annoyance, grievance, nuisance, bother)

relax-*v* loose, incoherence, immiscibility, looseness, laxity, loosening, freedom, disjunction, slacken, detach, disheveled, segregated, unconsolidated

relentless-*adj* resolved, determined, strong-willed, resolute, self-possessed, decided, definitive, peremptory, obstinate, persevering, (fickleness, levity, weakness, demur, hesitating, vacillation)

relief-*n* aid, assist, oblige,

accommodate, humor,
cheer, encourage, rescue,
deliverance, refreshment,
easement, softening,
alleviation, mitigation,
palliation, soothing,
consolation, (aggravate,
embitter)

relish-*n* desire, wish, fancy,
want, need, exigency,
mind, inclination, bent,
longing, hankering, inkling,
solicitude, anxiety,
yearning, coveting,
aspiration, (indifference,
cold, frigid, halfhearted,
neutrality)

remarkable-*adj* paramount,
essential, vital, all-
absorbing, radical,
cardinal, chief, main,
prime, primary, principal,
leading, foremost, vital,
significant, emphatic,
(ordinary, petty, frivolous,
insignificant)

remiss-*adj* careless,
neglect, trifling, omission,
default, supineness,
reckless, inconsiderate,
slovenly, erroneous,
nonchalant, inactive,
abandoned, disorderly,
(care, heed, watchful,
exact, attentive, vigil)

remote-*adj* distant, far,
elongation, background,
removed, telescopic,
yonder, farther, further,
beyond, apart, asunder,
wide apart, (nearness,
nigh, close, adjacent,
intimate, adjoin)

remove-*v* extract,
elimination extrication,
eradication,evolution,
extermination, ejection,
egress, extirpation, export,
evolve, squeeze out,
(insertion, introduction,
insinuation, injection,
immersion)

render-*v* restitution, return,
restoration, reinvestment,
recuperation, rehabilitation,
reparation, release,
replevin, redemption,
remit, revert, (take, catch,
capture, seizure,
subtraction, reception)

renovate-*v* restore,
reinstate, cure, repair,
reparation, recruit,
disinfection, redemption,
deliverance, restitution,
relief, recover, return to
original state,
(deterioration, retrogress,
fall back, relapse)

repair-*v* improve, amend,
betterment, mend,
advancement, progress,
ascent, promotion,
elevation, increase, reform,
correct, refinement,
elaborate, (deteriorate,
impair, injure, damage,
loss, detriment)

repel-*v* depart, cessation,
removal, exit, egress,
valediction, farewell,
outward bound, repulsive,
abduction, chase, dispel,
(attract, magnetism,
gravity, draw, adduce)

replace-*v* substitute,

commutation, supplant,
supersession, make-shift,
alternative, supersede, in
lieu of, redeem, change,
equivalent, shift,
(exchange, reciprocation,
transposition, shuffling,
barter, swap)

report-v description,
account, statement,
expose, disclosure,
specification, particulars,
abstract, narrative, history,
memoir, memorials,
annals, chronicle, relate,
recount, descriptive

repose-v rest, sleep,
relaxation, breathing time,
halt, pause, respite,
unbend, slacken, lie down,
recline, unstrained,
cessation, vacation,
recess, holiday, (exertion,
effort, strain, tug, pull)

represent-v express,
exposition, demonstration,
exhibition, production,
display, showing,
indication, publicity,
disclosure, indicate,
manifest, proclaim,
(allusive, dormant, hidden,
invisible, imply, conceal)

repress-v restraint,
hindrance, coercion,
compulsion, repression,
discipline, control,
confinement, durance,
duress, imprison, restrict,
(liberate, disengage,
release, enlarge, dismiss)

reprieve-v forgive, pardon,
condonation, grace,

remission, absolution,
amnesty, oblivion,
indulgence, conciliation,
reconciliation, pacification,
excuse, exonerate,
(revenge, vindictive,
unforgiving, ruthless,
retaliation, rancorous)

repudiate-v dissent,
discordance,
disagreement, difference,
diversity of opinion, non-
conformity, protest,
contradiction, rejection,
demur, (ratification,
confirmation,
corroboration, approval)

require-v need, want,
necessary, essential,
indispensable, urgent,
requisition, exactness,
demanding, compel, force,
make, drive, coerce,
enforce, oblige, (depletion,
vacancy, low, empty,
insolvency)

rescind-v abrogation,
annulment, canceling,
repeal, dismiss, depose,
abolish, retraction, destroy,
ignore, repudiate,
reconsecrate, divest,
(commission, delegate,
assign, ensign, entrust)

resist-v refuse, reject,
denial, decline,
peremptory, repulse,
rebuff, discountenance,
protest, dissent,
revocation, disclaim,
(present, bid, propose,
move, advance, start,
invite)

resolute-*adj* determined, strong-willed, decided, definitive, peremptory, obstinate, steady, intense, serious, relentless, inflexible, persistent, stability, (vacillating, changeable, weak, fluctuate, hesitate)

resolve-*v* interpret, explain, define, construe, translate, render, find out, illustrate, exemplify, unfold, expound, comment upon, annotate, popularize, disentangle, (misrepresent, garble, distort)

respect-*n* courtesy, good manners, behavior, breeding, politeness, gentility, polish, presence, humor, humility, obeisance, (disrespect, rude, insult, repulsive, bitter, acrimonious, sarcastic)

respire-*v* breathe, puff, gasp, wheeze, snuff, sniff, sneeze, cough, fan, ventilate, blow-up, air pump, lungs, bellows, hiccup

response-*n* answer, reply, replication, rejoinder, rebut, retort, repartee, rescript, examination, acknowledgement, password, discover, solution, explanation, rationale, respond, (question, analysis, query, problem, exploration, review, exploitation, ventilation, sifting, search, inquire, calculation, analysis)

restless-*adj* disturbance, fidget, disquiet, agitation, unstable, vacillation, fluctuate, vicissitude, alteration, oscillation, unrest, agitation, (stable, stand, keep, remain firm, establish, settled, solid)

restore-*v* repair, reparation, recruit, reaction, redemption, restitution, relief, reconstruct, redeem, redress, resuscitate, renovate, renew, reestablish, (deteriorate, mutilate, disfigure, blemish, deface)

result-*n* conclusion, upshot, deduction, inference, corollary, estimation, valuation, appreciation, estimate, deduce, derive, gather, collect, settle, (discover, detect, find, determine, evolve)

retain-*v* retention, keep, detention, custody, tenacity, firm hold, grasp, gripe, grip, clinch, clench, secure, withhold, detain, hold, reserve, possess, entail, settle, (relinquish, abandon, dispense)

retire-*v* seclusion, privacy, reclusion, recess, snugness, sequestered, delitescent, hermit, estrangement, voluntary exile, solitude, isolation, loneliness, (social,

companionship,
comradeship, hospitality)

retort-v retaliation, reprisal,
retribution, reciprocation,
recrimination, accusation,
revenge, reaction, turn
upon

retreat-v regress,
retirement, withdrawal,
recede, counter-motion, remigration, recession,
recidivation, deterioration,
(progression, advance,
improvement, proceed,
forward, forth)

return-v succession,
revolve, pulsate, alternate,
intermit, steady, punctual,
arrive, disembark, advent,
reception, welcome,
recursion, remigration,
(departure, cessation,
removal, exit)

revenge-n vengeance,
avenged, rancor,
vindictiveness,
implacability, malevolence,
ruthlessness, unforgiving,
rankling, (forgiveness,
pardon, conciliate,
condone, acquit, pacify)

reverse-v contrary,
opposite, counter, differing,
diametrically opposed,
inverse, antipodal, against,
annulment, dismissal,
remission, abolish, retract,
recall, dissolve.
(inaugurate, accredit,
engage)

revolt-v resistance, stand,
front, oppugnant,
opposition, renitency,

reluctant, repulse, rebuff,
insurrection, against,
strong, obstinate,
stubborn, (retaliate, retort,
turn upon, reciprocate)

rich-adj sufficient,
adequate, enough,
satisfaction, competence,
ample, abundant, wealthy,
luxuriant, fertile, affluent,
pregnant, inexhaustible,
(insufficient, deficiency,
incomplete, shortcoming)

rid-v liberate, disengage,
release, free, disband,
discharge, unfetter, untie,
loose, relax, escape,
redeem, deliver, extricate,
emancipate, acquit,
escape, (confine, imprison,
repress, control, hinder)

riddle-n instrument for
sorting, sieve, screen,
arrange, dispose, place,
form, put, collocate, pack,
marshal, range, size, rank,
group, enigma, puzzle,
charade, maze, (news,
information, advice, word)

ride-v chase, give chase,
course, hunt, hound, tread,
rush upon, run, direct,
pursue, quest, follow,
prosecute, prowl, engage
in, endeavor, search,
(retreat, recoil, depart,
avoid, evade, seclude)

ridiculous-adj folly, frivolity,
irrationality, trifling,
ineptitude, negaters,
inconsistency, conceit,
giddiness, inattention,
eccentricity, absurd, idiotic,

imbecile, (wise, sapient,
reasonable, rational,
sensible)

rift-n fissure, breach, rent,
split, crack, slit, incision,
dissection, decomposition,
cutting instrument, sharp,
divorce, part, detach,
separate, rescind,
segregate, (attach, fix,
bind, secure, join, hinge)

right-n privilege, allow,
sanction, warrant,
authorize, ordain,
prescribe, constitute,
charter, enfranchise,
prescribe, presume,
absolute, indefeasible,
unalienable, merit,
(infringe, encroach)

rigid-adj obstinate,
tenacious, stubborn,
obdurate, case-hardened,
inflexible, hard,
immovable, inert, arbitrary,
dogmatic, positive,
bigoted, prejudiced,
(recant, retract, revoke,
rescind, recall, withdraw)

rile-v annoy, grieve,
nuisance, vexation, bore,
bother, blow, distressing,
afflicting, disheartening,
depressing, deplorable,
undesirable, causing pain,
haunt, (pleasant,
charming, fascinating)

ring-n resonance, loud,
clang, clatter, noise, roar,
uproar, racket, sonorous,
powerful, thundering, ear-
splitting, deafening,
(inaudible, scarcely, low,

dull, faint, soft, soothing,
melodious)

riot-n violence, row,
rumpus, inclemency,
vehemence, impetuosity,
boisterousness, rage,
ferocity, fury, exacerbation,
turbulent, disorderly,
uproarious, frenzied,
(tranquil, mild, reasonable,
cam, still)

ripen-v completion,
accomplish, achieve,
fulfillment, performance,
execution, dispatch,
consummation,
culmination, conclusion,
close, final, finished,
(incomplete, neglect,
undone)

rise-v ascend, grow, begin,
slope, progress, stir, revolt,
rocket, climb, clamber,
mount, aspire, tower, soar,
hover, spire, excelsior, up
hill, flight, (decline, fall,
drop, lapse, tumble, dip,
descend, sink)

risk-v danger, chance,
speculation, venture,
stake, blind bargain,
gamble, fate, hazard,
wager, game, accidental,
indiscriminate, random,
(decision, determination,
purpose, resolution)

ritual-n rite, ceremony,
observance, duty,
solemnity, sacrament,
service, worship, duty,
officiate, transfiguration,
consecration, ostentation,
showy, pretentious,

pompous, palatial,
theatrical, dramatic

rival-*n* competition, contest,
opposition, strive, struggle,
scramble, wrestle, spar,
square, exchange,
belligerent, combative,
unpeaceful, quarrelsome,
pugilistic, (harmony,
peace, concord, tranquil)

rivet-*v* attach, join, close,
tight, taut, taught, secure,
set, intervolved, hinge,
unite, connect, fix, bind,
tie, string, pin, nail, bolt,
hasp, clasp, fuse-together,
jam, (separate, rupture,
shatter, carve, cut)

roast-*v* heat, calefaction,
increase of temperature,
melt, burn, combustion,
ignition, warm, chafe,
stove, kindle, toast,
inflame, stew, cook,
seethe, simmer, (cool, fan,
refrigerate, refresh,
congeal)

robust-*adj* strong, mighty,
vigorous, forcible, hard,
adamantine, stout, sturdy,
hardy, powerful, potent,
puissant, valid, resistless,
invincible, impregnable,
able-bodied, (weak,
delicate, soft, limp, feeble)

rogue-*n* cheat, knave,
scamp, bad man, wrong-
doer, evil doer, sinner,
rascal, scoundrel, villain,
wretch, viper, serpent,
monster, devil incarnate,
(paragon, hero, demigod,
saint, benefactor, angel)

rollick-*v* cheerful, genial,
gaiety, good humor,
liveliness, vivacity,
animation, jovial, pleasing,
laughter, amusement,
rejoicing, smile, rejoice,
enliven, exhilarate,
(depressed, dejected,
gloom, weariness)

romantic-*adj*
impressionable, sensitive,
gushing, impassioned,
tender, warm, enthusiastic,
highflying, spirited,
mettlesome, vivacious,
lively, expressive,
excitable, (nonchalance,
unconcern, callousness)

room-*n* spacious, extensive,
expansive, capacious,
ample, wide-spread, vast,
world-wide,
uncircumscribed,
boundless, capacity,
stretch, absence

root-*n* base, basement,
plinth, dado, wainscot,
foundation, support,
substructure, substratum,
ground, earth, pavement,
floor, paving, flag, carpet,
fundamental, built-on,
(summit, apex, zenith,
pinnacle)

rose-*n* fragrant, aroma,
redolence, perfume,
bouquet, sweet, aromatic
perfume, sachet, scent,
spicy, balmy, muscadine,
ambrosial, fragrant as a
rose, (stench, stick,
unclean, offensive, rank)

rot-*v* deteriorate, debase,

wane, ebb, recess,
retrogradation, decrease,
degenerate, impairment,
injury, damage, loss,
detriment, outrage,
pollution, poison, (relieve,
refresh, infuse, reform,
enhance)

rotation-*n* periodically,
intermittent, beat,
oscillation, bout, round,
revolution, turn, cycle,
stated time, routine,
succession, return,
revolve, pulsate, alternate,
(uncertain, capricious,
flicker, ramble, spasmodic)

rough-*adj* uneven,
scabrous, knotted, gnarled,
unpolished, rugged, grain,
texture, ripple, corrugated,
ruffle, crisp, crumble,
(smooth, even, plane,
shave, level)

round-*adj* circle, rotund,
circlet, ring, areola, hoop,
roundlet, annulet, bracelet,
armlet, ringlet, eye, loop,
wheel, cycle, orb, orbit,
ellipse, oval, necklace,
collar, noose

rouse-*v* stimulate, excite,
inspirit, animate, incite,
provoke, instigate, induce,
move, prompt, attract,
beckon, bribe, lure, inspire,
encourage, solicit,
(discourage, dampen,
hinder, restraint, repel)

routine-*n* custom, habit,
rule, standing order,
precedent, red-tape, rut,
groove, usual, general

accustom, naturalize,
repeat, prevalent, vogue,
etiquette, order of the day,
(breached, spontaneous)

row-*v* discord,
disagreement, jar, clash,
shock, broil, brawl, racket,
hubbub, embroilment,
disturbance, commotion,
quarrel, dispute, embroil,
entangle, (harmony,
agreement, conciliation,
peace, accord)

rub-*v* friction, attrition,
rubbing, scratch, scrape,
scrub, fray, graze, curry,
scour, polish, rub out,
gnaw, file, grind, difficult,
hard, tough, laborious,
awkward, unwieldy,
(lubricate, smooth, pat,
gentle touch)

rude-*adj* graceless,
inelegant, harsh, abrupt,
dry, stiff, cramped, formal,
forced, labored, artificial,
mannered, ponderous,
turgid, affected, barbarous,
uncouth, (graceful, easy,
temperate, gentle)

ruin-*n* waste, destroy,
dissolution, breaking up,
consumption, fall, downfall,
perdition, crash, smash,
havoc, extinct, annihilation,
demolish, suppress,
abolish, ravage, devastate,
(rectify, flower, evolve)

rumple-*v* disorder,
derangement, confusion,
disarray, jumble, huddle,
litter, lumber, mash,
muddle, complex, intricate,

unsymmetrical,
unsystematic, untidy,
slovenly, (order, uniform,
symmetry, arranged)

runagate-*n* absence of
pursuit, abstention,
forbearance, refrain,
inaction, neutrality,
avoidance, evasion,
elusion, seclusion, flight,
escape, retreat, departure,
rejection, (pursuit, chase,
hunt, follow)

rush-*v* haste, urgency,
acceleration, spurt, spurt,
forced, march, dash,
velocity, precipitancy,
impetuosity, hurry, drive,
scramble, bustle, fuss,
fidget, flurry, (leisurely,
slow, deliberate, quiet,
calm)

rusty-*adj* moldy, musty,
mildewed, moth-eaten,
mucid, rancid, bad, gone
bad, touched, effete,
rotten, corrupt, tainted,
unclean, dirty, filthy, sooty,
turbid, (wash, clean, pure,
disinfect, neat)

ruthless-*adj* revenge,
vengeance, vendetta,
retaliation, rancor,
vindictiveness,
implacability, malevolence,
avenge, unrelenting,
rigorous, (forgive, pardon,
conciliation, reconciliation,
absolution)

S

sack-*n* bag, receptacle,
enclosure, recipient,
receiver, reservoir, sac,
knapsack, satchel, take,
catch, hook, gain, acquire,
procure, collect, assemble,
bring home, secure,
derive, draw

saintly-*adj* piety, religious,
holiness, sanctimony,
reverence, humility,
veneration, devotion,
prostration, worship, grace,
unction, edification,
consecration, spiritual
existence, (hypocrisy,
irreverence, sin)

salute-*v* respect, regard,
consideration, courtesy,
attention, deference,
reverence, honor, esteem,
estimation, veneration,
admiration, homage,
command, (dishonor,
desecrate, insult, affront,
outrage)

salvage-*v* get back,
recover, regain, retrieve,
replevy, redeem, come by
one's own, come by,
receive, inherit, succeed,
realize, treasure up, clear,
produce, (loss, incur, rid,
forfeit, lapse)

sanctify-*v* moral, ethical,
casuistical, conscientious,
amenable, liable,
accountable, responsible,
answerable, allegiance,
(exempt, release, acquit,
discharge, remise, remit,
free)

satiate-*v* satisfy, saturate,
replete, glut, surfeit,

weariness, cloy, quench,
slake, pall, gorge, tire,
enough, complete,
altogether, wholly, totally,
laden, (exhaustive, regular,
consummate, sheer)

saunter-v creep, ramble,
dawdle, drawl, slacken,
mincing steps, linger,
loiter, sluggard, tortoise,
snail, move slowly, crawl,
lag, plod, lumber, drag,
grovel, waddle, shuffle
(move quickly, speed,
hasten)

savage-adj cruel, brutal,
inhuman, barbarous, fell,
untamed, truculent,
incendiary, bloodthirsty,
murderous, atrocious,
fiendish, demoniacal,
diabolic, devilish,
(benevolent, consideration,
kind)

save-v economy, frugality,
thrift, care, husbandry,
retrenchment, prevention
of waste, parsimony,
sparing, invest, miserly,
tightfisted, mercenary,
venal, greedy, (liberal,
generous, charitable,
bounty)

say-v speech, locution, talk,
parlance, verbal
intercourse, oral
communication, spoken,
lingual, phonetic,
unwritten, eloquent,
talkative, mouthpiece,
language, (stammer,
stutter, falter, mumble)

scaffold-n support,

foundation, base, bearing,
footing, hold, place,
platform, block, rest,
sustentation, aid, prop,
stand, truss, stilt, staff,
shaft, pediment, (pendant,
hanging, dependent,
suspended, loose)

scatter-v dispersion,
disjunction, divergence,
dissemination, diffusion,
dissipation, distribution,
apportionment, spread,
sow, strew, dismember,
interspersion, (accumulate,
heap, lump, pile, stack)

scold-v execrate, beshrew,
anathematize, denounce,
execration, proscribe,
excommunicate, fulminate,
threaten, abuse, cross,
grumpy, glum, morose,
(hug, cuddle, address with
affection, serenade)

scourge-v rod, cane, stick,
switch, truncheon, ship,
last, strap, thong, cowhide,
pillory, stocks, whipping-
post, brank, triangle,
wooden horse,
thumbscrew, guillotine
(reward, satisfy,
compensate)

scratch-v mark, line, stroke,
dash, score, stripe, streak,
tick, dot, point, notch, nick,
asterisk, red letter, jotting,
print, imprint, note,
annotation, maltreat,
abuse, bruise, hurtful,
injurious

scruple-n probity, integrity,
rectitude, uprightness,

honesty, faith, honor, good
faith, purity, clean,
fairness, fidelity, loyalty,
trustworthiness, candor,
dignity, (dishonesty, moral
turpitude, disloyalty)

scrutiny-n attention,
mindfulness, intentness,
thought, observance,
consideration, reflection,
heed, notice, regard,
circumspection, study,
(abstract, absence,
preoccupation, reverie)

scuttle-n destroy, move
quickly, trip, fisk, speed,
hasten, accelerate,
quicken, whisk, bolt,
bound, scamper, run,
spank, scour, scamper, run
like mad, fly, race, (slow,
slack, tardy, gentle, easy,
leisurely)

secure-v hope, desire,
sanguine expectation,
trust, confidence, reliance,
faith, belief, affiance,
assurance, reassurance,
promise, well-grounded,
presumption, anticipation,
(despair, lose, desperate)

seduction-n desire, wish,
fancy, fantasy, want, need,
exigency, mind, inclination,
attraction, magnet,
allurement, temptation,
fascination, devotee,
solicitant, (indifferent, cold,
frigid, half-hearted)

see-v view, vision, sight,
optics, look, espial, glance,
ken, glimpse, peep, gaze,
stare, leer, point of view,

demonstrate, eye, field of
view, contemplation,
regard, survey, (close,
blind, shut, cataract)

seethe-v hot, glow, flush,
sweat, swelter, bask,
smoke, reek, stew,
simmer, boil, burn, broil,
blaze, flame, smolder,
parch, fume, pant, sunny,
torrid, tropical, estival,
canicular, sultry,
oppressive

seize-v reception, carry,
bear sway, abstract, hurry
off, abduct, steal, ravish,
size, pounce, spring upon,
swoop, assault, confiscate,
sequester, despoil,strip,
(restitution, return,
restoration, atonement)

send-v delegate, consign,
relegate, turn over to,
deliver, ship, embark, waft,
shunt, transpose, propel,
project, throw, fling, cast,
pitch, chuck, toss, jerk,
heave, shy, (draw, pull,
haul, lug, rake, drag, tug)

sensation-n pleasure,
bodily enjoyment, animal
gratification, luxuriousness,
dissipation, titillation,
gusto, comfort ease,
refreshment, voluptuous,
cozy, snug, agreeable,
(torment, torture, rack,
agonize)

senseless-adj absurd,
imbecility, nonsense,
paradox, inconsistency,
blunder, muddle, bull, slipslop, anticlimax, farce,

rhapsody, farrago, jargon,
fustian, twaddle, no
meaning, (wise,
perception, belief)

sensuous-*adj* feeling,
warmth, glow, unction,
gusto, fervor, heartiness,
cordiality, earnestness,
eagerness, ardor, zeal,
passion, enthusiasm,
blush, flush, penetrating,
absorbing, impetuous

sequence-*n* coming after,
going after, order,
following, consecutive,
succession, posteriority,
continuation, sequential,
alternate, latter, posterior,
subsequently, (litter,
scatter, confound, tangle)

service-*n* useful, utility,
efficacy, efficiency,
adequacy, use, stead,
avail, help, applicability,
subservience,
instrumentality, function,
value, worth, productive,
(worthless, inefficient,
unskillful)

settle-*v* pay, discharge,
clearance, liquidation,
satisfaction, reckoning,
arrangement,
reimbursement, retribution,
reward, expenditure,
defray, quit, acquit,
(repudiate, protest,
dishonor, nullify)

several-*adj* many,
numerous, multitude,
profusion, large,
enormous, array, scores,
bushel, majority,

multiplication, diverse,
various, populous, crowd,
manifold, (few, small,
handful, paltry, minority)

severe-*adj* strict, harsh,
rigor, stringent, austere,
inclemency, absolute,
tyrant, disciplinarian,
stickler, despot, hard
master, oppressor,
inquisitor, extortioner,
vulture, (moderate, lenient,
tolerant, mild, soft)

shabby-*adj* poor, paltry,
pitiful, contemptible, sorry,
meager, miserable,
wretched, vile, scrubby,
scrannel, weedy, scurvy,
putrid, beggarly, worthless,
cheap, trashy, (essential,
vital, prime, main)

shade-*n* cover, screen,
cloak, veil, shroud, screen
from sight, draw close,
curtain, eclipse, mask,
disguise, ensconce, muffle,
smother, whisper, conceal,
(enlighten, open, impart)

shake-*v* oscillate, vibrate,
liberate, nutation,
undulation, pulsation,
alternation, flow, flux,
wave, swing, beat, wag,
dance, lurch, dodge,
fluctuate, to and fro,
brandish, (steady, unfurl,
unfold, without motion)

shame-*n* disgrace,
dishonor, tarnish, stain,
discredit, degrade, debase,
defile, expel, punish,
stigmatize, vilify, defame,
slur, reprehend,

despicable, unworthy,
(worthy, glorification, hero,
elevate)

shape-*n* form, figure,
fashion, carve, cut, chisel,
hew, cast, sketch, block,
hammer, frame, stamp,
build, mold, contour,
phase, posture, attitude,
sculpt, type, (destroy,
shapeless, unformed,
deface, mutilate)

shield-*n* defend, protect,
guard, ward, preservation,
resistance, safeguard,
shelter, fortification, hold,
armed, screen, shroud,
fence, ward off, hinder,
asylum, (attack, invade,
outbreak, assault, siege)

shift-*v* deflect, divert, shunt,
wear, draw aside, crook,
warp, stray, straggle, sidle,
diverge, digress, drift,
wander, twist, meander,
veer, rove, adrift, yaw,
(direct, aligned, straight,
straightforward)

shock-*n* false expectation,
disappointment,
miscalculation, surprise,
sudden burst, thunderclap,
blow, wonder, bolt of the
blue, electrify, astonish,
abrupt, startling, (foresight,
anticipate, reckon, waiting)

shoot-*v* death blow,
finishing stroke, execution,
gallows, fast, speedy,
rapid, quick, fleet, nimble,
agile, expeditious, express,
active, swift, (slow,
languor, drawl, retard,

relax, slow, slack, tardy)

short-*adj* concise, brief,
terse, close, to the point,
exact, neat, compact,
laconic, curt, pithy,
trenchant, summary,
compendious, compress,
summarize, (amplify,
profuse, drawn out,
ramble)

shrewd-*adj* cunning, crafty,
subtle, sharp, diplomatic,
artful, skillful, feline,
profound, designing,
contriving, intriguing,
strategic, underhanded,
hidden, (free, outspoken,
direct, downright, candid)

shrivel-*v* reduce, lessen,
shrink, consume,
condense, compress,
compact, squeeze,
strangle, corrugate,
astringent, dwindle,
narrow, collapse,
deteriorate, (expand, swell,
wide, fat, bulbous)

shudder-*v* cold, shiver,
gooseflesh, quake, shake,
tremble, diddle, quiver,
chill, frigid, nipping,
piercing, icy, glacial, frosty,
freezing, wintry, bitter,
(sunny, torrid, tropical,
seethe, broil)

shut-*v* close, enclose,
surround, imprison, enfold,
buy, encase, enshrine,
confine, desist, stop, give
over, break, relinquish,
abandon, renounce,
defect, withdraw,
renounce, desert, forsake

sick-*adj* ill, disease, ailing, infirmity, seizure, stroke, atrophy, disorder, malady, sore, fever, ulcer, corruption, abscess. consumption, eruption, rash, (healthy, sound, vigor, staunch, robust)

siege-*n* attack, assault, assail, aggression, offense, incursion, invasion, outbreak, storming, obsession, bombardment, fire, volley, beset, besiege, beleaguer, (defend, forefend, shield, screen)

signal-*n* insignia, banner, flag, colors, streamer, standard, eagle, post, rocket, important, momentous, salient, prominent, memorable, stirring, eventful, (subordinate,inferior, respectable, tolerable)

simple-*adj* mere, sheer, stark, bare, faint, light, slight, scanty, limited, meager, insufficient, sparing, so-so, modest, tender, subtle, inappreciable, unimportant, (extraordinary, important)

sincere-*adj* veracity, truthful, frank, candor, honesty, fidelity, plain dealing, genuineness, scrupulous, honorable, pure, unfeigned, outspoken, undisguised, (sham, pretense, false, forgery)

sink-*v* plunge, dip, souse, duck, dive, plumb, submerge, douse, engulf, bottom, wallow, descent, decline, fall, drop, cadence, subsidence, tumble, (ascent, rise, mount, arise, aspire, climb, clamber)

situation-*n* circumstance, phase, position, posture, attitude, place, point, terms, regime, footing, standing, status, occasion, predicament, event, juncture

skepticism-*n* disbelieve, discredit, doubtful, uncertainty, misgiving, demur, distrust, suspicion, jealousy, qualm, refuse to believe, dissent, hesitate, (believe, confide, assured, positive, satisfied)

sketch-*n* picture, drawing, draught, draft, trace, copy, photograph, image, likeness, icon, portrait, representation, illustration, delineation, depict, personification, (misrepresent, distort, bad)

skim-*v* recapitulation, resume, review, abbreviation, contraction, shorten, compress, abridge, abstract, epitomize, summarize, run over, (dissertation, essay, theme, discourse, memoir)

skittish-*adj* cowardly, fearful, shy, timid, poor spirited, soft, effeminate,

weak-minded, weak,
cower, skulk, sneak, slink,
frightened, dastardly,
(dare, venture, bold,
affront, confront, aweless)

slender-adj thin, small,
trifling, narrow, close, fine,
thread-like, finespun,
taper, slim, slight-made,
scanty, emaciated, lean,
meager, delicate, gaunt,
skinny, (thick, broad, wide,
ample, extended)

slink-v retreat, turn-tail, fly,
desert, elope, scamper,
sneak, flip, steal away,
decamp, flit, abscond,
levant, skedaddle, escape,
abandon, depart, (pursue,
follow, quest, hunt, seek)

slippery-adj dangerous,
precarious, critical, ticklish,
tumble down, threatening,
ominous, alarming,
crumbling, waterlogged,
top-heavy, unsafe,
hazardous, (safe, secure,
sure, shelter)

slow-adj idle, drone, droll,
dawdle, mope, truant,
lounge, loaf, indolent, lazy,
slothful, lust, remiss, slack,
inert, torpid, sluggish,
languid, supine, heavy,
dull, leaden, listless, (fast,
hasten, lively, agile)

smash-v failure, blunder,
mistake, fault, omission,
miss, oversight, slip, trip,
stumble, claudication,
botchery, scrape, mess,
mishap, collapse, blow,
explosion, misfortune,

(fortunate, attain, secure)

smite-v maltreat, abuse, ill-
use, buffet, bruise, scratch,
maul, scourge, violent,
stab, pierce, outrace,
mischief, nocuous,
malignant, noxious,
injurious, deleterious,
(beneficial, valuable,
serviceable)

smother-v repress,
suppress, restrain, stifle,
hush, bury, sink, keep
from, withhold, reserve,
ignore, silence, hoodwink,
mystify, puzzle, deceive,
(set right, awaken,
overhear, understand)

snag-v hindrance,
obstruction, interruption,
blockade, obstacle,
impediment, knot, bar,
stile, barrier, shackle,
restrain, bolt, cramp,
hamper, (relief, rescue,
help, aid, assist, give a
hand)

sneak-v contemptible,
abject, mean, shabby,
little, paltry, dirty, scurvy,
scabby, groveling,
scrubby, rascally, low-
minded, corrupt, venal,
mongrel, dishonest,
(upright, honest, veracious,
honorable)

snub-v short, brevity,
abbreviated, curtailment,
retrench, cut short, scrimp,
chop up, hack, hew, clip,
dock, prune, shear, shave,
mow, crop, compact, (long,
span, streak, prolong)

sober-*adj* moderate, wise, sane, grave, temperate, abstinent, serious, sedate, staid, solemn, demure, grim, visage, rueful, wan, long-faced, disconsolate, forlorn, (cheerful, happy, smiling, blithe)

soft-*adj* pliable, flexible, sequacity, malleability, plasticity, flaccidity, laxity, clay, wax, butter, dough, pudding, cushion, pillow, feather-bed, mollify, mellow, relax, temper, mash, (hard, rigid, durable)

solace-*n* relief, deliverance, refreshment, easement, softening, alleviation, mitigation, palliation, soothing, consolation, comfort, encouragement, (aggravation, exasperation, embitter, sour)

solution-*n* interpretation, definition, explanation, answer, rationale, meaning, translation, rendering, key, secret, clue, illustration, literal, translate, render, define, (distort, misrepresent, question)

soothe-*v* relieve, moderation, tranquilize, assuage, appease, swag, lull, compose, still, calm, cool, quiet, hush, quell, sober, pacify, alleviate, (violent, impetuous, uproar, riot, ferocity, rage, fury, row)

sore-*adj* pain, suffering, dolor, ache, smart, shooting, twinge, twitch, gripe, headache, hurt, cut, discomfort, spasm, cramp, torture, rack, agonize, (refreshed, regale, relish, treat, comforting, cordial)

sorry-*adj* trifling, care, anxiety, solicitude, trouble, grieved, concern, distress, affliction, woe, bitterness, heartache, broken-hearted, tribulation, desolation, despair, anguish, (overjoyed, entranced, at ease)

sound-*n* stable, unchangeable, constancy, immobility, vitality, fixed, steadfast, firm, fast, steady, balanced, confirmed, valid, immovable, riveted, rooted, settled, (restless, agitated, fitful, spasmodic)

span-*n* length, from end to end, outstretched, lengthy, wiredrawn, stretch out, extend, reach, stretch, elongate, prolong, (cut, chop hack, hew, crop, shave, mow, reap, nip, foreshorten)

spasm-*n* transilience, jump, leap, plunge, jerk, start, explosion, throe, revulsion, storm, cramp, nightmare, convulsion, throb, agitation, pang, (comfort, sensuous, palatable, cozy, snug)

spatter-*v* unclean, dirty,

spot, smear, daub, blot,
blur, smudge, slobber,
slime, grime, contaminate,
taint, leaven, corrupt,
sooty, smoky, thick, turbid,
(clean, rinse, wring, flush,
full, wipe, mop, sponge)

special-*adj* individual,
particular, peculiar,
specific, proper, personal,
original, private,
respective, definite,
determinate, certain,
esoteric, (general,
universal, impersonal,
miscellaneous)

speculate-*v* supposition,
assumption, postulation,
condition, hypothesis,
postulate, theory, proposal,
suggestion, surmise,
chance, venture, stake,
(decision, determination,
design, ambition,
intentional)

spicy-*adj* fragrant, aromatic,
redolent, balmy, scented,
sweet-smelling, perfumed,
thuriferous, muscadine,
ambrosial, (smell, odor,
stench, stink, rancid,
unclean, skunk, bad smell,
foul)

spiritless-*adj* dejected,
depressed, prostration,
lowness, oppression,
gloom, weariness, disgust
of life, melancholy, sad,
dismal, doldrums, vapor,
despondent, (cheerful,
amusing, hilarity, happy,
glad)

splendor-*n* form, elegance,
grace, beauty, unadorned,
symmetry, comeliness,
fairness, polish, gloss,
good effect, bloom,
brilliancy, radiance,
gorgeous, magnificent,
(ugly, deformed,
disfigured)

split-*v* divide, sunder, sever,
abscind, cut, saw, snip,
nib, nip, cleave, rend, slit,
splinter, chip, crack, snap,
break, tear, burst, rend,
rupture, lacerate, mangle,
gash, (join, unite, attach,
affix, bind, secure)

spout-*n* running water, jet,
spurt, squirt, splash, rush,
gush, stream, course, flow,
profluent, spring, overflow,
pour out, discharge,
shower down, drench,
(ingress, entrance, influx,
import, insert)

spread-*v* disperse, scatter,
sow, disseminate, diffuse,
shed, overspread,
dispense, disband,
disembody, dismember,
distribute, strew, straw,
cast, (assemble, collect,
locate, compile, levy)

spring-*v* hurry, hasten,
accelerate, leap, jump,
hop, bound, vault,
saltation, dance, caper,
curvet, caracole, capriole,
demivolt, buck, trip, bob,
bounce, flounce, start,
(plunge, dip, souse, duck,
dive)

sprout-*v* expand, grow,
offspring, posterity,

progeny, breed, issue,
brook, litter, seed, furrow,
spawn, family,
grandchildren, child, son,
daughter, shoot, olive
branch, spirit, descendant,
heir, heredity

squat-v place, situate,
locate, localize, put, lay,
set, perch, hive, bivouac,
burrow, encamp, establish,
reposit, cradle, moor,
tether, imbed, inhabit,
settle, abode, (displace,
eject, exile, abnegate,
remove)

staff-n director, manager,
governor, rector,
comptroller, supervisor,
intendant, attendant,
squire, usher, page,
servant, footman, flunky,
valet, orderly, messenger,
herdsman, maid,
housekeeper

stagger-v disincline,
indispose, shake,
discourage, deter, hold,
restrain, repel, turn aside,
deviation, chill, blunt, calm,
quiet, quench, deprecate,
dissuade, (stimulate,
inspirit, arouse, animate,
incite)

stand-v exist, behave,
subsist, live, breathe,
obtain, occur, event, have
place, prevail, find oneself,
vegetate, real, actual,
positive, absolute,
substantial, (perish,
annihilated, extinct,
exhausted, gone)

stare-v take an interest,
gape, prick up the ears,
see sights, lionize, pry,
curious, inquisitive, burning
with curiosity, curiosity,
inquiring mind,
(indifference, impassive,
have no curiosity)

start-v begin,
commencement, open,
outset, incipience,
inception, introduction,
initial, inauguration, rising
of the curtain, origin,
source, rudiment, genesis,
(end, close, terminate,
conclude, finale, edge)

state-n condition,
affirmation, statement,
allegation, assertion,
predication, declaration,
work, averment, remark,
observation, position,
certify, (contradictory,
deny, dispute, impugn,
repudiate)

station-n rank, standing,
brevet rank, precedence,
place, position, status,
order, degree, condition,
greatness, eminence,
height, importance,
primacy, dedication,
(disconcert, humble,
disgraced)

stay-v prolong, defer, delay,
lay over, suspend, shift,
waive, retard, remand,
postpone, adjourn,
procrastinate, dally,
protract, lengthen-out,
temporize, linger, loiter,
(premature, early)

steel-*n* strong, mighty, vigorous, forcible, hard, adamantine, stout, robust, sturdy, hardy, powerful, resistless, impregnable, sovereign, valid, potent, (frail, fragile, shatter, flimsy, unsubstantial, feeble)

step-*n* pace, rate, tread, stride, gait, port, cadence, carriage, velocity, angular velocity, progress, locomotion, journey, voyage, transit, nomadic, motor, erratic, (remain, stay, stand, ride, pause, rest)

stereotype-*n* indication, mark, note, stamp, earmark, label, ticket, docket, dot, spot, score, dash, trace, chalk, print, imprint, engrave, symbolize, typify, represent

stiff-*adj* rigid, hard, stubborn, firm, starched, stark, unbending, unlimber, unyielding, inflexible, tense, indurate, gritty, proof, petrify, crystallization, (soft, pliable, flexible, relax, tender, supple, pliant)

stimulate-*v* excite, provoke, arouse, inspirit, animate, incite, instigate, actuate, encourage, influence, sway, incline, persuade, overcome, engage, invite, procure, (discourage, dampen, hinder, repel)

stock-*v* accumulate, amass, hoard, fund, garner, save, reserve, keep, deposit, stow, stack, load, harvest, heap, collect, preserve, conserve, (spend, expend, use, consume, swallow up)

stoop-*v* low-minded, disgrace, dishonor, demean, degrade, derogate, grovel, sneak, lose caste, sell oneself, dishonest, unscrupulous, fraudulent, (scrupulous, respectful, reputable, candid)

story-*n* narrative, history, memoir, memorials, annals, chronicle, tradition, legend, tale, journal, life, adventures, experiences, confessions, anecdote, work of fiction

stow-*v* place, situate, locate, localize, put, lay, set, seat, station, lodge, quarter, post, install, house, establish, fix, pin, root, graft, plant, insert, (displace, exile, transposition, remove, transfer, banish)

straggle-*v* deviate, stray, sidle, diverge, digress, wander, wind, twist, meander, veer, ramble, rove, drift, adrift, step aside, scent, shift, shunt, wear, draw aside, crook, warp, (align, level, toward)

straight-*adj* rectilinear, direct, even, right, true, in a line, unbent, undeviating,

inflexible, align, (deviating,
errant, desultory, rambling,
stray, curved, arch)

strange-*adj* exceptional,
abnormal, irregular,
arbitrary, informal,
wandering, eccentric,
unusual, uncommon,
remarkable, noteworthy,
monstrous, wonderful,
unexpected, (typical,
normal, ordinary)

streak-*n* variegated,
iridescence, play of colors,
spottiness, spectrum,
rainbow, stripe, speckle,
sprinkle, stipple, maculate,
dot, tattoo, inlay,
polychromatic

stress-*n* labor, work, toil,
travail, manual labor,
exertion, effort, strain,
trouble, operoseness,
drudgery, slavery, flagging,
hammering, hardworking,
strenuous, (repose, rest,
sleep, relax, unbend,
slacken)

strict-*adj* exact, accurate,
definite, precise, well
defined, just right, correct,
close, rigorous, religiously,
punctual, mathematical,
faithful, constant,
authentic, (erroneous,
untrue, false, fallacious,
unsound)

strive-*v* endeavor, attempt,
speculation, probation,
experiment, tempt,
attempt, venture,
adventure,try hard, push,
exertion, contend, contest,

(tranquil, calm, peaceable,
harmony)

stronghold-*n* hold, asylum,
refuge, sanctuary, retreat,
fastness, keep, last resort,
ward, prison, covert,
shelter, screen, wing,
shield, umbrella, anchor,
(attack, assault, charge,
aggression)

strut-*v* ostentatious, showy,
dashing, pretentious,
jaunty, grand, pompous,
palatial, high-sounding,
splendid, magnificent,
sumptuous, theatrical,
gaudy, flaunt, (modest,
diffident, humble, timid,
bashful)

stumble-*v* tumble, trip,
titubate, lurch, pitch, swag,
topple, tilt, sprawl, plump
down, descend, fall, drop,
gravitate, slip, slide, settle,
decline, set, sink, (climb,
clamber, escalade,
surmount, tower, soar)

style-*n* tone, tenor, state,
condition, category, estate,
lot, case, trim, mood,
pickle, plight, fashion, light,
complexion, character,
structure, format,
(inconsequential,
unconformity, unrelated)

sublime-*adj* height, altitude,
elevation, eminence, pitch,
loftiness, tallness, stature,
prominence, colossus,
giant, tower, soar, (low,
depressed, underlie, squat,
prostrate)

substance-*n* matter, body,

stuff, element, principle,
materialistic, object, article,
thing, something, tangible,
substantial, unspiritual,
sensible, physical,
(immaterial, spiritual,
disembodied, subjective)

subterfuge-*n* untruth,
evasion, white lie, juggle,
device, plot, maneuver,
strategy, artful dodge,
trickery, deception, shift,
intrigue, contriving,
artificial, (innocence,
candor, sincerity, honest,
guileless)

subvert-*v* destroy,
demolish, overthrow,
suppression, abolish,
sacrifice, ravage,
devastate, revolution,
incendiarism, deterioration,
ruin, dispel, (flower,
fructify, teem, build, raise,
edify, erect, establish)

succulent-*adj* eatable,
edible, esculent,
comestible, alimentary,
dietetic, culinary, nutritive,
potable, bibulous, tasteful,
delicacy, gusto, (rank,
tasteless, repulsive)

sudden-*adj* instantaneous,
abrupt, moment, second,
minute, momentary,
instant, hasty, lightning,
spur of the moment,
(perpetual, eternal,
everlasting, continual,
endless, ceaseless)

suggest-*v* advice, council,
recommendation,
advocacy, persuasion,

mention, acquaint, instruct,
inform, authorize, inform,
(conceal, suppress,
evasion, silence, mystery)

summary-*n* short, brief,
curt, compendious,
compact, concise, curtail,
squat, reduce, (long,
lengthy, outstretched,
prolong, extend)

sunshine-*n* shine, glow,
glitter, glisten, twinkle,
gleam, flare, glare, beam,
shimmer, glimmer, flicker,
sparkle, scintillate, flash,
glance, bright, reflect,
sunny, cloudless, meteoric,
phosphorescent

T

tackle-*v* undertake, engage,
embark, volunteer,
promise, contract, take
upon one's shoulders,
begin, fasten, tie, ligament,
strap, rigging, standing,
trace, harness, yoke,
bandage, brace, roller

tactic-*n* game, policy,
execution, manipulation,
treatment, campaign,
career life, course,
conduct, behavior,
carriage, demeanor,
manner, direction,
transact, execute,
dispatch, proceed

tale-*n* description, account,
statement, report,
specification, particulars,
summary of facts, catalog,
information, fable, parable,

apologue, narrative, novel, work of fiction, journal, recital, sketch

talk-*n* speech, locution, parlance, verbal intercourse, oral communication, word of mouth, oratory, elocution, rhetoric, recitation, formal speech, (stammer, hesitation, impediment, stutter, falter)

tame-*adj* domesticate, acclimatize, breed, tend, break in, train, cage, bridle, restrain, pastoral, bucolic, veterinary art, teach, instruct, edify, school, tutor, cram, (bewilder, uncertain, misinform, deceive, mislead

tangible-*adj* material, bodily, corporeal, physical, somatic, sensible, ponderable, palpable, substantial, objective, impersonal, neuter, unspiritual, (personal, subjective, spiritualize, disembody)

task-*n* exercise, curriculum, explanation, teach, instruct, edify, fatigue, weariness, yawning, drowsiness, lassitude, tiredness, exhaustion, sweat, faintness, (restore, refresh, revive, repair, relief)

tattler-*n* narrator, scandal-monger, tale-bearer, gossip, many-tongued, rumored, currently,

reported, glad tidings, eavesdrop, (observe, swear, hide, close mouthed)

tear-*v* separate, destroy, over-turn, nullify, annul, demolish, crumple up, sunder, divide, cut up, carve, dissect, pull, disintegrate, nip, nib, cleave, snap, break, (join secure, inseparable)

tease-*v* annoy, displease, incommode, discompose, trouble, disquiet, disturb, perplex, molest, tire, irk, vex, mortify, harass, harry, badger, persecute, harrow, (please, agreeable, amusement, charm, delight)

technical-*adj* artistic, scientific, businesslike, talent, ability, ingenuity, cleverness, endowed, skillful, experienced, efficient, qualified, handy, capable, smart, proficient, (stupidity, inexperienced, ignorant)

tell-*v* influence, weight, pressure, preponderence, prevalence, sway, predominance, ascendancy, dominance, reign, authority, (impotence, inertness, irrelevancy, uninfluential, unconducing)

temper-*n* pervading, penetrating, absorbing, strong, sharp, acute, cutting, piercing, incisive, caustic, violent, vehement, warm, rough, boisterous, rampant, (moderate, gentle, mild, cool, sober, calm)

tempt-*v* seduce, entice, allure, captivate, fascinate, bewitch, carry away, charm, conciliate, coax, lure, tantalize, cajole, deceive, bribe, influence, prompt, instigate, (dissuade, discourage, hinder)

tender-*adj* offer, proffer, present, bid, propose, move, advance, start, invite, hold out, put forward, overture, bribe, give, (refuse, reject, repulse, rebuff, deny, decline, nill, repudiate)

tendril-*n* filament, line, fiber, fibril, funicle, vein, hair, capillary, gossamer, wire, string, thread, packthread, twine, ribbon, splinter, yarn, hemp, jute, strand

tenor-*n* direction, bearing, course, set, drift, tendency, incidence, bending, trending, dip, tack, aim, collimation, steer, bend, trend, verge, incline, (deviation, swerve, digress, depart, aberration, sweep)

tenure-*n* possession, ownership, occupancy, monopoly, retention, sanction, authority, warranty, charter, permission, constitution,

security, claimant, appellant, (infringe, encroach, exact, relax)

term-*n* time, duration, period, stage, space, span, spell, season, era, limit, boundary, confine, frontier, word, vocabulary, name, nomenclature, verbal, literal

terrorist-*n* coward, poltroon, dastard, sneak, recreant, weak-minded, effeminacy, timidity, oppressor, tyrant, firebrand, incendiary, anarchist, destroyer, iconoclast, savage, (benefactor, savior, courage)

text-*n* copy, design, type, matter, subject, meaning, signify, convey, imply, breathe, indicate, bespeak, expressive, declaratory, (nonsense, jargon, gibberish, jabber, absurd, vague, balderdash, trash)

thankless-*adj* bitter, distasteful, uninviting, unwelcome, undesirable, obnoxious, unacceptable, unpopular, distressing, disheartening, depressing, (bless, beatify, satisfy, gratify, thankful, flatter)

thaw-*v* melt, liquefy, heat, dissolution, run, dissolve, resolve, fuse, burn, combustion, ignition, inflammation, roast, singe, incinerate, smelt, boil, (cool, refrigerate, refresh, congeal, freeze, chill)

thesis-n supposition, assumption, postulation, condition, hypothesis, postulate, theory, proposal, plan, association of ideas, topic, proposition, (perception, image, sentiment, reflection, abstract idea)

thick-adj dense, solid, impenetrable, cohesion, constipation, consistence, condense, substantial, lump, massive, (rarefy, expand, dilate, subtilize, sponginess, thin, fine, flimsy, slight)

thin-adj insufficient, inadequate, deficiency, imperfection, scarcity, want, need, lack, scanty, small, stingy, meager, poor, spare, starve, stricken, (sufficient, ample, abundant, enough, adequate, full)

thorn-n point, spike, spine, needle, pin, prick, spur, rowel, barb, spit, cusp, horn, antler, snag, tag, bristle, nib, tooth, tusk, spoke, cog, ratchet, barbed, spurred, (blunt, obtund, dull)

thoughtless-adj negligent, omission, careless, inattentive, nonchalance, insensibility, heedless, remiss, perfunctory, unmindful, inconsiderate, (careful, regardful, prudent, considerate, provident, cautious)

thread-n pass, perforate, penetrate, permeate, enfilade, traverse, journey, worm, passage, wire, string, slip, strip, filament, line, fiber, splinter, ribbon, soft, fragile, inactivity

threaten-v inspiring fear, alarming, formidable, perilous, danger, portentous, fearful, dread, shocking, terrible, horrid, ghastly, revolting, awful, terrorize, startle, (hopeful, confident, secure, enthusiastic)

threshold-n beginning, entry, inlet, orifice, mouth, portal, portico, door, gate, vestibule, border, edge, commence, rise, arise, conceive, initiate, open, dawn, (end, close, terminate, conclude, finale, finish)

thrill-n provoke, summon, raise, rouse, arouse, stir, fire, kindle, inflame, excite, stimulate, inspire, infect, agitate, passion, stun, astound, electrify, galvanize, (insensible, disregard, neglect, unaffected)

throw-n fling, toss, discharge, shy, propel, project, cast, pitch, chuck, jerk, heave, hurl, dart, lance, tilt, ejaculate, send forth, expel, shot, (draw, drag, tug, tow, trail, train, pull together)

tickle-v please, cause

pleasure, delight, gladden,
make cheerful, captivate,
fascinate, enchant,
entrance, enrapture,
regale, amuse, stimulate,
excite, (irritate, annoy,
grieve, vex, displease)

tidy-adj orderly, regularity,
uniformity, symmetry,
methodically, ship shape,
routine, arrangement,
array, series, neat,
spruced, primp, prepared,
classified, (disorderly,
derange, ruffle, untidy,
shapeless)

tight-adj firm, fast, joined,
close, taut, secure, set,
intervolved, drunk, tipsy,
intoxicated, inebriation,
mellow, groggy, (sobriety,
teetotaler, water-drinker,
separate, scission, loose)

tilt-v obliquity, incline, slope,
slant, crooked, leaning,
bevel, bias, list, twist,
swag, cant, lurch,
distorted, bend,
recumbent, skew, (parallel,
coextension, alongside,
straight)

timid-adj modest, humble,
diffident, timorous, bashful,
shy, nervous, skittish, coy,
sheepish, shamefaced,
blushing, reserved,
constrained, demure,
quiet, private, (self-
satisfied, airs, pretentious)

tinsel-n luster, sheen,
shimmer, reflection, gloss,
spangle, brightness,
brilliancy, splendor, lucid,

illuminate, shine, glow,
glimmer, sparkle, dazzle,
(dark, dim, dingy, gloomy,
shady, obscure, black)

title-n name, style, baptism,
appellation, designation,
surname, description, call,
term, denominate, entitle,
christen, characterize,
specify, distinguish, label,
(anonymous, nameless,
misnomer, pseudonym,
alias, nickname)

tolerate-v lenient, mild,
gentle, soft, indulgent,
easy-going, clement,
compassion, forbearing,
favor, moderation,
merciful, spoil, (severe,
strict, harsh, domineer,
rigid, stern, rigorous,
uncompromising)

tone-n state, condition,
category, estate, lot, case,
trim, mood, pickle, plight,
temper, aspect,
appearance, tenor, turn,
guise, fashion, light,
complexion, style,
character, (circumstantial)

tonic-n remedy, help,
redress, antidote,
prophylactic, antiseptic,
corrective, restorative,
sedative, cure, physic,
medicine, potion, salve,
ointment, (poison, leaven,
virus, venom, arsenic,
fungus, rot, canker)

tool-n instrument, organ,
implement, utensil,
machine, engine, lathe,
gin, mill, gear, tackle,

apparatus, appliance,
equipment, harness,
hammer, fittings

top-*n* supreme, superior,
major, greatest, higher,
exceed, distinguished,
vault, important, first-rate,
excellent, unparalleled,
culmination, foremost,
(inferior, smaller, bottom
diminish, short-coming)

topple-*v* unbalanced,
unequal, difference,
uneven, countervail,
disparate, over-balanced,
top-heavy, lop-sided,
inferior, (equal, matched,
reach, balanced, equate,
adjust, accommodate,
level)

torture-*v* punish, chastise,
castigate, cruelty, brutality,
savagery, ferocity,
barbarity, inhumanity,
vivisection, outrage,
persecution, atrocity,
(benevolent, kind, well-
meaning, amiable,
obliging)

total-*n* complete,
integration, entirety,
perfection, entire, whole,
full, thorough, plenary,
undivided, altogether,
beginning to end,
saturated, limit, sufficient,
(deficient, shortcoming,
omit, incomplete)

totter-*v* fluctuate, vary,
waver, flounder, flicker,
flitter, flit, flutter, shift,
shuffle, shake, tremble,
vacillate, wamble, sway,

oscillate, changing,
alternating, mobile, (fixed,
steadfast, firm, immovable,
tethered)

touch-*v* contact, abutment,
osculation, meet, close,
adjoin, graze, coincide,
coexist, adhere, deed, act,
overt act, gesture,
transaction, job, maneuver,
(remote, distant, far off,
away, apart, asunder)

tower-*n* pillar, column,
obelisk, monument,
steeple, spire, minaret,
campaniles, turret, dome,
cupola, pole, pikestaff,
maypole, flagstaff,
mountain, height, (low,
depress, concave, lowland,
underlie)

trace-*v* discover, recognize,
realize, verify, make
certain of, identify, get at,
solve, resolve, unriddle,
unravel, interpret, disclose,
unearth, (obliterate,
extinct, no trace of,
deletion)

trade-*n* commerce, buying
and selling, bargain, sale,
traffic, business, custom,
shopping, commercial
enterprise, speculation,
jobbing, dealing,
transaction, negotiate

tradition-*n* old, ancient,
antique, maturity,
prescription, prime,
primitive, customary,
immemorial, old-fashioned,
time honored, long
standing, (new, novel,

recent, fresh, green, young, immature, late)

train-v prepare, make ready, educate, novitiate, cultivate, mature, evolve, pioneer, instruct, edify, tutor, direct, guide, qualify, drill, practice, explain, lecture, task, school, (deceive, conceal, misrepresent)

trample-v destroy, waste, dissolve, break-up, consume, disorganize, fall, downfall, ruin, crash, smash, annihilation, demolish, ravage, devastate, (produce, perform, operate, construct, fabricate)

tranquil-adj calm, moderate, relax, remission, mitigation, gentleness, sedative, assuage, appease, swag, lull, soothe, compose, still, cool, quiet, hush, quell, sober, (fury, dragon, demon, tiger, violent)

transcendent-adj super-excellence, goodness, superiority, perfect, complete, immaculate, spotless, unblemished, sound, scathless, intact, harmless, paragon, (indifferent, middling, secondary)

transport-v ship, tender, transit, remove, displace, relegation, deportation, conveyance, draft, carriage, transition, send, delegate, consign, relegate, (hold, store, retain, keep, preserve)

transpose-v exchange, interchange, reciprocate, shuffle, castling, barter, retaliate, commute, mutual, communicative, intercurrent, (substitute, supplant, supersede, instead of, redeem, equivalent)

trash-n useless, inefficacy, futile, inaptitude, inadequate, insufficient, unskillfulness, unproductive, litter, rubbish, lumber, refuse, rubble, (useful, value, worth, fruitful, serviceable, prolific)

travesty-n imitate, mock, mimic, ape, simulate, impersonate, act, represent, counterfeit, parody, caricature, burlesque, plagiarism, forgery, echo, duplication, repeat, (originality, unique)

tremor-n agitation, stir, shake, ripple, jog, jolt, jar, jerk, shock, succussion, trepidation, quiver, quaver, disquiet, perturbation, commotion, turmoil, turbulence, fuss, racket, fits, (calm, quiet, disentangle)

trenchant-adj strong, energetic, forcible, active, intense, deep-dyed, severe, keen, vivid, sharp, acute, incisive, brisk,

rousing, irritating, poignant,
caustic, corrosive, (inert,
inactive, passive, torpid,
dull)

trespass-*v* transgression,
infringement,
transcendence,
redundance, surpass, go
beyond, over-step, exceed,
surmount, encroach,
infringe, (default, collapse,
extricate, eliminate)

tribute-*n* observe,
respectful, deferential,
decorous, obsequious,
regard, revere, venerate,
worship, duty, devotion,
salute, inspire, impose,
dazzle, (ridicule,
disrespectful, irreverent,
disparaging)

trickle-*v* ooze, emerge,
emanate, issue, pass, pour
out, pass off, evacuate,
spout, gush, dribble,
perspire, vent, filter, filtrate,
distill, discharge,
extravagate, (absorb,
ingest, inhale, swallow,
engulf)

trim-*v* equalize, match,
balance, cope with, dress,
adjust, poise, fit,
accommodate, adapt,
establish equality, readjust,
co-ordinate, (unequal,
countervail, advantage,
disparate, partial, over
balanced)

trip-*n* journey, excursion,
expedition, tour, grand
tour, circuit, peregrination,
discursion, ramble,

pilgrimage, course,
ambulation, march, walk,
promenade, constitutional,
(rest, pause, lull, bivouac)

trouble-*n* difficulty, irksome,
laborious, arduous,
awkward, unwieldy,
unmanageable,
impossible, complicated,
impracticable, hopeless,
embarrassing, perplexing,
(easy, facilitate, smooth,
submissive)

true-*adv* verity, gospel,
authentic, veracity,
accuracy, exactness,
precise, delicacy, rigor,
mathematical, punctuality,
plain, honest, sober,
naked, real, actual,
(mistake, fault, blunder,
error, fallacy, untrue)

trump-*n* perfect, faultless,
immaculate, spotless,
impeccable, sound,
superior, transcendence,
model, best, inimitable,
paragon, superhuman,
divine, (bearable,
imperfect, below par,
indifferent)

trunk-*n* house, stem, tree,
stock, stirps, pedigree,
lineage, line, family, tribe,
sect, race, clan,
genealogy, descent,
extraction, birth, ancestry,
forefathers, patriarchs

truss-*n* support, aid, prop,
stand, anvil, stay, shore,
skid, rib, bandage, sleeper,
stirrup, stilts, shoe, sole,
heel, splint, outrigger,

(suspend, hang, sling,
hook up, hitch, fasten to,
append)

trust-*n* believe, credit, give
faith, credence, esteem,
confide, certain, sure,
assured, positive,
unhesitating, convinced,
accredited, persuasive,
impressive, (disputable,
uncertain, unworthy)

try-*v* experiment, endeavor,
tempt, attempt, venture,
adventure, speculate,
tempt fortune, assay,
contend, contest, strive,
struggle, scramble,
wrangle

tube-*n* channel, passage,
way, path, pipe, vessel,
tubule, canal, gut, fistula,
chimney, flue, tap, funnel,
gully, tunnel, shaft, alley,
mine, (closure, occlusion,
blockade, obstruction)

tug-*v* effort, exertion, strain,
pull, stress, throw, stretch,
struggle, spell, spurt,
labor, work, toil, travail,
drudgery, trouble, pains,
duty, exert, strive, (repose,
rest, slacken, inactive,
recline, halt, pause)

tumble-*v* trip, stumble,
titubate, lurch, pitch, swag,
topple, tilt, sprawl, plump,
descend, dismount, alight,
swoop, stoop, titubation,
drop, (climb, clamber,
surmount, scale, tower,
soar, hover, spire)

tumultuous-*adj* violent,
inclemency, vehemence,

might, impetuosity,
boisterousness,
effervescence, turbulence,
severity, ferocity, rage,
fury, exacerbation, strain,
(moderation, relaxation,
tranquilize)

turbulence-*n* disquiet,
perturbation, commotion,
turmoil, tumult, hubbub,
rout, bustle, fuss, racket,
spasm, throe, throb,
palpitation, convulsion,
disturbance, disorder,
restlessness

turgid-*adj* expanded,
increase, enlarge,
extension, augmentation,
amplification, spread,
increment, growth,
development, pullulating,
dilatation, inflation,
(condense, lessen, shrink,
collapse, atrophy)

turn-*v* rotate, revolution,
gyration, circulation,
convolution, whir, vortex,
whirlpool, whirligig, roll,
axis, axle, spindle, pivot,
mandrel, swivel, (vibration,
alternation, up and down,
fluctuation)

turpitude-*n* dishonor,
disgrace, shame,
humiliation, scandal,
baseness, vileness,
improbity, infamy, tarnish,
taint, defilement, pollution,
stain, blot, blur, (elevate,
ascent, dignify,
consecrate, enthrone)

turret-*n* tower, pillar,
column, obelisk,

monument, steeple, spire,
minaret, dome, cupola,
pole, pikestaff, maypole,
flagstaff, top, mast,
skyscraper, (low, debased,
underneath, below, flat,
level)

tutelage-n safe-conduct,
escort, convoy, guard,
shield, defense, guardian
angel, deity, protector,
warden, preserver,
custodian, chaperon,
sentinel, sentry, (danger,
peril, insecurity, jeopardy,
risk)

twaddle-v absurd, jargon,
fustian, exaggeration,
moonshine, stuff, vagary,
tomfoolery, mummery,
nonsensical, preposterous,
egregious, senseless,
quibbling, punning, foolish

twist-v distort, contort,
warp, writhe, deform,
misshape, contortion,
crooked, grimace,
irregular, unsymmetrical,
grotesque, deformed,
misbegotten, (symmetrical,
shapely, uniform, classic,
uniform)

twitch-v traction, draw,
draught, pull, haul, rake,
tow, haulage, lug, trail,
train, take in tow, wrench,
jerk, tousle, tactile, (dart,
propel, project, throw, fling,
cast, pitch, discharge, bolt,
shoot)

type-n form, figure, shape,
conformation, make,
formation, frame,

construction, cut, set,
build, trim, stamp, cast,
mold, fashion, contour,
outline, structure, feature,
lineament, posture, attitude

tyranny-n assume, usurp,
arrogate, domineer, bully,
inflict, wreak, sever, strict,
hard, harsh, rigid, stiff,
stern, rigorous,
uncompromising, (lenient,
tolerant, mild, indulgent,
clement, compassionate,
forbearing)

U

ugly-adj deformity,
inelegance, disfigured,
blemish, squalor, eyesore,
frightful, hideous, odious,
uncanny, forbidding,
repellent, repulsive,
shocking, (form, elegance,
grace, beauty, gorgeous)

ulterior-adj
extraneousness,
extrinsically, foreign, alien,
strange, ultramontane,
excluded, inadmissible,
exceptional, (component,
integral, element,
constituent, ingredient)

ultimatum-n decision,
determination, resolve,
purpose, resolution, with
motive, settled, intent,
undertaking,
predetermination, design,
ambition, (speculation,
venture, stake, gamble,
chance)

unabashed-adj bold,

spirited, daring, audacious,
fear, daunt, dread,
aweless, undaunted,
enterprising, adventurous,
ventures, dashing,
chivalrous, soldierly, fierce,
(courage, bravery, valor,
resolute)

unadorned-adj simple,
plain, homely, ordinary,
unaffected, chaste, severe,
ungarnished, disarrange,
untrimmed, unvarnished,
bald, flat, dull,
(ornamented, beautified,
ornate, rich, gilt)

unanswerable-adv
categorical, decisive,
crucial, demonstrated,
proven, deducible,
consequential, inferential,
following, established,
verify, (refutation, answer,
disproof, conviction,
invalidation)

unassisted-adv encumber,
stop, prevent, load,
burden, lumber, pack,
difficulty, dampen,
obstruct, stay, bar, bolt,
unaided, hinder, block,
impede, (assist, aid,
rescue, help, contribute,
furnish, relief)

unaware-adv uninformed,
ignore, unexplored,
unknown, blind,
unconsciousness, shallow,
superficial, (aware,
cognizant, conscious of,
acquainted, versed,
learned, instructed,
proficient)

unblushing-adj dignity, self-
respect, pride,
haughtiness, vainglory,
arrogance, supercilious,
disdainful, bumptious,
magisterial, imperious,
overweening,
consequential, (humble,
lowly, meek, modest)

unborn-adv non-existence,
absence, abeyance, nullity,
negative, annihilation,
extinction, destruction,
abrogate, uncreated,
perished, exhausted, gone,
lost, departed, (real,
actual, positive, absolute)

uncertain-adv incertitude,
doubt, dubiety, hesitation,
suspense, perplexity,
embarrassment, dilemma,
bewilderment, timidity,
fear, vacillation,
indetermination, vague,
obscure, (certain, unerring,
infallible)

unclog-adv liberate,
disengage, release,
enlarge, emancipate,
enfranchise, discharge,
dismiss, deliver, redeem,
extricate, acquit, absolve,
set free, unfetter, untie,
(confine, restraint, hinder,
repress)

uncommendable-adj
dispraise, disapprobation,
censure, obloquy, detract,
condemnation, ostracize,
criticism, sarcasm,
insinuation, innuendo,
poor, (approval, sanction,
advocacy, applause)

uncomplying-*adj* refuse,
reject, deny, decline, nill,
negative, discountenance,
recusancy, abnegation,
protest, disclaimer,
dissent, revocation,
unconsenting, (offer,
present, tender, advance,
invite, bid)

unconditional-*adj*
unrestricted, unlimited,
absolute, discretionary,
unassailed, unforced,
unbiased, spontaneous,
free, autonomous,
unclaimed, (dependence,
employ, constraint, liability)

unconscious-*adj*
insensible, impassive,
blind to, unimpressionable,
unfeeling, apathetic,
phlegmatic, dull, frigid,
cold, obtuse, inert, torpid,
sluggish, inactive, languid,
(sentimental, sensible,
romantic)

uncouth-*adj* bad taste,
vulgar, awkward, coarse,
indecorum, misbehavior,
low life, boorishness,
gaudy, unkempt,
unpolished, incondite,
rude, outlandish, (tasteful,
pure, chaste, classical,
artistic)

uncover-*v* divulge, reveal,
break, split, utter, blab,
acknowledge, allow,
concede, grant, admit,
own, avow, disclose,
transpire, confess, visible,
(ambush, hide, mask,
disguise, masquerade)

under-*v* low, underneath,
below, down, neap,
crouched, squat, prostrate,
horizontal, depress,
concave, molehill,
underlie, wallow, (high,
elevated, eminent, exalted,
tall, gigantic)

underhand-*adj* reticence,
reserve, mental,
suppression, evasion,
white lie, silence,
misprision, secretive,
seclusion, hidden, sneak,
skulk, prowl, (inform,
enlighten, acquaint,
communicate)

undermine-*v* cunning,
crafty, artful, skillful, subtle,
feline, profound, contriving,
intriguing, strategic,
diplomatic, artificial,
insidious, stealthy, hidden,
underhand, (free, plain,
outspoken, blunt, direct)

understand-*v* knowledge,
acquaintance, insight,
familiarity, apprehension,
recognition, appreciation,
intuition, perception,
enlightenment, impression,
philosophy, (ignorance,
bewilder, uncertain)

underwrite-*v* execute,
stamp, sign, seal,
evidence, grant, lease,
hold in pledge, security,
acceptance,
authentication, verification,
warrant, certificate,
voucher, docket, record,
discharge, release

undone-*v* lost, ruined,

broken, bankrupt, dead
beat, destroy, frustrated,
crossed, unhinged,
disconcerted, dashed,
unattained, uncompleted,
(succeed, prosper,
triumphant, flushed, well
spent)

unearthed-*v* exhume,
disinter, autopsy,
examination, inhume, lay
out, mummify, look,
inquire, peer, hunt, leave
no stone unturned, seek,
search, explore, rummage,
ransack, (answer, reply,
respond)

unerring-*adj* unblamed,
blameless, above
suspicion, irreproachable,
venial, harmless, pure,
virtuous, innocent, model,
paragon, perfection,
impeccable, (guilt,
misbehave, sinful, fault,
failure, atrocity)

uneven-*adj* diverse, varied,
irregular, rough,
multifarious, multiform,
various kinds, all sorts, not
uniform, lop-sided,
unequal, different, partial,
over-balanced, (even,
level, equal, balance,
monotony)

unexplored-*v* hidden,
silence, mystery,
concealed, darkness,
unknown, invisible,
impenetrable, undisclosed,
unexposed, dormant,
unsuspected, (apparent,
prominent, flagrant,

notorious, distinct)

unfamiliar-*adj* unusual,
uncommon, rare,
remarkable, unexpected,
unaccountable,
unconventional,
unparalleled, newfangled,
grotesque, outlandish,
(conventional, ordinary,
common, usual)

unfit-*adj* objectionable,
unreasonable,
unallowable, unjustified,
improper, illegal, immoral,
wrong, inequitable, partial,
unfair, injustice, (right, fit,
impartial, moral, reward,
recompense, good, just)

unforeseen-*v*
miscalculation,
unexpected, unaware,
pounce, abrupt, sudden,
startle, instantaneous,
surprised, shock, wonder,
fall upon, (expect,
foreseen, prospective,
impending, prepared,
count on)

unfortunate-*adj*
unsuccessful, abortive, at
fault, inefficient, ineffectual,
foiled, defeated, ruined,
broken, unattained,
uncompleted, frustrated,
disconcerted, (successful,
prosperous, triumphant,
victorious)

unfriendly-*adj* hostile,
inimical, discord,
alienation, estrangement,
dislike, hate, heartburning,
animosity, malevolence,
disaffected, (familiarity,

intimacy, fellowship,
friendly, welcome,
harmony)
unguided-*v*
extemporaneous,
impulsive, improvised,
unprompted, unnatural,
unguarded, spontaneous,
voluntary, flash, spurt,
improvisation,
(predetermined,
aforethought)
unhappy-*adj* mope, brood,
fret, sulk, pine, yearn,
repine, regret, despair,
refrain from laughter,
depressed, gloomy,
unlively, melancholy,
dismal, somber, (cheering,
inspiriting, jovial, hilarious)
uniform-*adj* homogeneous,
consistency, conformity,
agreement, regularity,
constancy, routine, even
tenor, monotony,
assimilate, level, smooth,
dress, invariable,
(diversified, varied,
uneven, rough)
union-*n* combination,
mixture, junction,
unification, synthesis,
incorporation,
amalgamation,
embodiment, coalescence,
fusion, blending,
(decompose, separate,
dissect, unravel)
unique-*adj* non-conformity,
unconventional, abnormal,
eccentricity, rarity, freak,
individual, originality,
exceptional, exclusive,

eccentric, irregular,
(conform, typical, normal,
formal, ordinary)
unite-*v* gather, assemble,
collect, convene, draw,
conclave, accumulate,
heap, converge, pile,
pyramid, conglomeration,
muster, meet, join, cluster,
(unassembled. broadcast,
stray, disperse, sow)
unlucky-*adj* unfortunate, ill-
timed, intrusive,
inopportune, inauspicious,
unfavorable, unsuited,
inexpedient, premature,
unpunctual, (opportune,
timely, well timed,
fortunate, lucky, suitable)

V

vacant-*adj* absence,
inexistent, nonresidence,
absenteeism, empty, void,
vacuum, truant,
unoccupied, uninhabited,
devoid, deserted, (present,
occupied, inhabited, dwell,
fill, domiciled)
vacate-*v* depart, cessation,
decampment,
embarkation, outset, start,
removal, exit, egress,
exodus, flight, valediction,
adieu, farewell, good-bye,
abandon, leave, (arrive,
welcome, reception,
return)
vacillate-*v* unsteady,
changeable, unsteadfast,
fickle, capricious, volatile,
frothy, light, giddy, weak,

feeble-minded, fidgety,
tremulous, hesitate,
uncertain, (steady, sound,
inflexible, hard, resolute)

vacuous-*adv* absent, not
present, away, non-
resident, gone from home,
missing, lost, wanting,
omitted, nowhere to be
found, nonexistent, empty,
void, vacant, untenanted,
(fill, pervade, permeate,
present)

vagabond-*n* bad man,
wrong-doer, worker of
iniquity, evil-doer, sinner,
bad example, rascal,
scoundrel, villain,
miscreant, wretch, reptile,
viper, serpent, scamp,
(model, paragon, hero,
saintly)

vagrant-*n* roving, vagrancy,
marching, nomad,
gadding, flitting, migration,
travel, journey, take wing,
emigrate, prowl, roam,
range, patrol, traverse,
wander, (stagnate, stick,
pause, anchor)

vague-*adj* indefinite,
indistinct, perplexed,
confused, undetermined,
loose, ambiguous,
mysterious, mystic,
transcendental, occult,
recondite, abstruse,
crabbed, (understand,
comprehend, grasp)

vain-*adj* vanity, conceit,
self-conceit, self-
complacency, self-
confidence, selfishness,

airs, pretensions,
mannerism, egotism,
priggish, gaudery,
vainglory, elation, (modest,
reserved, demure,
blushing)

value-*n* price, amount, cost,
expense, prime cost,
charge, figure, demand,
damage, fare, hire, wage,
remuneration, dues, duty,
toll, tax, impose, tallage,
levy, gabelle, excise,
assessment, benevolence

vanish-*v* disappear,
dissolve, fade, melt away,
pass, go, avant, be-gone,
leave, no trace, retire from
sight, efface, evanescent,
missing, lost, gone,
(appear, view, vista,
spectacle, guise, look,
visible)

vary-*v* differ, diverse,
heterogeneous,
distinguishable, modified,
other, another, unequal,
not the same, unmatched,
distinct, characteristic,
(uniform, regular, level,
always, without exception)

vast-*adj* great, immense,
enormous, extreme,
inordinate, excessive,
extravagant, exorbitant,
outrageous, preposterous,
swinging, monstrous, over-
grown, (small, diminutive,
minute, paltry)

veer-*v* change, alter, vary,
wax and wane, modulate,
diversify, qualify, tamper
with, turn, shift, tack, chop,

shuffle, swerve, warp,
deviate, turn aside, overt,
introvert, resume,
(permanent, stationary)

vehemence-_adv_ feeling,
emotion, excitability,
impetuosity,
boisterousness,
turbulence, impatience,
intolerance, non-enduring,
irritability, agitation,
(serene, calm, placid,
composure, quiet, tranquil)

vein-_n_ tend, contribute,
conducive, lead, dispose,
incline, verge, bend to,
trend, affect, carry,
gravitate, promote,
subservient, instrumental,
nature, temperament,
mood, drift, cast

velocity-_n_ speed, swiftness,
rapidity, expedition,
activity, acceleration,
haste, spurt, rush, dash,
race, lively, gallop, move
quickly, hasten, whisk,
sweep, (retard, relax,
slacken, gentle, easy,
linger)

vent-_v_ divulge, reveal,
break, split, tell, breathe,
utter, allow, acknowledge,
concede, grant, admit,
own, confess, avow,
disguise, transpire, come
to light, (screen, cover,
shade, blinker, veil,
curtain)

ventilate-_v_ gust, blast,
breeze, squall, gale, storm,
tempest, hurricane,
whirlwind, wind, blow, fan,

respire, breathe, waft,
flatulent, issue, bellows,
blow-pipe

venture-_n_ trial, endeavor,
attempt, essay, adventure,
speculation, probation,
experiment, try, strive,
tempt, gamble, bet, risk,
hazard, accidental, (intend,
purpose, design, propose)

verdict-_n_ result, conclusion,
upshot, deduction,
inference, egotism, illation,
estimation, valuation,
appreciation, judicature,
assessment, ponderous,
judgment, (discover, find,
determine, evolve)

verge-_n_ edge, brink, brow,
brim, margin, border, skirt,
rim, flange, side, mouth,
jaws, cops, chaps, lip,
muzzle, threshold,
marginal, conducive, tend,
incline, affect, gravitate
toward, promote

vernacular-_n_ indigenous,
native, domestic,
domiciled, naturalized,
home, indoor, endemic,
interior, intrinsic, closed,
inward, within, (exterior,
outside, surface, skin,
superficial, external)

versatile-_adj_ changeable,
mutable, checkered, ever
changing, inconstant,
unsteady, fluctuate,
restless, agitated, erratic,
fickle, irresolute,
capricious, vagrant,
vibratory, alternating

very-_adv_ fact, reality,

existence, nature, truth,
gospel, authenticity,
veracity, accuracy,
exactness, precise,
unalloyed, regularity,
principal, (error, fallacy,
mistake, fault, blunder,
heresy, deceit)

vessel-*n* receptacle,
enclosure, recipient,
receiver, reservoir,
compartment, vase,
bushel, barrel, canister, jar,
bottle, basket, hopper,
crate, cradle, bassinet,
hamper, douser, cistern

vexation-*n* disappointment,
mortification, cold comfort,
regret, repining, taking on,
inquietude, soreness,
heartburning, lamentation,
hypercriticism, malcontent,
(comfort, resignation,
content)

vibrate-*v* fluctuation,
vacillation, swing, beat,
shake, wag, see-saw,
lurch, dodge, oscillate,
alternate, undulate,
pulsate, beat, dance,
curvet, reel, (fixed,
steadfast, firm, fast,
steady, balanced)

vicious-*adj* vice, evil-doing,
wickedness, iniquity,
demerit, sin, immorality,
impropriety, indecorum,
scandal, laxity, infirmity,
weakness, frailty,
imperfection, (virtuous,
good, innocent,
meritorious, deserving)

victim-*n* pigeon, April fool,

laughing stock, flat,
greenhorn, fool, dupe, gull,
gudgeon, cull, deceived,
swallow up, bite,
credulous, mistaken,
(cheat, swindler, thief,
knave, rogue, decoy-duck,
trickster)

view-*v* see, observe, watch,
attend to, eye, survey,
scan, inspect, glance,
behold, discern, perceive,
discover, distinguish,
recognize, spy,
contemplate, (blind,
hoodwink, dazzle, dim
sighted, wall-eyed)

vigilance-*n* watchful,
surveillance, vigil, look out,
care, solicitude, heed,
alertness, activity,
attention, prudence,
circumspection, caution,
preparation, accuracy,
(neglect, carelessness,
trifling, omission)

vigor-*n* healthy, well, sound,
hearty, hale, fresh, green,
whole, florid, flush, hardy,
stanch, staunch, brave,
robust, unscathed, perfect,
excellent, (fever, calenture,
inflammation, ailing,
disease, sick)

villain-*n* rascal, scoundrel,
miscreant, wretch, reptile,
viper, serpent, urchin,
delinquent, criminal,
malefactor, culprit, thief,
murderer, jail-bird, (good,
paragon, hero, innocent,
good example)

vincible-*adj* powerless,

impotent, unable,
incapable, incompetent,
inefficient, inept, unfit,
disqualified, harmless,
defenseless, unfortified,
indefensible, pregnable,
(powerful, puissant, potent,
capable)

vinaigrette-*n* fragrance,
aroma, redolence,
perfume, bouquet, sweet
smell, aromatic perfume,
incense, musk,
frankincense, spicy, balmy,
ambrosial, perfumed,
(stench, stink, fetid, strong
smelling, putrid,
suffocating, nidorous)

vindicate-*v* justification,
warrant, exoneration,
exculpation, acquittal,
whitewashing, extenuation,
softening, mitigation, reply,
defence, recrimination,
(accusation, charge,
imputation, slur,
inculpation, exprobration)

vindictive-*adj* resentful,
cantankerous, pugnacious,
perverse, querulous, fiery,
peppery, passionate,
choleric, shrewish, quick,
hot, testy, touchy,
animosity, exasperation,
bitterness

violate-*v* seduction,
defloration, defilement,
abuse, rape, incest, social
evil, adultery, harem,
intrigue, debauch, defile,
rampant, lustful, carnal,
erotic, voluptuous, (pure,
undefiled, modest,

delicate)

viper-*n* snake, serpent, asp,
vermin, beast, poison,
leaven, virus, venom,
arsenic, antimony,
nicotine, demon, sting,
fang, (remedial,
restorative, corrective,
palliative, balsamic,
narcotic)

virgin-*n* new, immaculate,
immaturity, novel, recent,
youth, restore, evergreen,
untried, modern, neoteric,
new born, (old, ancient,
antique, long standing,
prime, primitive)

virile-*adj* strength, power,
energy, force, physical
force, stamina, muscle,
sinew, vitality, athletic,
adamant, steel, iron, oak,
might, stout, robust, (weak,
frail, fragile, languid, poor,
rickety, cranky)

virtual-*adj* inexistence,
negative, blank, missing,
omitted, absent, unreal,
potential, baseless,
unsubstantial, vain,
uncreated, exhausted,
annihilated, gone, lost,
departed, (actual, real,
positive, absolute,
prevalent)

virtue-*n* good, innocent,
meritorious, reserving,
worthy, correct, moral,
righteous, well-intentioned,
creditable, laudable,
commendable,
praiseworthy, admirable,
(vicious, corrupt, atrocity)

visible-*adj* perceptibility, conspicuousness, distinctness, appearance, exposure, manifestation, ocular, ocular evidence, demonstrate, field of view, (invisible, indistinct, conceal, hidden)

visit-*n* courtesy, light, alight, dismount, debark, disembark, cast anchor, arrive, land, reception, welcome, destination, harbor, haven, port, refuge, (depart, removal, exit, egress, adieu, farewell)

vitality-*n* life, ability, animation, vital, spark, flame, respiration, wind, breath of live, existence, vivification, nourishment, subsist, quick, tenacious, (die, expire, meet one's death, end, pass away)

vivacious-*adj* cheerful, genial, gaiety, good humor, glee, light hearted, mirth, merriment, hilarity, exhilaration, amusement, winsome, pleasing, (dreary, flat, dull, mournful, dreadful, depressing)

vivid-*adj* strong, energetic, forcible, active, intense, deep-dyed, severe, keen, sharp, acute, incisive, trenchant, brisk, rousing, exciting, (inert, inactive, passive, torpid, sluggish, dull, heavy, flat, slack)

vixen-*n* shrew, virago, termagant, dragon, scold, porcupine, spit-fire, fire-eater, blusterer, fury, violent-person, irascible, bad, ill-tempered, irritable, susceptible, excitable, fretful, fidget, hasty, passionate

vocabulary-*n* word, term, vocable, name, phrase, root, etymon, derivative, part of speech, grammar, dictionary, lexicon, index, glossary, thesaurus, concordance, literal, verbal, titular, conjugate, exact

vocation-*n* calling, profession, cloth, faculty, industry, art, industrial arts, craft, mystery, handicraft, trade, commerce, perform, observe, fulfill, obligation, (exempt, free, neglect, relax, excuse, fail)

vociferation-*n* hullabaloo, loud noise, clang, clatter, noise, bombination, roar, uproar, racket, hubbub, raucous, resonance, thunder, bellow, powerful, (inaudible, low, muffled, hoarse, husky, gentle, soft)

void-*n* vacant, vacuous, empty, eviscerated, blank, hollow, nominal, null, inane, vanish, evaporate, fade, dissolve, melt away, disappear, nothing, (substantial, exist, object, tangible, being, substance)

volatile-*adj* gaseous, aeriform, ethereal, aerial, airy, vaporous,

evaporation, flatulent,
distillation, sublimation,
exhale, transpire, emit,
fume, reek, (dissolve,
resolve, liquate, liquefied,
soluble)

volcano-*n* reverberatory,
forge, fiery furnace,
brazier, salamander,
heater, warming-pan,
boiler, cauldron, kettle,
crucible, alembic, still,
furnace, (refrigerate, cool,
dampen, freezing mixture)

volitant-*n* aeronautics,
balloon, flying, flight,
voyage, sail, put to sea,
navigate, warp, luff, scud,
boom, drift, course, cruise,
row, paddle, pull, maritime,
(walk, march, step, tread,
pace, plod, wend)

volley-*n* shower, storm,
cloud, group, cluster,
clump, repeated sounds,
report, thud, burst,
explosion, discharge,
detonation, squib, cracker,
rap, snap, (rolling,
monotonous)

volume-*n* size, magnitude,
dimension, bulk, large,
great, quantity, expanse,
amplitude, mass,
proportions, mammoth,
capacity, ton, obesity,
(small, little, thin, dwarf,
pygmy, minute,
microscopic)

voluntary-*adv* willing,
disposition, inclination,
leaning, mood, vein, free,
without reluctance,

graciously, assent,
spontaneous, unasked,
unforced, (unwilling,
grudgingly, under protest,
qualm)

voluptuous-*adj* impure,
concupiscent, prurient,
lickerish, rampant, lustful,
carnal, lewd, lascivious,
lecherous, social, evil,
smut, unchaste, wanton,
debauched, (vestal, virgin,
prude, pure, undefiled)

vouch-*v* assert, declaatory,
predictor, pronunciation,
affirmative, positive,
certain, express, explicit,
absolute, emphatic,
distinct, decided, confident,
dogmatic, (dispute,
impugn, traverse, rebut,
deny)

vow-*v* promise, undertake,
engage, commit, assure,
warrant, guarantee,
covenant, bear witness,
troth, plight, pledge, word
of honor, oath, affirmation,
compromise, votive,
obligation

vulnerable-*adj* expose, risk,
hazard, venture,
precarious, instability,
defenseless, forlorn,
hopeless, threaten,
tottering, ominous,
unprepared, (safe, sure,
guard, shield, protect,
precaution, refuge)

W

wade-*v* gather, learn,

acquire, gain, receive,
drink in, obtain, collect,
knowledge, information,
peruse, pore, industrious,
studious, (teach, instruct,
edify, tutor, enlighten)

waggle-v oscillate,
alternate, undulate, wave,
rock, swing, pulsate, beat,
nod, bob, courtesy, curtsy,
play., fluctuate, dance,
curvet, reel, quake, shake,
flicker, wriggle, roll, toss,
pitch, flounder

wait-v put off, defer, delay,
lay over, suspend, shift,
waive, retard, remand,
postpone, adjourn,
procrastinate, dally,
prolong, protract, knee
back, (early, prime, timely,
punctual, forward, prompt)

wall-n bar, barrier, turn-stile,
gate, portcullis, barricade,
defense, breakwater,
bulkhead, block, buffer,
stopper, dam, weir,
drawback, objection,
stumbling block, (relief,
rescue, lift, aid)

wallop-v strike, punish,
chastise, castigate, slap,
smack, spank, thump,
beat, swing, buffet, thresh,
thrash pummel, drum,
leather, trounce, baste,
belabor, pelt, stone,
lapidate, torture

wander-v move, motion,
transitional, motor, motive,
shifting, mobile, mercurial,
unquiet, restless, nomadic,
erratic, drift, flow, stream,

(remain, stay, stagnate,
rest, pause, lull, stop,
repose)

want-v desire, wish, fancy,
fantasy, need, exigency,
mind, inclination, leaning,
bent, longing, hankering,
inkling, solicitude, anxiety,
yearning, coveting,
aspiration, (indifferent,
cool, unconcerned)

wanton-adj capricious,
erratic, eccentric, fitful,
hysterical, full of whims,
maggoty, inconsistent,
fanciful, fantastic,
whimsical, crotchety,
particular, humorism,
freakish, skittish, wayward,
contrary, arbitrary

ward-n region, sphere,
ground, soil, area, realm,
hemisphere, quarter,
district, beat, orb, circuit,
circle, pale, limit,
department, domain, tract,
territory, parish,
(boundless,
uncircumscribed,
extensive)

warehouse-n storehouse,
closet, depository,
repository, stock,
accumulate, hoard, stack,
promontory, reservoir,
receptacle, amass, collect,
harvest, save, reserve,
(spend, expend, use,
consume, spill)

warn-v discourage,
dampen, disincline,
indispose, stagger, repel,
quench, deprecate, induce,

deter, dissuade, obstinate, restrain, keep back, (prompt, persuade, bribe, lure, stimulate)

warrant-*n* dictate, mandate, caveat, decree, writ, ordination, bull, edict, decretal, dispensation, citation, permit, authorize, admission, grant, empower, (prohibit, forbid, disallow, bar, withhold, shut)

wash-*v* lavatory, laundry, clean, pure, purification, defecation, lustration, abstersion, ablution, disinfect, fumigate, deodorize, immaculate, (mud, mire, quagmire, sludge, slime, slush)

watch-*v* observe, attend to, peep, peer, pry, look, witness, contemplate, speculate, cast, discover, distinguish, recognize, spy, behold, demonstrate, (blind, hoodwink, undiscerning, dim sighted)

way-*n* method, manner, wise, form, mode, fashion, tone, guise, procedure, path, road, route, course, trajectory, orbit, track, beat, means of access, channel, passage, avenue, approach, artery, lane

weak-*adj* feeble, insipid, illogical, frail, fragile, flimsy, unsubstantial, rickety, cranky, drooping, tottering, broken, lame, withered, shatter,shaken,

crazy, shaky, (strong, might, vigorous, forcible, hard)

wear-*v* impair, injure, damage, loss, detriment, laceration, outrage, havoc, deteriorate, degenerate, decay, dilapidation, rotten, blight, (improve, refine, rectify, enrich, mellow, elaborate)

weave-*v* produce, perform, operate, do, make, form, construct, fabricate, frame, contrive, manufacture, forge, twine, entwine, twist, interlace, (destroy, ruin, dilapidation, deteriorate, wreck)

wedge-*n* fusiform, wedge-shaped, triangular, angular, bent, crooked, firm, fast, close, tight, taut, secure, hinge, tether, pin, nail, rivet, jam, dovetail, (sunder, divide, sever, carve, dissect, detach)

ween-*v* think, hold, opinion, conceive, trow, fancy, apprehend, embrace, assured, positive, satisfied, confident, nurture, credence, secure, impress, (dispute, fallible, uncertain, untrue, distrust, doubt)

weigh-*v* influence, tell, have a hold upon, magnetize, bear upon, pervade, prevail, dominate, gain, important, rampant, regnant, reign, (irrelevant, unconducive, impotence, inert, powerless)

well-intentioned-*adj* merit,
worth, excellence, credit,
self-control, resolution, self
denial, virtuous, creditable,
laudable, commendable,
exemplary, (vicious, sinful,
wicked, immoral, lawless)

wheedle-*v* coax, persuade,
prevail, bring round, tempt,
seduce, entice, allure,
captivate, fascinate,
bewitch, carry away,
charm, conciliate, lure,
tantalize, (remonstrate,
dissuade, discourage,
averse)

where-*v* seek, inquire,
search, look for, scan,
reconnoiter, explore,
sound, rummage, ransack,
pry, peer, hunt, canvass,
investigate, examine,
probe, fathom, scrutinize,
(answer, respond, reply,
rebut)

whet-*v* sharpen, hone,
strop, grind, point,
aculeate, picul, set, acute,
prickly, thorny, bristling,
studded, spike, cutting
edge, (obtuse, dull, bluff,
render blunt)

whim-*n* caprice, fancy,
humor, crotchet, quirk,
freak, maggot, fad, vagary,
prank, erratic, eccentric,
fitful, hysterical, frivolous,
fickle, giddy, volatile,
skittish, inconsistent,
fanciful, fantastic,
whimsical

whine-*v* complain, lament,
murmur, mutter, grumble,

groan, whimper, sob, sigh,
mourn, grieve, weep,
complain without cause,
frown, scowl, (smile,
giggle, titter, cheer,
chuckle, shout, sing,
triumphant)

whisk-*v* sweep, rapid,
speed, hasten, rush, dash,
race, lively, swift, gallop,
skim, hurry, accelerate,
quicken, spring, fast, agile,
expeditious,
instantaneous, (gradual,
slow, languid, sluggish,
slow-paced)

whisper-*n* inaudible, low,
dull, stifled, muffled,
husky, melodious, speak
imperfectly, mutter, under-
tone, faint sound, hoarse,
gentle, (blast, loud, swell,
clang, holler, scream,
piercing, deafening)

whittle-*v* sunder, divide,
subdivide, sever, abscind,
cut, snip, nib, nip, cleave,
rend, slit, split, rupture,
shatter, shiver, crunch,
cop, hack, hew, slash,
haggle, hackle, lacerate,
scramble, mangle, slice

whole-*n* entire, total,
integral, complete, one,
individual, unbroken,
wholly, altogether, sum
total, gross amount,
embody, (fractional,
fragmentary, section,
divided, break, piece,
compartment)

wholesale-*adj* trade,
commerce, market, buying

and selling, bargain, traffic, business, commercial enterprise, speculation, jobbing, broker, negotiation, dealing, transaction, (retail, over the counter)

whopping-*adj* huge, enormous, giant, immense, monstrosity, corpulent, stout, fat, plump, thumping, thundering, overgrown, puffy, mighty, stupendous, infinite, (small, little, dwarf, unimportant)

wide-*adj* broad, ample, extended, expanded, breadth, latitude, amplitude, diameter, thickness, crassitude, expansion, thicken, dumpy, squab, squat, (narrow, coarctate, taper, slim, scanty)

wield-*v* agitate, shake, convulse, toss, tumble, bandy, brandish, flap, flourish, whisk, jerk, hitch, jolt, joggle, buffet, hustle, disturb, stir, hake up, churn, jounce, wallop, whip, vellicate, palpitate

will-*n* voluntary, volitional, free, optional, discretionary, freedom, spontaneity, originality, of one's own accord, by choice, purposely, deliberately, (compulsory, necessary, needful, compel, requisite)

win-*v* triumph, exultation, proficiency, skill, conquer, victor, succeed, gain, attain, secure, accomplish, master, conquest, carry, secure, effect, complete, (failure, lose, ruined, defeated, broken down)

wince-*v* pain, suffering, physical pain, aching, smart, twinge, twitch, gripe, headache, hurt, sore, discomfort, malaise, spasm, cramp, nightmare, convulsion, writhe, agonize, (sensual, sensuous, pleasure, bodily enjoyment, gratification, creature comforts)

winch-*n* lever, crane, derrick, instrument, tool, implement, utensil, handle, hilt, haft, shaft, shank, blade, trigger, helm, treadle, capstan, lift, heighten, elevate, (crouch, stoop, bend, bow, sink, reduce)

wing-*n* leave, depart, exit, egress, exodus, farewell, good-bye, quit, retire, withdraw, remove, wing one's flight, spring, fly, flit, outward bound, (arrive, welcome, here, return, overtake, join)

winsome-*adj* charming, delightful, felicitous, exquisite, lovely, beautiful, ravishing, rapturous, heart-felt, thrilling, ecstatic, beatific, seraphic, heavenly, attractive, (repel, disgust, revolt, nauseate, sicken)

wipe-*v* dry, soak up, sponge, swab, drain, parch, anhydrous, napkin, cloth, handkerchief, towel, sudary, doily, duster, mop, wash, launder, spruce, tidy, (sludge, slime, slush, grime)

wise-*adj* intelligent, keen, acute, alive, awake, bright, quick, sharp, sage, sapient, sagacious, reasonable, rational, sound, sensible, judicious, strong-minded, unprejudiced, calculating

wish-*n* desire, fantasy, want, need, grasping, longing, hankering, anxiety, yearning, aspiration, vaulting, ambition, eagerness, zeal, ardor, impatience, (indifferent, undesired, neutral)

wistful-*adj* thinking, thoughtful, pensive, meditative, reflective, museful, contemplative, speculative, deliberate, studious, sedate, introspective, philosophical, (vacant, unintellectual, unoccupied)

wither-*v* decrease, dwindle, shrink, contract, narrow, shrivel, collapse, lose flesh, fall away, waste, wane, decay, deteriorate, lessen, pare, reduce, strangle, restrain, file, (expand, spread, extend develop)

withstand-*v* resist, repugn, reluctant, stand up, strive, bear up, stand firm, refractory, oppose, strike, revolt, front, repulse, insurrection, (reprisal, retort, reaction, reciprocate)

witness-*n* spectator, beholder, observer, on-looker, eye-witness, bystander, passer by, sight-seer, spy, sentinel, be present, contemplate, survey, curiosity, (retire from sight, disappear, vanish)

woe-*n* beshrew, confusion, damn, confound, blast, curse, devil take, hang, plague, scold, denounce, proscribe, excommunicate, fulminate, threaten, (benevolent, kind, well-meaning, amiable, obliging)

wonder-*v* astonish, amazement, marvel, bewilder, admiration, awe, stupor, fascination, sensation, surprise, wondrous, electrify, stun, confound, dazzle, baffle, stupendous, miraculous, overwhelming

word-*n* maxim, aphorism, saying, adage, saw, proverb, sentence, motto, axiom, reflection, conclusion, term, name, phrase, part of speech, vocabulary, literal, concordance

work-v labor, toil, travail, manual labor, sweat of one's brow, trouble, pains, sweat, drudge, slave, wade through, strive, strain, pull, exert, effort, struggle, (relax, unbend, slacken, refresh, sleep, rest)

workmanship-n produce, perform, operate, flower, bear fruit, fructify, create, beget, generate, hatch, develop, form, prolific, labor, build, edify, pride, (destroy, perish, demolish, tear up, dispel, nullify)

worldly-adj atheist, septic, unbeliever, deist, infidel, heathen, alien, gentile, freethinker, rationalist, materialistic, agnostic, disbelieve, doubt, (worship, inspire, revere, adore, bow down and worship)

worn-v weak, battered, shattered, pulled down, seedy, altered, fatigued, weary, drowsy, drooping, haggard, toil, footsore, weatherbeaten, faint, exhausted, prostrate, (reinvigorate, freshen up)

worse-adv deteriorate, degenerate, wane, decrease, retrograde, decline, droop, sink, from bad to worse, recession, decay, decrepitude, (improve, mend, advance, reform, ripen, better, correct)

worthy-adj virtuous, good, innocent, meritorious, deserving, righteous, well-intentioned, creditable, laudable, commendable, praiseworthy, excellent, admirable, sterling, pure, noble, admirable

wrangle-v discord, quarrel, dispute, tiff, squabble, altercation, words, jangle, babble, broil, brawl, racket, disturbance, dissent, dissension, (agree, accord, harmonize, concord, united, allied)

wreck-n smash, crash, quell, squash, squelch, shatter, sink, swamp, scuttle, shipwreck, engulf, submerge, raze, level, lay waste, ravage, gut, dismantle, (create, construct, form, put together)

write-v record, pen, scribe, transcribe, copy, scribble, scrawl, scrabble, scratch, interline, write down, compose, print, publish, compositor, manuscript, shorthand, handwriting

wry-adj slope, slant, lean, incline, shelve, stoop, decline, descend, bend, heel, careen, sag, swag, slouch, cant, sidle, poke, askew, askant, oblique, (parallel, coextension, alongside, laterally)

Y

yarn-n exaggeration,
expansion, hyperbole,
stretch, strain, coloring,
caricature, extravagance,
nonsense, fringe,
embroidery, traveler's tale,
overestimate, wire, string,
thread, twine, cord, rope

yawn-n nod, get sleepy,
snooze, nap, dream,
sleepy, indolent, lazy,
slothful, idle, lust, remiss,
slack, inert, sluggish,
languid, supine, heavy,
dull, leaden, listless,
(active, quick, prompt,
alert, spry, sharp)

yearling-n infant, babe,
child, youth, stripling,
youngster, younker,
weanling, papoose,
bambino, seedling,
whipper-snapper, (veteran,
old man, seer, patriarch,
centenarian, old stager,
forefathers)

yearn-v pity, compassion,
commiseration, sympathy,
tenderness, forbearance,
humanity, mercy,
clemency, leniency,
charity, touched, soften,
(unmerciful,
uncompassionate, severe,
unrelenting)

yeast-n leaven, ferment,
barm, light, subtile, airy,
imponderable, astatic,
weightless, ethereal,
sublimated,
uncompressed, volatile,

buoyant, floating, portable,
(heavy, massive, lead,
millstone)

yell-v cry, vociferate, raise,
shout, roar, bawl, brawl,
hop, whoop, bellow, howl,
scream, screech, screak,
shriek, squeak, squall,
whine, pule, pipe, cheer,
hoot, grumble, moan,
groan

yield-v succumb, submit,
bend, resign, defer,
submissive,
surrender,capitulate,
retreat, downtrodden,
pliant, undefended, permit,
relinquish, sanction,
(overpower, struggle,
unbending, forbid, refuse)

yoke-n lock, latch, belay,
brace, hook, grapple,
leash, couple,
accouplement, link,
bracket, bridge over, span,
pin, nail, bolt, hasp, clasp,
clamp, (sever, rupture,
segregate, breach,
rescind, divide)

yokel-n bungler, blunderer,
marplot, fumbler, lubber,
duffer, awkward, squad,
greenhorn, clod, muff,
(proficient, expert, adept,
connoisseur, veteran)

yokemate-n spouse,
consort, husband, wife,
better half, mate,
helpmate, match,
betrothment, promise,
(unmarried, bachelor,
virgin, single, celibacy)

yonder-adj distant, far-off,

remote, telescopic, distal, stretching, ulterior, transmarine, span, stride, faraway, farther, further, beyond, far and wide, (near, close, no great distance, nigh, within reach)

yore-*adj* formerly, of old, last, latter, retrospective, ancient, time immemorial, olden, forgotten, extinct, gone by, ancestral, (anticipate, millennium, advent, look forward, eventual)

young-*adj* youthful, juvenile, green, callow, budding, sappy, beardless, under age, junior, infant, minor, pupilage, puberty, prime, rising generation, (seniority, elder, longevity, aged, antiquated, decay)

Z

zany-*adj* fool, idiot, tomfoolery, wiseacre, simpleton, witling, donkey, ass, ninny, nincompoop, lout, loon, gabby, trifler, babbler, dullard, doodle, clod, lack-wit, (authority, luminary, wise man)

zeal-*adj* quick, prompt, yare, instant, ready, alert, spry, sharp, smart, fast, swift, expeditious, awake, forward, eager, strenuous, enterprising, industrious, diligent, (indolent, lazy, slothful, idle, remiss)

zealot-*n* bigot, intolerant, obstinate, immovability, inflexibility, prejudgement, opinionist, enthusiast, tenacious, (changeful, idle, withdraw from, relinquish)

zealous-*adj* eager, animated, resolute, steadfast, vivacious, diligent, fiery, brisk

zero-*n* nothing, naught, cipher, none, no one, nobody, never, unsubstantial, blank, void, immaterial, groundless, nonentity, (substantial, thing, object, something, being

zest-*n* pleasure, gratification, enjoyment, fruition, delectation, relish, gusto, satisfaction, content, well-being, snugness, comfort, amusement, happiness, (concern, grief, sorrow, distress, affliction, woe)

zigzag-*v* diversion, digression, departure, aberration, divergence, detour, circuit, wander, vagrant, by-paths and crooked ways, oblique motion, deviate, swerve,(toward, aim, line, path, road, range)

zone-*n* region, sphere, clime, climate, meridian, latitude, territorial, local, arena, precincts, district, domain, tract, parish, province, township, field, plot, (unlimited space, wilderness, waste, free space)